Fields
of
Little America

To the 6,032

Fields
of
Little America

BY MARTIN W. BOWMAN

WENSUM BOOKS (NORWICH) LTD
33 ORFORD PLACE, NORWICH

First published November 1977
Second impression December 1977
ISBN 0 903619 19 9 (paperback)
ISBN 0 903619 20 2 (casebound)

Printed by Euromedia Print Limited, Norwich
Binding by Hunter and Foulis, Edinburgh

Acknowledgements

This book encompasses the memories of the men who flew and maintained the B-24 Liberators of the Second Air Division. Remembered too are the countless East Anglians who came into contact with the Americans during the 'invasion' of 'Little America'. Their evocative memories extol with pride the sacrifice the young American aircrews made during three years of war. I would like to extend my sincere thanks to each and every contributor, without whose prolific donations of photographs and memorabilia this book could never have been written.

I would especially like to thank Bill Robertie for his Foreword and encouraging correspondence over a number of years, sustaining me through many difficulties; Tony North and Mike Bailey for their endless patience in providing me with material and technical advice; Vernon D. Burk, Historian, United States Third Air Force, for material of rare extraction and continual assistance; Alan Healy for allowing the excellent photos used in his 1947 publication to be used again, and all those listed below who provided me with more information and photos than I could have expected. Finally, my wife Paula, who despite scant knowledge of the Liberators, learned more and more as she typed, proofed, and listened, to help ensure that the demands of the book were met.

Second Air Division personnel
Tom Allen, Ray A. Betcher, Rudolph Birsic, Lt. Col. Don Baldwin, William A. Berry, Waldo D. Butler, Lt. Col. Tom S. Belovich, Bob Bishop, Thompson H. Boyd, Bill Cameron, Lt. Col. Thomas Cardwell, Ed Chalifoux, Curt Crouch, William L. Case, Col. John Driscoll, Richmond Henre Dugger, Albert D. Franklin, Lt. Col. Charles H. Freudenthal, Gene Gaskins, Sol Greenberg, Pete Henry, Charles J. Halbert, Russ D. Hayes, Alan Healy, John Hildebran, Ben C. Isgrig, Jim Kotapish, John Knox, Jake D. Krause, James Kidder, Lt. Gen. M. Keck, Col. Myron H. Keilman, Louis Lawrence, Art Livingston, Newton L. McLaughlin, James J. Mahoney, Floyd H. Mabee, George Mazzara, Roxy Marotta, George Matecko, Wiley S. Noble, Art Nanas, Lt. Col. Harlan Oakes, Jim O'Brien, Ted Parker, George H. Parker, Bill Robertie, Roy L. Rainwater, Rick Rokicki, Francis X. Sheehan, Col. Albert E. Shower, Bob Shaffer, Marty Schreck, Fred Sissenstein, Paul Surbaugh, Lloyd T. Smith, Keith C. Schuyler, James V. Tootell, Frank Thomas, Lt. Col. John H. Woolnough, Dan Winston, C. Joe Warth, Lt. Gen. Charles B. Westover, Earl Zimmerman.

The East Anglians
John Archer, Francis Allen, May Ayers, Jack Bunkell, Muriel Colborn, Barbara Dowdeswell, Neil Evans, Russell Foster, Molly Giles, Chris Gotts, Steve Gotts, A.F. Moore, Ian McLachlan, Norman Ottaway, Ernie C. Powell, Cliff Poole, Phyllis Smales, Jack Turner, Mrs. H. Watson, Tony Walker.

and also
Don Olds, George Reynolds, Russell K. Wagner, United States Embassy in London, United States 3rd Air Force NCOIC Officers, The Imperial War Museum (Air Historial Branch), The Ministry of Defence (Air), The Department of the Environment, The Norfolk and Suffolk Aviation Society, The Cambridge Aircraft Preservation Society, The Friends of the Eighth and Ronald Blake.

Preface

Although the United States did not enter the war until December 1941 it soon became clear after the outbreak of hostilities in Europe that American intervention would only be a matter of time. American Chiefs of Staff used the time wisely and, partly on the initiative of President Roosevelt, the Army Air Corps was scheduled for expansion. On 20 June 1941 the Army Air Force was formed under the leadership of Major-General Henry 'Hap' H. Arnold. The American plan was to develop a heavy bomber force to specialize in high-level daylight bombing. To this end a new liquid-oxygen system for airmen at high altitude had been developed in 1928. To enable high altitude precision bombing the Norden bomb-sight was also developed.

The aircraft, too, were made available. The Boeing B-17 Flying Fortress prototype was developed in 1935 and the B-24 Liberator was ordered in late March 1939. These two four-engined heavy bombers formed the mainstay of the Eighth Air Force, activated on 28 January 1942 and destined for Great Britain. It was composed of the First, Second and Third Bombardment (later Air) Divisions and it is with the Second which was based in Norfolk and Suffolk that this book is concerned.

The Second Air Division was activated at Detrick Field, Maryland, as the Second Bombardment Wing on 7 June 1942. It was redesignated the Second Bombardment Division on 13 September 1943 and remained so until 1 January 1945 when it became the Second Air Division. All three Divisions came under the control of Eighth Bomber Command (later Eighth Air Force) Headquarters at High Wycombe near London. The Second Bombardment Wing (later Division) set up its Headquarters at Old Catton, Norwich, on 7 September 1942 under the command of Major-General James P. Hodges. It later moved to the near-by airfield of Horsham St Faith, finally moving across Norwich to Ketteringham Hall near Hethel in December 1943. On 1 August 1944 Major General William E. Kepner moved from command of Eighth Fighter Command to Commanding General Second Bombardment Division. On 13 May 1945 Brigadier-General Walter R. Peck, assumed command.

The Second Air Division was the only one of the three Divisions to use Liberators throughout hostilities. The First used Fortresses and the Third converted, on Doolittle's orders, from Liberators to Fortresses. The Second resisted General Doolittle's (Commanding General, Eighth Air Force) attempt to make the Eighth an all-Fortress command and by the end of the war comprised twelve Heavy Bombardment Groups (one having been disbanded and another having been rotated Stateside).

Each Group had its own airfield and normally comprised four Squadrons. For the purposes of formation flying the Groups were assigned to one of five Combat Bombardment Wings (later four). At the height of the war its maximum strength was 8,870 officers and 43,884 enlisted men. During operations from 'Little America' the Second Air Division lost 1,458 Liberators and 6,032 airmen killed. It flew a total of 95,948 sorties on 493 operational missions, dropping almost 200,000 tons of bombs on enemy targets throughout Europe and the Mediterranean theatre. Six Presidential Unit Citations were awarded to Second Air Division Groups and five individuals received the Medal of Honor.

Martin W. Bowman, Norwich, June 1977

Contents

Foreword

This book, *Fields of Little America*, can best be described as both the official and unofficial history of the men and planes of the 2nd Air Division based in England during WW II.

In compiling this history the author has read his way through miles of official documents. In addition he has corresponded with hundreds of men who served in the Division during those trying times. The result is a history of incomparable magnitude and a testament to the B-24 as a very rugged bomber, the men who flew it under impossible conditions and those very important people on the ground who performed miracles in order to keep 'the show on the road'.

It details the role the 2nd Air Division personnel played in turning East Anglia into 'Little America' if only for a short time. It is the first definitive history of the B-24 units in England and will be a welcome addition to the library of every Air War enthusiast.

WILLIAM ROBERTIE
Editor, 2nd Air
Division Association

Chapter One

The Eagle Spreads Its Wings

The origins of the English-based B-24 Liberator force began with the formation of the 44th Heavy Bombardment Group on 15 January 1941, almost twelve months before the United States declared war on Japan. Although at the time the United States was still officially neutral it had already become involved in the protection of Atlantic convoys. In April 1941 the first United States overseas air base was established in Greenland, with the agreement of the Danish Government, and by May the Germans had started their first U-boat attacks on American shipping. These attacks remained fairly sporadic until the end of August when an increase in their activity prompted President Roosevelt to warn Germany and Italy that if their vessels of war entered waters whose protection was deemed vital to America's security then they would do so at their peril. The last pretence of American neutrality was finally abandoned in November 1941 when Congress repealed the remaining neutrality statutes. The world had only to wait until 7 December 1941 when Japan, with her attack on Pearl Harbor, resolved the position.

It was against this backcloth of unofficial war activity that during late 1941 the 44th began receiving its first B-24Bs and B-24Cs. In February the following year the Group moved to Barkesdale Field, Louisiana, where it embarked on anti-submarine patrols in the Gulf of Mexico. By this time the 44th had become so proficient that its movement overseas was delayed and instead it was used to train other urgently needed units. Like a gigantic game of pool the 44th was broken up and pocketed round the world, leaving only a nucleus of the original personnel who called themselves the 'Eightballs'. The 93rd Heavy Bombardment Group ('The Travelling Circus'), soon to become the 44th's keenest rival in England, was created from 44th personnel and was activated at Barkesdale Field on 1 March 1942. Later two further splits formed 'Killer' Kane's 98th Heavy Bombardment Group — the 'Pyramiders' — which was dispatched to North Africa, and the 90th Heavy Bombardment Group, which went to the South West Pacific, where it became famous as the 'Jolly Rogers'. The 44th and 93rd would be united later with the 'Pyramiders' in North Africa under somewhat strained circumstances.

The 93rd Heavy Bombardment Group under the command of Colonel (later Brigadier-General) Ted Timberlake, completed its first phase of training on 15 May 1942 when it moved to Fort Myers, Florida. There it remained for almost three months while Staff secured supplies and organized the men into combat crews. The 93rd, like the 44th, became involved in anti-submarine duties and flew many patrols over the Gulf of Mexico and along the coast of Cuba. In all, three U-boat kills were credited to the Group, one of which went to Lieutenant John Jerstad.

On 2 August the 93rd began leaving Fort Myers for Fort Dix and the journey on slow troop trains took about thirteen days. The ground echelon's stay was a short one and on 31 August they embarked on the *Queen Elizabeth* and sailed for Greenock in Scotland. The air echelon, however, did not follow overseas immediately but was transferred to Grenier Field, New Hampshire, where it was to make its final preparations for overseas duty and to receive its brand-new B-24Ds. Here on 17 August Lieutenant John H. Murphy of the 328th Bombardment Squadron and his crew of four spent a restless and expectant morning sitting around the operations-room awaiting the arrival of their new aircraft. It was eventually ferried in about midday and Lieutenant Murphy and his men went out to inspect it. They were not told that the ferry pilot had been glad to get out of it, claiming that it was 'jinxed' — which was perhaps just as well. Having completed their inspection they were confronted with the problem of finding a name for it. It so happened that a current pursuit of the men on the base was that of rolling dice and this was often accompanied by the expression, 'Shoot Luke, you're faded.' After some discussion one member of the crew offered this phrase as a name and eventually, abbreviated to 'Shoot Luke', it was adopted; a typically informal beginning for one of the most famous B-24s in the E.T.O. (European Theatre of Operations).

On 5 September the B-24s of the 93rd began leaving Grenier Field on the long journey to England. However the crews soon ran into bad weather and were forced to seek shelter for four days at Newfoundland. At 18.30 hours on 9 September the weather cleared and *Shoot Luke* took off to lead seventeen Liberators into a flaming red sunset and across the inhospitable North Atlantic. Shortly after dark they again encountered bad weather but this time tried to climb above it. At 12,000 feet ice began to form on the wings and propellers, only to be dislodged by the slipstream and hitting the fuselages with cracks that sounded 'like gunfire'. Arch Rantala, the navigator aboard *Shoot Luke*, became ill when his oxygen-supply failed and to make matters worse the wind, which was stronger than anticipated, took the Liberators northwards and off course. Landfall at Prestwick was finally made eight hours and fifteen minutes after leaving Newfoundland.

The 93rd's ground echelon in the *Queen Elizabeth* docked at Greenock on the night of 4 September. Unloading commenced the following day and by 16.30 hours the last of the men had arrived at Greenock railway station where they were piped aboard their train by a Scottish band. They were heading for the village of Alconbury, Huntingdonshire, where they were to be reunited with the air echelon.

B-24Ds on the line during training, preparatory to flying to England.

The airfield was only partially completed on their arrival and afforded little luxury with only a few billets having been erected. This caused widespread problems, not least for the two Squadrons which had to sleep under canvas in a field of mud. Shortly after their arrival the men attended various lectures and received briefings on English social customs, mail security, and R.A.F. operational procedures. The 93rd was at that time the first and only B-24 Liberator Group stationed in England and it would not be until October 1942 that they would be supplemented by the 44th Group. (The only other Eighth Air Force bomber units present were three B-17 Groups.)

Amid rumours of yet another 'split', on 26 July 1942, the Eightballs were suddenly ordered to move to Will Rogers Field, Oklahoma, and pick up some LB-30 Liberators to begin training for overseas duty. On 30 August the air echelon moved to Grenier Field while the ground echelon prepared to move to Fort Dix two days later. While still at Grenier Field, the 44th's Commanding Officer, Colonel Frank H. Robinson (who had succeeded Lieutenant-Colonel Asp and Lieutenant-Colonel Rush by May 1941) decided that the Eightballs should have their own insignia. Predictably a winged eightball was painted on the nose of each aircraft. When the 44th began flying in England the Group became known as 'The Flying Eightballs'.

An echelon of the 66th Squadron left Grenier Field in August 1942 for Cheddington, England. It remained there until it was reunited with the 67th Squadron and the 68th Squadron at Shipdham in early October that same year. The 404th Squadron had been redeployed during training and it was not until March 1943 that the 506th Squadron was to join the 93rd Group.

Bill Cameron, a co-pilot in the 44th, awaited his Squadron's deployment from Grenier Field to England. 'I was assigned to the 67th Squadron and met my pilot, First Lieutenant Chester "George" Phillips. Phillips called everyone "George" so the name stuck. He was a typically rugged Texan and a fine pilot. At Grenier we had only four B-24s and about six "first" pilots for the entire Group. We later received twenty-seven new Liberators along with additional "first" pilots. We made a shakedown flight to Florida and back in our new planes and on 4 October flew off one by one for Gander, the first leg of the long trip to England. By the time we arrived over Gander the clouds were on the ground and there were no instrument landing systems. However we got down after several attempts. After a few days' waiting for good weather we took off again for England on 9 October 1942 in *Little Beaver*.'

Another crew member of the 67th Squadron who made the same crossing was First Lieutenant Bob Bishop, the navigator aboard *Suzy Q*, flown by Howard 'Pappy' Moore and named after his three-year-old daughter. A little older than most of his contemporaries, Moore was an exceptional pilot. Later at Shipdham he was to take bets on the number of times he could spin his wheels on the grass before landing on the concrete runway.

Bishop and all the other navigators were forced to navigate the 2,800-mile journey using stars because electrical storms ruled out the use of instruments. St Elmo's fire lit up the instruments of *Suzy Q* and the Northern Lights were also in evidence as, half-way across, Bishop navigated using the R.A.F. method of predetermined star paths charted on graph paper so that only a single star shot would give some indication of the aircraft's position. The combined storm and overcast

Early wartime photograph of Shipdham airfield showing the 'stave and crochet' design of runways and taxi-ways. Bottom right is the technical site and bottom left is the bomb dump stretching into the grounds of Letton Hall. Some conversion work from 'frying pan' to 'spectacle' type dispersals can be seen. IWM

had ruled out celestial navigation.

Although *Suzy Q* made its projected landfall at Prestwick, others were not so lucky. Lieutenant Cameron in Phillips's B-24 veered off course and landed at Bally Herbert in Northern Ireland while Lieutenant John Long overflew Scotland having been misdirected by a spurious German radio signal. Fortunately R.A.F. Spitfires managed to intercept him and he turned back. From Prestwick on 11 October the 67th Squadron flew to Shipdham to rejoin the other B-24s that had flown in from Cheddington. At Shipdham the 44th replaced Marauders of the 319th Medium Bombardment Group who had been in Norfolk since September. During mid November the Marauders began to leave for Operation Torch in North Africa.

The October winds had brought rain turning the airfield into a sea of mud. One by one the Liberators touched down to the voice of 'Axis Sally', or the 'Berlin Bitch' as the Americans called her, welcoming the new arrivals over the German radio. One B-24 ran off the runway and became stuck fast.

Shipdham air base, situated on Patterson Farm, was originally constructed by the Air Ministry for R.A.F. use at a cost of £1,100,000. The over-all picture it presented was one of depression. There was no grass; just mud in which stood scraps of buildings. There were three cavernous hangars, a 216,000 gallon fuel dump, and three runways — two of 1,400 yards and the main one of 1,975 yards. Round the runways ran a perimeter track bordered with fifty dispersals. The living areas were widely dispersed and comprised a number of small one-storey barracks each with about five rooms on either side of a central corridor. Eventually the base was to accommodate 3,120 men in this primitive type of housing. Bill Cameron discovered a large single room at one end of his hut and this became the community sitting-room called the '200 Club' after the barracks number.

The 44th was confined to base for five weeks before being permitted to visit Norwich and the surrounding villages although the R.A.F. liaison officer on the base did invite some W.A.A.F.s over for a party from near-by Swanton Morley in an attempt to alleviate the boredom of such confinement. Having thus invaded this quiet and parochial corner of England, the Americans expected the 'locals' to be very reserved. In fact many of the Americans soon struck up friendships with the Norfolk people and often accepted invitations to join them in their homes. Bill Robertie, an airman at the base, remembers that '. . . relationships were generally better at the beginning but by the middle of 1944 things became rather strained because by then the locals were being inundated with Americans. Generally speaking relationships remained amicable throughout the war.'

Crews were separated from their Liberators for six weeks while modifications were made at Langford Lodge in Northern Ireland. The quaquaversal armament underwent several field modifications. Machine-guns on the early B-24Ds had to be reloaded by hand with drums containing only thirty-six rounds of ammunition. These were changed to automatic belt-feed systems which increased the rate of automatic fire to several hundred rounds. New 0.50 calibre machine-guns were installed in the vulnerable nose section and even 'twin fifties' fitted

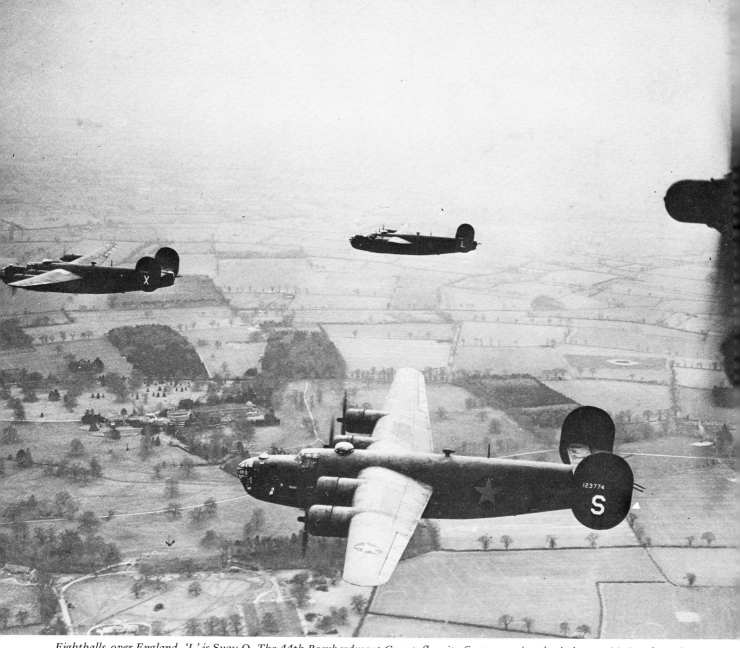

Eightballs over England. 'L' is Suzy Q. *The 44th Bombardment Group flew its first operational mission on 22 October when six B-24Ds made a diversionary sweep on Cherbourg-Marqutus airfield in France. The target was clouded over and the 44th brought its bombs home.*

in the field were made to protrude from the glasshouse. Either the bombardier or the navigator had to lie on his stomach to fire them. However they had the advantage of offering very little wind resistance and were much lighter than the later nose turrets which were installed to combat head-on attacks. Bill Cameron viewed the makeshift gun installations with some scepticism but they proved effective and the Luftwaffe soon learned the lesson they taught and reverted to conventional pursuit tactics.

Meanwhile, at Alconbury on 9 October 1942 the 93rd flew their maiden mission to 'the Fives-Lille steelworks in Belgium. This mission was also the first ever flown by Liberators from an English base and the first in which over a hundred heavy bombers participated. Crews remember Colonel Ted Timberlake's address at that first briefing. He said, 'I know you Joes can do it', and indeed it was up to the 93rd to 'do it' for the 44th would not fly its first mission until almost a month later. The briefing finished, Colonel Timberlake in *Teggie Ann* led twenty-four of the Liberators behind a bigger force of B-17s.

As the formation approached the French coast Lieutenant Janic, the bombardier aboard *Shoot Luke*,

reported over the intercom that the navigator had been taken ill and that to proceed could prove fatal. The pilot turned back. One of the Group's B-24s was lost over France and *Ball of Fire Junior* made the five-hour flight only to crash-land at another airfield on its return. In all only ten of the Group's Liberators bombed the target and the results were considered generally poor.

On 25 October 1942 the 330th Squadron was transferred to Holmsley South, Hampshire, for anti-submarine duties with R.A.F. Coastal Command over the Bay of Biscay. Similarly, the 409th operated from St Eval in Cornwall, and both Squadrons provided long-range convoy protection duties for the Operation Torch invasion fleet, scouring the Bay of Biscay for up to twelve hours at a time looking for elusive U-boats. Despite a handful of sightings no attacks were made but two Luftwaffe incursions were countered in November. The most memorable clash occurred on the 21st when Major Ramsay D. Potts of the 330th was faced with an onslaught of five Junkers JU-88s. Undaunted, the Liberator gunners, aided by the Germans' cumbersome approach, dispatched two and damaged a third. On another occasion the 409th participated in a fruitless search for a Fortress which had disappeared with

Liberators of the 44th Bombardment Group taxi from their muddy dispersals at Shipdham for one of the Eightballs early missions.
USAF

Brigadier-General Asa Duncan, the first Eighth Air Force Commanding General, aboard.

The two Squadrons returned to Alconbury in late November. Sandwiched between the 409th's arrival on the 26th and the 330th's on the 28th, the 329th Squadron was transferred to Hardwick, Norfolk, to operate in conjunction with the 44th. Until the Squadron's move to Norfolk, the 93rd had not suffered any further operational losses in its eight missions following the first to Lille. However an entire crew perished on 30 October when their Liberator crashed on an internal flight in Somerset. During November the Second Bombardment Wing, with its Headquarters at Old Catton, Norwich, was charged with training air units for eventual posting to North Africa. However it was soon selected to control all B-24 Groups and in early November it was announced that the 93rd would soon transfer to that Wing.

In November 1942 the very future of the Eighth was in jeopardy and even instructors doubted the crews' ability to bomb in daylight and survive against German opposition. The Americans had to convince the R.A.F. and themselves that daylight precision bombing was both practicable and effective. It fell to the 44th and 93rd, the only two Liberator Groups in England at that time, and four Fortress Groups, to prove that it was within their capability. If successful this nucleus would grow. On 7 November the Eightballs got their first opportunity to prove themselves when eight B-24s, each displaying the characteristic Eightball emblem, flew a diversionary sweep for Fortresses attacking positions at Cap de la Hague in Holland. The crews, having been in the penumbra of the 93rd and the Fortress Groups since their arrival in England, were pleased at last to have flown over enemy territory. Their introduction to combat would probably have been sooner had it not been for the unserviceability of some of their Liberators and the transfer of several machines to anti-submarine duties.

By now the 44th had gained enough strength and on 9 November it was given its first opportunity to bomb the enemy. Saint-Nazaire, at the mouth of the Loire in Brittany, the home of one of Germany's most notorious U-boat pens, was the target for a combined force of twelve B-24s drawn from both the 44th and the 93rd supplemented by a further thirty-five B-17s. The plan called for the entire force to fly in over the sea at 500 feet to avoid enemy radar and then to climb to heights ranging from 7,500 feet to 18,000 feet before turning on to the target. The B-17s suffered extensive flak damage and the 306th Group flying in trail, lost three aircraft. The B-24s were more fortunate. They bombed from 18,000 feet and came through intact although some crews reported instances of frostbite caused by lack of protective clothing. The problem was aggravated by the fact that crews often wore their flying-clothes some time before entering their aircraft causing moisture to form inside their uniforms before they took off. At altitude this moisture became ice and added to the inherent frostbite problem caused by icy blasts sucked through the open waist-window positions. Later electrically heated flying-suits solved the problem.

The intense flak over Saint-Nazaire succeeded in breaking up the formations which flew back across the sea in disarray. Debriefing confirmed that the Eighth could never again flaunt itself over such a heavily defended target at such a low altitude. The losses would have been higher had it not been for the Luftwaffe's inability after the attack to intercept and shoot down stragglers. Not unnaturally future missions to 'Flak City', as it became known, did not venture below four miles high and the truth of the motto 'the higher the fewer' was established.

Missions against the U-boat bases continued with attacks on Saint-Nazaire on 17 November and two missions to Lorient on the 18th and 22nd. *Shoot Luke* shrugged off three flak shells which exploded under the port wing almost turning the aircraft upside-down on the Saint-Nazaire mission of the 17th. On the homeward flight the formation was attacked by JU-88s for forty-five minutes. *Shoot Luke* dispatched one of the fighter-bombers which burst into flames and crashed into the sea.

On 27 November the 93rd's 329th Squadron transferred to Station 104, Hardwick, eleven miles south of Norwich, in order to evaluate the R.A.F.-inspired Gee navigational device. A special force, consisting of selected crews from all four Squadrons, was to test the device on behalf of the U.S.A.A.F., which at the time was considering various R.A.F. operational radar equipment for bombing in overcast skies. In October 1942 the Eighth had agreed to spare eight valuable Liberators to help in the work. Originally the 44th Group had been provisionally selected but the 93rd was finally chosen, a decision which increased tension between the two Groups. The 329th Squadron moved to Flixton airfield, just outside Bungay, after only a week at Hardwick. Flixton was still in the throes of development when the 329th arrived. Its task was one of an experimental nature involving 'intruder' or 'moling' flights over Germany in an attempt to disrupt working schedules in German factories by causing air-raid warnings to sound, upsetting civilian morale, and impairing industrial output.

The first intruder or 'moling' mission was undertaken on 2 January 1943 when four Gee-equipped B-24s took off for various parts of the Ruhr. Radio transmitters spaced at intervals throughout Great Britain beamed out given radio signals which were picked up by the Gee-carrying bombers. The time-lag between the signals received, after certain calculations, indicated the B-24s' exact position. Operating singly, because of the flight's experimental nature, the 329th lost the concentrated fire-power that formation flying afforded it. However diminishing cloud on this first 'moling' mission forced the Liberators to return to Flixton. Six more attempts were made, the last on 28 March 1943. The project was subsequently abandoned and the 329th supplemented the 44th on conventional missions after its secret equipment had been removed. The experience had been rewarding, however, and some crews later formed the nucleus of the U.S.A.A.F. Pathfinder units set up to perfect blind-bombing techniques.

While the 329th was engaged in 'moling' missions, General Ira Eaker telephoned Colonel Timberlake on 5 December 1942 ordering his Group to fly to North Africa on 7 December to participate in ten days of disruptive raids against Axis ports and shipping. On the morning of 6 December twenty-four Liberators belonging to the 328th, 330th, and 409th Squadrons took off from Alconbury for Portreath in Cornwall where they were refuelled for the long oversea flight to Oran. A few ground crews had been carried with them for this purpose while those that remained at Alconbury prepared to travel to Hardwick.

On the morning of 7 December the formation droned out over the sea and headed south. Crews stripped off their heavy combat clothes as they flew through bright sunny skies. The 328th and 409th Squadrons broke off and headed for Tafaroui airfield but the 330th experienced difficulties. Three Liberators deviated from their course heading and were fired upon by Spanish Moroccan coastal batteries. All three Squadrons had

rendezvoused successfully off the coast of North Africa and had waved to one another after descending from 10,000 feet. One 330th Liberator, however, crashed into a mountain south of Tafaroui and all aboard were killed.

At the Algerian airfield personnel of the United States Twelfth Air Force equipped with B-25 Mitchells and B-17 Fortresses were waiting to greet them. There were also infantrymen bivouacked around the surrounding countryside, which was anything but dry. In fact persistent rain had made taxiing impossible and the field was a sea of mud. To make matters worse the runways were too short and the base facilities non-existent. Three missions were mounted and subsequently abandoned. The 93rd came under the command of the embryonic Twelfth Air Force who wanted to use the Liberators at the first available opportunity. It ordered a mission to be flown on 12 December despite Colonel Timberlake's fears that take-off would prove dangerous in the prevailing conditions. His fears were realized when the first B-24 tried to take off only to finish up with its nose wheel embedded in the mud. The mission was subsequently cancelled. At midnight on 15 December 1942 the Travelling Circus headed eastward for Gambut Main, a dust-ridden escarpment in the Libyan desert. This was its home where it came under the command of the U.S. Ninth Air Force.

John H. Murphy, pilot of *Shoot Luke* wrote about some of the African missions: 'The middle of December we took off at midnight and flew east till dawn, at which time *Shoot Luke* had a change of diet, from mud to sand: we had arrived at our base in the Libyan desert. The field where we sat *Luke* down was a strip of desert the Jerries had just vacated. Christmas Eve found the crew of *Luke* gathered round a camp fire in the middle of the desert singing Christmas carols and drinking Canadian Club.

'On 31 December we bombed Sfax in what was one of the Group's most successful raids. Every bomb hit a vital military target and it was a good way to end up the old year. On the way home we listened to the B.B.C. and sang "Auld Lang Syne" with them.

'Dust-storms that lasted for three days set in and made life miserable for all concerned, even *Luke* looked strange with a coat of dust all over the inside and outside. (It's in this type of weather that the Liberator will continue to operate and the almighty Fortress will bog down and cause nothing but grief.) The wind at times would reach 45 to 50 miles per hour and several of the crew who went to bed in a hut woke up with just the stars for a roof.

'On 6 January while raiding Sousse *Luke* was hit by a piece of flak about the size of a cigar that passed harmlessly between the legs of one of the gunners. The man kept it as a souvenir. Aside from a few holes that did no real damage, we still continued to operate without injury. As was our custom while in the desert, we would go raiding one day, rest and do maintenance on the ships the next day, and then go out raiding the following day.

'On 7 January we went to Palermo, on *Luke*'s thirteenth mission, and climbed to altitude [over 22,000 feet] where it was minus 46 degrees Centigrade and stayed there for three and a half hours, at the end of which time we had to administer first aid to some of the men, the worst being our tail gunner who had nearly frozen to death in his turret. On our way home we managed to make some hot coffee on the heaters and this soon brought him round. The ship received no damage on this raid even though we were buzzed by some Italian fighters who broke off their attack before they came within shooting range of us. Despite the cold the ship functioned perfectly and the more we flew in it the better we liked it.

'Shortly after this *Luke* took the crew to a town on the Suez Canal for a much-needed bath. There were no facilities in the desert and not enough water anyway. We were rationed to one canteen of water a day! The only chance we "Desert Rats" had to get cleaned up was to fly over 500 miles to where people lived like human beings. While in Egypt all the crew bought souvenirs of every kind. These included a native puppy, which we naturally called "Luke", even if she was the only female on the crew.

'On our return to base we took *Shoot Luke* on a sightseeing tour. We flew around gazing at the Nile and over Cairo. We saw the Sphinx and the Pyramids and we took pictures that we shall always treasure. It was almost dark when we returned to base. After we had put *Luke* to bed the Jerries thought we might be lonesome and paid us a call, as a result of which we spent the greater part of the night in our slit trenches. The British night-fighter pilots shot down two of the six enemy planes that came over, which helped us a good deal.

'*Luke* next had a chance to see how tough the flak was over Tripoli and came out of that fine with no hits, no runs, and no errors. However the next time out we were not so lucky. This was on 19 January and the target was Sousse. Nothing much happened over the target but when, after dropping our bombs, we headed for home the fighters attacked and all Hell broke loose. One FW-190 got through the guns of our formation and managed to put a burst into *Luke*. Four 20 mm explosive cannon shells and half a dozen machine-gun bullets tore into *Luke*'s wings and fuselage. The cannon shells severed eight spars and made two ribs look like a piece of cheese cloth and blew the skin away from the spar and ribs underneath, destroying the air foil characteristics. One cannon shell lodged in the fuel cells and ignited them. Another cannon shell penetrated the control cabin and exploded, badly wounding two men and damaging the hydraulic system and radio. The badly damaged plane limped into Malta with one wing in very bad shape and three fuel cells smouldering: it was here we really appreciated the wonderful work done by Consolidated Aircraft Factory workers.

We landed and the Maltese immediately began hacking away at the wing in order to make a hole so that they could get inside the wing and put out the fire. The smouldering fuel cells were extinguished, the wounded taken to hospital, and the ship left till the morning. The preliminary diagnosis figured that it would take four days to repair *Luke* but a week later they were still tearing the wing apart and had not begun repairing. Finally all the ragged edges were cleaned up and rebuilding began. There were no power tools available so all the work had to be done by hand, including the cutting and riveting of over 3,000 rivets, not to mention the strengthening of the ribs and splicing of the spars. The crew of *Luke* helped as much as possible but the six Maltese that had been detailed for the job had to work twelve hours a day in order to complete their task. For a while we thought they would never quit tearing down and start building but eventually they did and on 5 February we were told that the next

day *Luke* would be once again ready to fly. On the original test flight we took about thirty people for a ride. On landing I was thanked by at least ten people I know I never said could come along.

'The afternoon of 6 February found *Luke* on the way to the Middle East with the wounded aboard and Malta fading into the distance. Within a week *Luke* was on the way to Naples where the crew again heard the harps calling. Until we were attacked by fighters we didn't realize that two gun turrets were frozen stiff. We were under attack for one hour and fifteen minutes and also extremely accurate flak was bursting around us continually for fifteen minutes. One fighter closed to within fifty feet of *Luke*'s tail and just sat there: the tail gunner trained his guns round but couldn't fire because the intense cold had frozen them, and the Italian pilot waved his hand in front of his nose. Finally the fighter pulled up and one of the other ships in our formation shot him down. (It was a constant source of argument with us as to just why this guy didn't shoot us down.)

'I know that this was one of the most nerve-racking times of my life and the other fellows all said they felt the same way. There were several times that day when I looked out and saw the sky red with tracers, and they weren't ours either; the Italians were sitting back and literally spraying our formation with bullets. When we got home we were amazed to discover that the total damage sustained by *Luke* was two tiny flak holes causing almost no damage.'

In late February the 93rd received orders for a return to England and on 22 February the Travelling Circus flew its twenty-third and final mission of the first African Liberator campaign. During its three-month stint in the desert the Group had flown missions in support of the First Army's advance on Tunis and others in support of the British Eighth Army, the 'Desert Rats'. Seven Liberators had been lost on missions, which were switched to Italian ports such as Palermo, Naples, Messina, and Cretone, after Rommel had been prised out of Tripoli. Lack of replacements, flight fatigue, and shortage of spare parts strained efficiency to the utmost. The desolate desert air bases, with their steel-meshed runways, were rife with dust which infiltrated the aircraft engines and the men's billets. Servicing of the Liberators was agony. Despite these adverse conditions the ground crews managed to have twelve bombers available for a mission every other day, weather permitting.

During the 93rd's absence, the 44th had suffered over the U-boat pens. At the time of the Saint-Nazaire missions some 44th Liberators, including *Little Beaver*, were still undergoing modifications in Northern Ireland. But by early December 1942 the 67th Squadron had received its full quota of B-24s. The 67th was the last Squadron at Shipdham to receive them.

In the days that followed the U-boat pen missions the Eightballs flew more practice missions. Late on 6 December the new aircraft made possible the first full Group mission; a diversionary raid for the Fortresses on the airfield at Abbeville-Drucat in Picardy. Crews had flown so many diversionary missions for the B-17s by now that they had painted ducks on their B-24s' fuselages, each representing a decoy mission. Nineteen Liberators, including *Little Beaver* flying her first mission, were dispatched but shortly after take-off things began to go wrong. *Little Beaver* lost an engine when the supercharger controls were over-advanced

Insignia of Little Beaver — *lost on the fateful Kiel raid of 14 May 1943.*   Cameron

A painting of the famous Eightball emblem discovered in the 14th Combat Bombardment Wing Headquarters building thirty-two years after the war.   Author

during their climb to altitude. When the throttle was pulled back to slow down in formation the superchargers rammed in too much air and the engines were starved of fuel. The other B-24s continued to the target as *Little Beaver* returned to base.

Nearing the French coast an abort signal was radioed to the Group after British radar tracked oncoming enemy aircraft. Unfortunately only the 66th and 67th Squadrons received the signal leaving six B-24s of the 68th Squadron to continue to the target alone. The small force bombed the airfield and was then bounced by thirty yellow-nosed FW-199s. This crack Luftwaffe fighter unit was dubbed the 'Abbeville Kids' by the R.A.F. This *force majeure* shot down Lieutenant Dubard's Liberator in flames and it crashed in the Channel. Five other Liberators all received hits. The other crews were saved by the Germans' overestimation of the Liberators' fire-power. They did not press home their attacks and losses were not as high as they might have been. *Little Beaver*'s supercharger failures would plague her crew for some time to come. Inexperience was the main problem, as Bill Cameron remembers:

'Fortresses had a larger wing area than the B-24s and were somewhat easier to fly in formation, especially at high altitude. Straight and level, as on a bomb run, both were good platforms, but in formation there was probably more jockeying of controls and throttles in the B-24s. We often had one pilot on the controls and the other on the throttles for this reason. We had problems to begin with on the superchargers because we made heavy corrections, pulling off power while flying formation to keep from overrunning the aircraft. However the superchargers continued to ram air into the closed carburettors and the engines would then cut out completely. We later overcame the problem to some extent by trying to fly using the supercharger controls rather than the throttles for such speed adjustments. This was difficult and not always successful.

'All this was necessary when the Group was flying a tight formation, but if the lead ship started evasive action, then we had problems. Later when we had power controls (usually referred to as the "formation stick") and the superchargers were changed from levers to rheostatic-type controls, these problems were eliminated. But they were real at the time and many aircraft turned back because their superchargers had been blown out trying to stay in formation. We were untrained in formation flying at high altitude until we arrived in England but with experience the problem was eventually solved after a few months.'

The Eightballs made an unsuccessful attempt to bomb Abbeville-Drucat on the 12th and eight days later twenty-one Liberators took off from Shipdham for a raid on Romilly-sur-Seine Air Park, south-east of Paris. Its sprawling hangars and marshalling yards offered an excellent target. Nine B-24s were forced to abort with troubles ranging from supercharger to oxygen and machine-gun failures. *Little Beaver* again experienced supercharger failure and was forced to abort after flying for three and three-quarter hours. Twelve Liberators continued to the target where Spitfires from a Polish R.A.F. squadron played a cat and mouse game with the Luftwaffe, boxing them in before shooting them down.

Lieutenant Clyde Price crossed the target on his bombing run but the bombs failed to release. No Liberators were lost over the Air Park but one crewman was killed and another two were wounded when their Liberator took a direct hit. This time it was the Fortresses, flying slower and below the Liberators, who soaked up all the punishment. Acrimony developed between the B-24 and B-17 crews who had to run the gauntlet of the Liberators' bombs descending on them. Strong headwinds on the homeward journey made it a long crawl for the bombers. The raid had achieved very

Original crew of Shoot Luke. *Left to right (back row) Ed Janic, Bombardier; John Murphy, Pilot; Frank Lown, Co-pilot; Arch Rantala, Navigator. Left to right (front row) James Cowan, Tunnel-gunner; Arville D. Sirmans, Engineer; Paul Slankard, Tail-gunner; William Mercer, Radio-operator; Floyd Mabee, Left waist-gunner; Mahlon Cressey, Right waist-gunner.*   Mabee

Eager Beaver of the 93rd being 'bombed up' shortly after arrival in England. USAF

little but crews were told later that the German officers' mess had been hit at dinner-time and there had been many casualties. Major Algene Key, Commanding Officer of the 66th Squadron, was awarded the Distinguished Service Cross for his leadership on the raid. Major Donald MacDonald treated his Squadron's malfunctions with scepticism and recriminations followed. The crew of *Little Beaver* were not credited with the mission because of their abort. Bill Cameron wrote: 'I began to realize that the price of a ticket back to the ZI might be pretty high.'

Because of the high rate of ammunition expended the 44th began carrying boxes of additional ammunition on the catwalk of the bomb bays. They had to wait two weeks before their adoption was complete. There then followed an unbroken series of scrubbed missions for the Group. Bad weather was a prime cause and morale began to slump. Over the next few months the 44th remained in the wings of the European theatre while Fortress units attacked in strength. Any aspirations the 44th had of doing the same were thwarted by requests for diversionary sweeps and then by attrition meted out by the Luftwaffe. Spares were slow getting through and the 67th Bomb Squadron felt the squeeze most in the coming weeks.

Christmas 1942 was the Eightballs' and the 93rd's first in England. In an attempt to integrate the English and American communities, General Eisenhower instructed all units where possible to have Christmas dinner in English homes. The 44th reciprocated with parties on the base.

On 3 January 1943 the target was again Saint-Nazaire. It was planned to overfly the Brest Peninsula on the outward trip and to return by a different route. To avoid recrossing France the 44th was to fly due south out over the Bay of Biscay and then swing wide right towards England. Mechanical failures, however, accounted for many Liberators returning to base early, leaving only eight B-24s to accompany the sixty-eight B-17s to the target. Visibility was unlimited so an unusually long bomb run was ordered. The run was

made into the wind, which was blowing a 115 m.p.h. gale above 20,000 feet, reducing the bombers' speed by more than half despite their flying with reduced fuel loads.

The Liberators, being some 20 m.p.h. faster than the Fortresses, started out behind the B-17s but by the time they had reached the target the Liberators had caught up with the Fortresses and were ready to bomb at a higher altitude.

For ten minutes the bombers flew almost straight and level and so the enemy had ample time to concentrate their guns on the formation. At this stage of the war the destruction of the U-boat pens came high on the list of Allied priorities because Britain was being starved of supplies by the intensification of German submarine warfare. The Germans, also realizing the importance of Saint-Nazaire, moved in more than seventy-five anti-aircraft guns, later increasing them to over a hundred. They put up a box barrage at the release-point thus forcing the Fortresses to fly through intense flak. It was on this mission that the Eighth Air Force abandoned individual bombing in favour of Group bombing. Each aircraft released its bombs simultaneously with the lead ship. This method, if the aim was true, could produce the concentration of bombs needed to destroy the twelve feet of concrete protecting the U-boats.

However, Colonel Robinson, seeing that the Fortresses were being decimated, was forced off the target and the eight Liberators headed out to sea jettisoning their bombs as they went. They made for home at a height of 200 feet above sea-level. The weather over the target had been clear but the return over the sea was made in thick fog. Crews could only see a few feet in front of them. When the Liberators neared the Brest Peninsula, however, it began to clear. Unfortunately the navigators' reports were ignored and later the Isles of Scilly were mistaken for Brest. Consequently the small formation flew farther and farther up the Irish Sea. It was only when the Irish coast and the very real threat of internment loomed before them that Colonel Robinson led the formation into a turn towards the Bristol

Channel. Fuel in the tanks, which had been reduced before take-off, was getting low and in any case had only allowed for landfall at Lizard Point. Crews, realizing that they had missed Land's End, searched for airfields in Wales. Not many were to be found in this part of Britain. Lieutenant John Long in *Texan* discovered Talbenny airfield only to have his last engine fail through fuel starvation just as he made his approach. Fortunately all the crew managed to escape from the Liberator, which was destroyed in the crash. Others were not so fortunate, including two Liberators which crashed into stone walls obscured by hedges. Three crewmen were killed and three were injured. The survivors flew into near-by airfields. *Little Beaver* eventually landed at Talbenny airfield, at the time occupied by a Czech squadron and remained there for five days, buffeted by snowstorms. Eventually all elements returned to Shipdham on 8 January. When the crews landed and climbed out of their B-24s they were met by a stranger. Colonel Leon Johnson had been sent by Eighth Air Force Headquarters to replace the well-liked and respected Colonel Robinson.

Bill Cameron recalls: 'The Saint-Nazaire débâcle was the official reason given for Colonel Robinson's dismissal. Eighth Air Force Headquarters blamed him for not ensuring that the aircraft had enough fuel for the mission. However some believed Headquarters used the incident to relieve Robinson of his command because he continually complained of the lack of sufficient replacements in the light of increasing losses. He could not always send out the Group on missions although ordered to do so by Headquarters because at the time the 44th was losing aircraft and crews faster than they could be replaced. Six months later Colonel Leon Johnson said much the same thing but by then the arguments were much better understood and he was respected for them rather than sacked.''

On 23 January six Liberators from the 44th accompanied forty-eight Fortresses to the U-boat pens at Lorient. Four bombers were shot down by German fighters employing head-on attacks for the first time, and one other bomber was lost to flak. By the end of the month casualties exceeded replacements with only twenty-four B-17 and B-24 crews arriving to replace sixty-seven lost on missions during January.

As a result of the Casablanca Conference in mid January 1943 Ira Eaker, who since November 1942 had been Acting Deputy Commanding General of the Eighth Air Force, decided that, because of the experience gained in bombing the U-boat pens, he was ready to attack Germany. The U-boat construction yards at Vegasack on the Weser had long been earmarked as a possible target although the R.A.F. had plastered the port throughout 1942. The Americans were to attempt to finish off the U-boat pens and the adjacent shipyards that had escaped destruction.

The raid on 27 January 1943 was intended to be a maximum effort. While the main spearhead of Fortresses attacked Vegasack itself the Liberators flew a diversionary raid on Wilhelmshaven, where an earlier photo reconnaissance had revealed the pocket battleship, the *Admiral Scheer* to be in dry-dock and also that considerable construction was being carried out to the docks themselves. The Liberators flew out over the North Sea in clear visibility which began to deteriorate when the German coast was reached. Crews soon realized

that bad weather conditions would prevent effective bombing. Guns and turret mechanisms failed as they froze solid and crews had to rub their oxygen-masks with salt to prevent them also freezing up in the intense cold. Camera shutters became clogged and windscreens were made opaque by rime. The Eightballs failed to locate their target, so crews bombed through cloud somewhere near the German-Dutch border. Navigation went uncorrected and the 44th continued out over Friesland. Unfortunately the Group met very heavy fighter opposition. Lieutenant Sullivan's B-24 was shot down and Lieutenant Cargyle's ship was destroyed in a mid-air collision when a FW-190 careered into it after being hit by machine-gun fire from another B-24. First Lieutenant Jim O'Brien barely made it home. His bombardier, Lieutenant Reg Grant and his assistant radio-operator, Staff Sergeant M. Deal had both been killed and his navigator, Second Lieutenant Leroy Perlowin, was severely wounded by a 20 mm shell which also slightly injured one of his gunners, Sergeant Guilford.

The Fortresses had better luck and were fêted by the Press for their part in the first American raid on Germany. The Eightballs received barely a mention. The newspapers neglected the Liberators that had borne the brunt of the Luftwaffe's attack allowing the Fortresses to slip through and drop their bombs. The 44th resented being used as bait while the Boeing boys captured the headlines. Conversely the B-17 crews were becoming positively hostile to the B-24s dropping their bombs through their formations as they had done over Romilly-sur-Seine and Saint-Nazaire.

February 1943 brought some respite when missions were cancelled through bad weather. The Liberators were out on the 2nd and 4th, however, with visits to Hamm. There were also some shallow penetration diversionary missions to aid the Fortresses. The 44th flew so many that it was scornfully referred to as the 'Second Bombardment Diversion'. Its mission on the afternoon of the 15th, another maximum effort, was to prove no exception. The B-24s were required to make a diversionary attack on Dunkirk. Their target was the *Tojo*, a surface raider disguised as a slow freighter.

The 67th Squadron, led by Major MacDonald, headed the formation. *Little Beaver* flew on his left wing in the number three position in the lead element. Just beneath them were three B-24s of the second element, with six more to the right and six more to the left. The formation crossed the Channel to Le Havre. MacDonald's navigator, Lieutenant 'Ben' Franklin, plotted a course to make the Germans believe that the Liberators were headed inland. However they changed direction and flew straight and level up the coast of France to Dunkirk where, three years before, the Royal Navy and an armada of small boats had rescued the British Expeditionary Force from its beaches.

But their long straight run had enabled the German gunners to determine their speed and height. From their high altitude the B-24s could release their bombs some distance out over the Channel and let their trajectory carry them in. Aboard MacDonald's Liberator the bombardier, Second Lieutenant Paul D. Caldwell, cried out 'target in view'. Arthur Cullen, the pilot, flew P. and I. for a few seconds, changing direction a few degrees right. Flak enveloped the formation and just as the bomb-release light came on at 15.40 hours, the B-24 took a direct hit.

B-24Ds of the 44th Bombardment Group bomb Dunkirk on 15 February 1943. They failed to hit the Tojo *which was berthed in the harbour.*
USAF

When Cullen had recovered from the shock the Liberator was in a dive with no other ships in sight. There was no roof on the cabin, just a windshield. The cowlings were blown off number two and three engines, which were smoking. He could not operate the rudder because his leg was broken. MacDonald, sitting in the co-pilot's seat, had a bad stomach gash but signalled to bale-out. For a few moments the noseless bomber flew on, only to fall away to starboard with the port inboard engine aflame and the right inboard ripped from its mounting. Finally the starboard wing fell off and a huge explosion scattered debris among the formation, hitting another Liberator whose pilot managed to recross the Channel and force-land at Sandwich. MacDonald baled out in extreme pain, Cullen helping him by pushing him through the hole where the roof had been. He then followed MacDonald, hitting the tailplane and breaking his arm and then breaking his leg a second time. MacDonald died later in a German hospital but Cullen was eventually repatriated in September 1944 after having broken his leg a third time. Lieutenant Oliphant's

B-24 was hit by flak, exploded, and was finished off by fighters. Despite all the Eightballs' endeavours the *Tojo* remained afloat.

The following day Howard Moore assumed command of the 67th Squadron and led them to Saint-Nazaire. Colonel Leon Johnson flew Group lead. Shortly after leaving the English coast, Lieutenant Fred Billings's Liberator, flying in front of Lieutenant Long's B-24, developed a fault and slowed down. Falling away to port it hit Long's port wing tip, and locked there. Both aircraft were engulfed in the ensuing fire and seconds after impact they exploded. Debris was scattered, some even reaching the Fortress formation flying below. Four men were amazingly thrown clear but Air-Sea Rescue, found no trace of them in the murky sea.

When the remaining Liberators arrived over the target it was shrouded by a smoke-screen. Over the target First Lieutenant 'George' Phillips lined up *Little Beaver* for a bomb run, but the bomb-bay doors refused to open. Lieutenant Bill 'Bus' Hill, the bombardier, leaped from the nose and scrambled into the bomb bay by way

Pistol Packin' Mama *lifts off from Shipdham. It was forced to land in Sweden on 9 April 1944 after sustaining damage on the Berlin - Marienburg mission.*   Robertie

of the radio compartment. The doors still remaining closed he decided to release the bombs anyhow. The bombs hit the doors with a splintering impact leaving jagged edges flapping beneath the bomber which threatened to break off and damage other B-24s. Bursts of flak jostled the B-24 and German fighters sparred for an opening. Phillips commenced to take violent evasive action. Tom Bartmess, the navigator, hunched over his tiny table in the nose, steadied himself against the bulkhead. Meanwhile, clinging precariously to the catwalk, Hill realized that the flapping doors must somehow be tethered and as the gunners opened up on the German fighters he went to work with pieces of wire. For a time Hill hung in the bomb bay, some 20,000 feet above the earth. The remnants of the doors were eventually secured in what must have been the highest trapeze act of the war.

On the homeward journey the formation escaped virtually unscathed although they suffered further attacks by the Luftwaffe. Despite the intense flak over the target the Eightballs managed to hit the dock areas. The raid was notable in that it was the first occasion in which the Eighth Air Force had bombed the enemy on two successive days and the Liberators' effectiveness was noted.

The 44th's continuing losses had increased doubts in certain circles as to the value of the Liberator in the E.T.O. The Group itself and its ability to continue operations also lay in the balance. Lack of adequate numbers was a prime consideration and could be largely attributed to maintenance and replacement problems. The B-17 crews, however, saw the Liberators in a completely different light, claiming with some justification that with them along the Luftwaffe had completely forsaken the Fortresses.

However, the number of Liberators was about to be increased by the return of the Travelling Circus.

Some of the crew of Little Beaver. *Back row left to right: Mike Denny, Engineer; George Price, Radio-operator; Unknown; Dale Glaubitz; Charles Forehand; Bill Cameron, Co-pilot. Bottom row: Ed Phillips; Tom Bartsmess, Navigator; 'George' Phillips, Pilot; and Jim DeVinney, Bombardier.*
                                                                    Cameron

Chapter Two

Kiel

On the night of 25 February 1943 the 93rd took off from Gambut and headed back to England. Only Major K. K. Compton, the Group's Operational Officer, remained behind. He was promoted to full Colonel and assumed command of the Ninth Air Force's 376th Bombardment Group based in Egypt. Most of the crews were not sorry to leave because their original ten-day detachment had extended to almost three months. The homeward flight was marred by the loss of the eighth Liberator of the campaign.

The men of the 93rd went to Hardwick — their new base — to be greeted by a blaze of publicity, their African exploits having preceded them. Soon the bronzed veterans were exchanging experiences with the 329th Squadron which had flown into Hardwick during early March. Preparations for a return to the air war over Europe began almost at once and combat-worn and dusty Liberators were overhauled while their crews took seven days' leave.

Meanwhile, the 44th were battling with the Luftwaffe and the elements over Europe. On 26 February the Eightballs flew to Wilhelmshaven where they encountered fierce opposition. The ubiquitous ME-109s ventured so close that crews could not only easily see the pilots but could count the number of guns and gauge their calibre. Aboard one of the two B-24s lost on the raid was Robert B. Post, a *New York Times* reporter. He was the only one of seven journalists — the writing 69th — who chose to fly with the 44th on that mission. Those who flew with the Fortresses returned safely.

On 4 March Colonel Leon Johnson, flying in First Lieutenant Jim O'Brien's B-24, led the 44th to Brest. Four days later sixteen B-24s from the 44th were dispatched to the marshalling yards at Rouen in northern France. This was a diversionary mission to aid Fortresses attacking Rennes. Several squadrons of R.A.F. Spitfires and, for the first time, the 4th Fighter Group's P-47 Thunderbolts, flew interdiction strikes against airfields ahead of the bombers.

Bob Bishop recalls that 'The sky was like a black cloud of fighters.' Unfortunately, unknown to the bomber crews, the American fighters had encountered heavy opposition, leaving the B-24s to fend for themselves. However some Liberators had their own problems. First Lieutenant Jim O'Brien had started out leading the Group with Lieutenant-Colonel Posey, the future 44th Commanding Officer, aboard. But one of the gunners, Sergeant Husseltine, had passed out through lack of oxygen and the B-24 was forced to return to base. Captain Clyde E. Price took over the Group lead and First Lieutenant Bob W. Blaine the deputy lead. With their fighter cover gone the 44th was exposed to a Gruppe of FW-190s which attacked the fifteen Liberators from head on. At first the American crews took them for Thunderbolts because of the similarity in radial engines. All too late they realized their mistake and Captain Price's ship and Lieutenant Blaine's went down immediately. There were no survivors from Price's ship and only two from Blaine's. Price's ship crashed in flames with the bombs still in their racks. Both aircraft were from the ill-fated 67th Squadron, now reduced to only three original crews and aircraft. (Jackson Hall had been grounded for medical reasons leaving only the crews of *Suzy Q*, *Little Beaver*, and that of 'Bucky' Warne's of the original nine crews.) The Spitfire escort finally showed up in time to prevent further losses. Even so, two B-24s barely made it back to England.

The 93rd's period of inactivity on its return to Norfolk was brief, and on 12 and 13 March some crews joined with the Eightballs on two diversionary missions to aid the Fortresses. Although the return of the 93rd met with some disfavour among the Eightballs, most would have been quick to admit that its inclusion strengthened the Liberators' cause in the E.T.O. On 18 March the Liberators struck at Vegasack in Germany. Leading the 44th on that day was the 67th Squadron, led by Major Moore in *Suzy Q*. Over the target his gunners claimed six enemy fighters. It was a running fight throughout but, while the 44th encountered heavy opposition, the only B-24 shot down belonged to the 93rd. Lieutenant John H. Murphy flew *Shoot Luke* out of Hardwick with Lieutenant George Black in the co-pilot's seat. (Lieutenant Frank Lown now commanded his own B-24.) Their trip was uneventful until the formation, flying 2,000 feet below the Fortresses, reached their bombing altitude fifty miles from the German coast. For almost one and three-quarter hours the Liberators came under constant fighter attack. However the run into the target was good and the bombing successful.

On the return leg the Luftwaffe stepped up its attacks, sometimes with as many as thirty fighters taking part. They engaged the nine-ship element of the 93rd and succeeded in hitting Frank Lown's number four engine and blowing a hole in his vertical stabilizer. Next it was the turn of the twin-engined ME-110s and JU-88s. Their attacks were more nerve-racking, taking longer to complete and break away. Just as the B-24 crews thought themselves safe, the German pilots would skid their fighters and fire longer bursts. When, at last, the German fighters broke off their attacks, the crew of *Shoot Luke* saw Frank Lown's engine beginning to smoke and vibrate badly. The B-24 dropped from formation and Lieutenant Murphy and his crew decided to help Lown home. *Shoot Luke* broke formation and took up position off the stricken Liberator's wing. Unfortunately

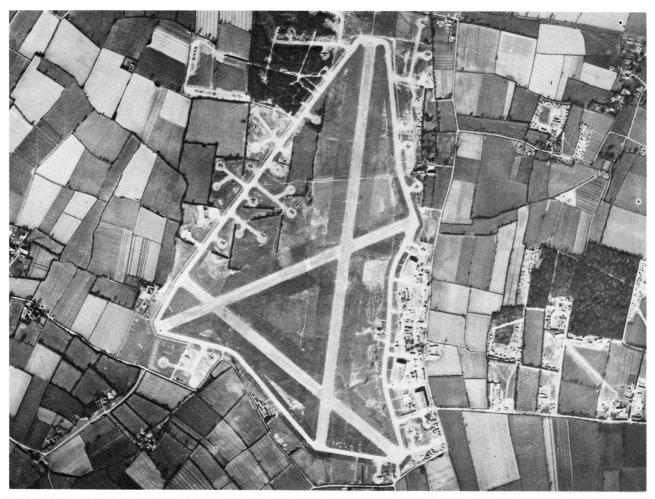

Hardwick airfield, showing (top left) *Spring Wood and bomb dump,* (top right) *Topcroft village* (bottom right) *Bush Wood and living sites and* (bottom left) *Shelton Common. Living accommodation centred around Topcroft while the MT section lay to the bottom left of Bush Wood. Above it more living accommodation and to its right the communal sites. Station Headquarters is to the right of the two hangars.*   IWM

the stragglers attracted the attention of a lone FW-190. Its pilot surveyed the situation and made his attack from nine o'clock with his four machine-guns and cannon blazing. Three bullets missed Frank Lown's head by less than eighteen inches.

Shortly afterwards *Shoot Luke* bucked with a sudden explosion in the rear section. Although hit in the eye by fragments, Staff Sergeant Floyd H. Mabee in the waist remained at his gun and succeeded in shooting down the fighter. Staff Sergeant Paul B. Slankard, the tail gunner, was blasted through the top of his turret by a direct hit from a 20 mm shell. Slankard flew for interminable minutes at 22,500 feet with the upper part of his body protruding from his turret. His left foot, which had caught in the gun controls, was all that had prevented him from being shot, projectile fashion, through the turret roof.

Floyd Mabee made his way to the bomber's tail, pulled Slankard back into the aircraft, and applied an oxygen-mask to his face. Lieutenant Edmund J. Janic, the bombardier, crawled to the rear of the ship despite severe head wounds and applied sulphonamide to Slankard's wound. Janic and Mabee together dragged the severely wounded tail gunner to a hole in the fuselage where the frigid air entering the plane at a temperature of some 45 degrees below zero sealed the wound. The hypodermic needles had frozen and no amount of warming in the crew's mouths could thaw them enough

to enable drugs to be administered. Slankard remained in his precarious position for two and three-quarter hours while Mabee massaged his hands to maintain circulation. Lieutenant Janic returned to the flight deck and collapsed through loss of blood and shock. Lieutenant Arch Rantala, the navigator, successfully navigated the two bombers home. Frank Lown landed and thanked Murphy's crew, which completely filled an ambulance, for saving him and his crew from certain destruction. Paul B. Slankard, who had made medical history, eventually recovered from his terrible wounds.

This had been the largest B-24 force hitherto dispatched. On 22 March the two Groups merged for another raid on Germany, this time on Wilhelmshaven. First Lieutenant Jim O'Brien and Major Francis McDuff, the 68th Squadron Commander, led the Eightballs in *Rugged Buggy* behind five B-24s from the 93rd. Jim O'Brien described the mission as 'hot as my first' and later counted twenty-nine separate holes in *Rugged Buggy*. Despite a thorough going over by ME-110s and FW-190s, it was flak rather than fighters which claimed the sixth original 67th Squadron crew. Captain Gideon W. 'Bucky' Warne's Liberator and a 506th Squadron replacement ship both went down. Lieutenant Robert Walker was the sole survivor from the two B-24s. This left *Little Beaver* and *Suzy Q* as the only remaining original Liberators in the Squadron. Colonel Ted Timberlake, who was leading the 93rd in *Teggie Ann*, narrowly escaped

Lord Trenchard. 'Father of the R.A.F.', inspects a 93rd B-24D at Hardwick. In the background is Colonel Ted Timberlake. USAF

death when a 20 mm shell entered the cockpit and missed him by only a few inches.

Four days later Colonel Ted Timberlake assumed command of the 201st Provisional Combat Bombardment Wing. The 44th and 93rd were later joined by the 389th Bombardment Group in June 1943 and the Second Bombardment Wing was reorganized into provisional Combat Wings. Meanwhile Lieutenant-Colonel Addision T. Baker had assumed command of the Travelling Circus on 17 May 1943.

Shoot Luke with a patched-up crew was out in the lead again on 31 March on a mission to Rotterdam and again on 5 April to Antwerp. The 93rd had flown a diversionary mission on the 4th but the mission to Brest on the 6th was one of the worst Murphy's crew ever experienced. Frank Lown was shot down over the target and *Shoot Luke* was hit by a 20 mm shell which missed the tail gunner by a few inches. Almost a month later a postcard from Lown arrived at Hardwick via the Red Cross — he was a prisoner of war in Germany.

During April 1943 some important visitors arrived in Norfolk. Lord Trenchard, the 'Father of the Royal Air Force', visited Station 104 on 6 April and personally congratulated the air crews. Lieutenant-General Frank Maxwell Andrews, Commanding General of the E.T.O., visited Hardwick on 27 April. One week later, on 4 May, General Andrews was killed along with the first crew at Hardwick to complete its tour. Lieutenant Shannon and his crew in *Hot Stuff* crashed into a bleak Icelandic mountain on their way home to America. Only Sergeant George Eisel, the tail gunner, who had escaped two similar disasters, survived after being trapped in the wreckage for fourteen hours. Andrews Field in Essex was named in honour of the late Commanding General on 17 May 1943.

Apart from such important visitors, several new crews arrived in England during April 1943. Among those who arrived at Shipdham was Lieutenant Horace Austin and the men of *Southern Comfort*. This crew was assigned to the Group's 506th Squadron which had only been formed in March. Like most American bombers this brand-new B-24 was decorated with artwork on its

Lieutenant-General Frank M. Andrews (centre), with Brigadier-General James P. Hodges (second from right) and Colonel Timberlake (far right), inspect the crew of Shoot Luke. Left to right: *John Murphy, Pilot; George Black, Co-pilot; Arch Rantala, Navigator; Ed Janic, Bombardier; Floyd Mabee, Engineer top turret-gunner; William Mercer, Radio-operator; James Cowan, Left waist-gunner; Mablon Cressey, Right waist-gunner; Adam Hastack, Tail-gunner; George Foster, Tunnel-gunner.*
Mabee

B-24Ds of 93rd Bombardment Group. Nearest aircraft is Joisey Bounce (41-124228).   USAF

nose. At first the design presented a problem because the crew's favourite drink, Southern Comfort, was mixed with other ingredients and the name given to it was 'cesspool'. 'No artist could be found who could paint such a design,' recalls Joe Warth, the aircraft's twenty-year-old tail gunner, 'so we came up with "Southern Comfort", the prime ingredient of our drink. A fellow in the 506th, talented at drawing the female body in various attitudes and dress, was found. Thus a bomber dedicated to a brand of liquor and not to any girl or place was born.'

In addition to the regular bombing sorties, in March and April 1943 the 44th flew some night-training missions over England for possible night-bombing assignments with the R.A.F. Several B-24s were also seconded to R.A.F. Coastal Command for raids on German shipping and naval forces. At Shipdham twelve new Liberators were forthcoming but there were no trained men available to fly them. Crews had to be begged and borrowed from the R.A.F. while others came from Fortress Groups. Lieutenant Roach became the 67th's first replacement to arrive direct from the States. Group Staff decided that the surviving co-pilots had acquired sufficient combat experience and they were promoted to become first pilots. Bill Cameron was among those who soloed. His crew was made up of

Major James E. O'Brien, Commanding Officer, 68th Bomb Squadron of the 44th Bombardment Group at Shipdham in April—May 1943. Major O'Brien was shot down on the Kiel raid and made a prisoner of war.   O'Brien

R.A.F. transferees and five members of *Little Beaver*'s ground crew. They were sent to gunnery school for two weeks. When they returned they found Bill Dabney and Tom Clifford had joined the crew from the R.A.F. The former as co-pilot and the latter as navigator. Gola Gibby and Roy Winters became the flight engineers while Gerald 'Sparky' Sparks, a 'reject' from a B-17 unit, became the radio-operator. His guitar-playing became a real morale-booster to the crew. 'Gentleman' Jim DeVinney was the last to join the green crew, as bombardier. Before the new crew became operational they took a three-day leave. Howard Moore went with them to London. While Cameron and his crew were in London, Jim O'Brien returned to Shipdham, on 13 May 1943. He had previously been on detachment with R.A.F. Coastal Command 300 miles out in the North Sea with feathered engine shadowing German shipping. O'Brien's arrival coincided with Major Francis McDuff, the Commanding Officer of 68th Squadron, being rotated home.

It was a hectic homecoming for O'Brien. He recalls: 'On return from this flight I found that I had been appointed Squadron Commander of the 68th. Somehow date of rank had come through with new responsibilities.

Major James E. O'Brien's Rugged Buggy (B-24D-5-CO; 41-123819)   O'Brien

(I received orders on 6 May dated 29 April that I had been promoted to Major.) My only squadron experience other than flying had been some additional duty as Engineering Officer back at Barkesdale Field. I had no sooner found out what a squadron commander was supposed to do when word came on the calm night of 13 May recalling all the Group crews for a maximum effort on the French port of Bordeaux, entailing a long oversea flight, a short quick climb to drop bombs on U-boat pens, and then out. Other than the hurry to install bomb-bay tanks, this didn't seem to be too much of an order. However, at 02.00 hours the field order changed to remove bomb-bay tanks and load up with 4,000 pounds of new-type incendiary clusters for Kiel in Germany. The obvious question was, "What good would incendiaries do at Kiel?" The explanation given at the briefing on the following morning at 05.00 hours was that the B-17s were going to bomb the hell out of the U-boat pens, aircraft factories, and seaport facilities and the B-24s were to kindle the fires. It was all very logical but it was a long trip without fighter escort.'

Following the change in orders, Major O'Brien cancelled the recall of Lieutenant Cramer and Lieutenant Phillips that had been put out earlier. It was decided that

The B-17 Groups at last got their wish — they flew behind and above the B-24s for the first time in the E.T.O. This resulted in heavy losses for the Liberators. USAF

the 68th Squadron could put up six B-24s without calling upon either of them provided that the Major flew with his usual co-pilot, 'Mac' Howell, to check him out as first pilot for combat flying. 'The morning of Monday, 14 May, arrived (like most others) with the night orderly banging on my door and shouting "Mission briefing at 05.00." I had only got to sleep at 04.00! After the ground crews under Captain Landrum and the armament crews under Lieutenant Thompson had worked all night taking out the bomb-bay tanks from the racks and re-loading them with 1,000-pounders, we were briefed and ready for take-off about 09.00. The 44th was putting up twenty-four ships for the mission. I showed up at the briefing not so much as the squadron commander but as co-pilot of the *Rugged Buggy* in a Tail-end Charlie slot. What a glorious way to go!'

Meanwhile, Bill Cameron and his crew arriving in Norwich at about four o'clock in the morning of 14 May met an airman trying to get back to Shipdham. He had word that the Group was to fly a mission that day. Cameron and his crew, plus Major Moore, hired a taxi and were back at the base within an hour. They were in time for the briefing but just too late to take part in the raid on Kiel. Lieutenant Westbrook became first pilot on a new Liberator, *Q for Queenie*, and Lieutenant Robert Brown, *Suzy Q*'s normal pilot, filled in as co-pilot. *Suzy Q* was undergoing maintenance in Northern Ireland. Bob Bishop, the navigator plus seven others, all

from the *Suzy Q* completed the scratch crew of *Q for Queenie*, which was to fly at the very tail of the formation. Lieutenant Roach flew with the only replacement crew while 'George' Phillips flew *Little Beaver*. In the circumstances it was decided to leave the line-up unchanged. In all, the 44th would put up nineteen aircraft but the 93rd could not supplement it because of damage and maintenance problems.

On previous missions the Liberators had bombed through the Fortress formations. However, High Command decreed that on the Kiel mission the Liberators would have to reduce their speed and fly behind the B-17s. Colonel Leon Johnson and First Lieutenant Bob Bishop were up most of the night planning the mission. It was mooted that if the B-24s tried to slow down to the speed of the Fortresses 'they would drop out of the sky'. The B-24D's cruising speed was 180 to 185 indicated airspeed while the B-17s cruised at 160 m.p.h.

Jim O'Brien wrote, 'I shall always remember rolling down the taxi strip behind Lieutenant George R. Jansen's *Margaret Ann*. I thought, too, about Howard Moore's remark at the briefing, "I wouldn't go on this mission if I were you." '

After assembly the 44th headed out over Cromer as the low formation at 21,000 feet. They rendezvoused some fifty miles off Cromer with a hundred plus B-17s stacked upwards to 32,000 feet. The B-24s cruised at 180 m.p.h. but they had to continuously zigzag twenty

Ground crews and those too late to go on the Kiel raid peer skyward waiting for the survivors to return. Major Moore is in the foreground wearing sunglasses. He sat in on the briefing but was too late to go on the raid. Cameron

miles in one direction and forty miles in the other in order to remain behind the Fortresses. The B-24s were briefed to go over Kiel at 21,000 feet but their constant zigzagging brought them over Heligoland Bay at 18,000 feet and down to 160 m.p.h. — almost stalling speed.

The Eightballs were to have avoided the Friesian Islands but the constant zigzagging had caused them to veer off course and they crossed them at 19,000 feet and were met with sporadic bursts of flak. Major O'Brien observed flames emanating from the bomb bay of the B Flight leader of 68th Squadron, piloted by

Original crew of the Suzy Q *with friends. Back row, left to right:* Millhouse, Ullrich, Wanadtke, Bishop, Susan, Collie. *Bottom row, left to right:* Unknown, DeVinney, Brown, Moore, Klingler. *Lieutenants Brown and Bishop were shot down over Kiel and made prisoners of war. Roy Klingler the tail-gunner was killed.* Cameron

Tom Holmes. The 66th Squadron flew lead, flanked by the 68th Squadron on its left and the 67th on its right and to the rear. Four B-24s of the 506th were flying their first mission in a diamond position. Tom Holmes managed to maintain height and cross the North Sea again to England. The flak had also hit the *Rugged Buggy*. OBrien recalls: 'All of a sudden our ship was rocked by two explosions. A real indication of trouble was the manifold pressure on the two left engines which dropped to 15 p.s.i. and there was a sudden drag to the left which Howell and I struggled to correct. I thought about feathering the two left engines but that would have been an invitation to the German fighters who were waiting to come in for the kill.'

Unknown to Major O'Brien flak had also blown a hole in the tail, knocking Sergeant Castillo out of his turret and amputating his foot. Three crew members in the tail came to his aid and quickly realizing his plight pushed him out of the plane, pulling the ripcord of his parachute for him, and then they too baled out. One of the three, Sergeant Van Owen, was drowned in Kiel Bay despite wearing a Mae West. Jim O'Brien lost communication with the five men in the rear of his ship and continued to the target.

The 44th's cargo of incendiaries required a shorter trajectory and a longer bomb run than the B-17s'. Flying a scattered formation the Liberators were exposed to fighter attack. Five Liberators were shot down before they had time to release their bombs. Three of these belonged to the 67th Squadron which brought up the rear of the formation. The first to go down was Lieutenant Roach and his replacement crew. There was only one survivor. Lieutenant Westbrook's Liberator had all four engines shot out over the target and went into a

First Lieutenant Bill Cameron (left) and Major Howard Moore (right) walk sadly away knowing that their crews had been lost over Kiel. Phillips' Little Beaver was lost and Moore's usual crew had gone down in a replacement B-24. Behind them is Victory Ship, (41-123813).
Cameron

flat spin. Mulhausen, the engineer, and Roy Klingler, the tail gunner, were both killed. Bob Bishop was in the nose with the bombardier, Second Lieutenant Holden R. Hayward. Bishop spotted a fighter boring in and shouted at Hayward to duck, but he did not hear him and was struck in the face by fragments and Bishop had the paint stripped from his steel helmet by the blast. The survivors proceeded to bale out. The time was just one o'clock. Westbrook picked up a parachute and baled out. Brown searched the aircraft for a parachute and he also baled out. Bishop, meanwhile, had made his way to the nose-wheel bay where he looked out and saw a 'red carpet of tracer'. He paused for a moment until the German fighter ceased firing and then jumped. (Bishop knew the German pilot could not fire for long without his guns

seizing up.) Feet up and head down in case the German should open fire on him Bishop folded his arms into 'wings' thinking it would aid his descent, but the reverse happened and he tumbled. Quickly reverting to his former position he groped for the ripcord and was horrified to discover it was not there! In his haste to leave the stricken Liberator Bishop had put his R.A.F. chest parachute on upside-down! However he located and pulled the ripcord after free falling to about 5,000 feet to avoid being fired upon by German fighters. 'It was like standing on a motor bike doing 120 miles an hour, when suddenly a little handkerchief came out. I thought it was rather small for a parachute: then the big parachute opened out and reduced my speed to practically nil in a split second.' His flying-boots went

Shipdham airfield taken later in the war and showing the technical site and in foreground, the control tower.
Robertie

93rd combat crews at mess at Hardwick. Because of the specialized diets they messed separately from the remainder of the base.   USAF

spinning off. Bishop decided to inflate his Mae West before he hit the water — a dangerous manoeuvre as the sudden force could have broken his ribs. Nevertheless he hit the water safely and was hauled aboard a Danish trawler where he collapsed on top of a bundle on the deck. The Danes shouted and gesticulated and he found he was sitting on a wounded German fighter pilot who had been shot down in the same raid!

The Liberators proceeded to the target despite the losses but not without a good many hazards befalling Major O'Brien and the others. Jim O'Brien continues: 'The 44th let go their cluster of matchstick incendiaries but they only held together for about 200 feet before they broke up. As soon as they hit the slipstream they were all over the sky in a negative trajectory and added to the confusion by passing back through the formation and bouncing off wings and propellers. The formation aided the German defences by scattering. We became separated from the Group after leaving the target. I noticed at least two other stragglers off to the right: one was Captain Jack Oliphant from the 67th Squadron and the other was Captain "Swede" Swanson of the 506th. We were all in the bad company of German single-engined fighters. "Mac" McCabe in the top turret repeatedly yelled through his oxygen-mask to dip the wing so that he could hit them with a few 0.50s. Howell and I were concerned only in keeping the ship flying for we were practically stationary in a hundred mile an hour headwind on a 285 degree heading and still overflying Germany.

'The German fighters opened up with a steady flow of cannon and 0.30 calibre fire. I heard several 0.30s zing into the cockpit and bounce off the armour-plated seats. The cockpit smelled of gasoline and incendiary bullets quickly ignited the fumes and started a roaring furnace in the bomb bay. I leaped from my seat and pulled the hatch in front of the top turret. However the slipstream blew off my steel helmet (worn before the introduction of flak helmets) so I decided to try another exit. Ralph Ernst, the radio-operator, desperately kicked the bomb-bay door open through the dense smoke and flame. In the rush I mistakenly snapped on a life-raft dinghy. I threw it aside and found my snap-on R.A.F.-type chest pack and jumped. Above me I saw another chute with one nylon panel torn open from top to bottom but could not determine whose it was. On the ground I found seven crew members, including Castillo,

who was lying on a stretcher. "Mac" Howell must have been using the torn chute because he did not show up. The first indication I had that he was dead was when a German medic inquired, "Do you know a little man in a yellow suit — he is dead." I thought he was bluffing to induce me to talk carelessly during my interrogation but it turned out to be true.'

The third 67th Squadron Liberator and the sixth lost over all was *Little Beaver*. 'George' Phillips was killed in one of three explosions which rocked the B-24 after leaving the target. Mike Denny, the engineer, could not get the bomb-bay door open and was forced to crawl right through the bomb bay and escape by way of the rear hatch. He last saw Phillips and his co-pilot standing on the flight deck. William 'Bus' Hill, the bombardier, and Second Lieutenant Tom Bartmess, the navigator, both baled out. Unfortunately Bartmess was drowned in Kiel Bay before he could be rescued. Of the nineteen Liberators only thirteen returned. Major Moore's *Suzy Q* was now the sole survivor of the original 67th Squadron.

Major O'Brien and the surviving members of his crew joined up with the other shot-down crews rounded up by the Germans. Bishop was landed from the Danish trawler and he and Jim O'Brien were sent to prisoner of war camps. In their absence the Eightballs were awarded the Distinguished Unit Citation for their part in the Kiel raid, the first such award made to an Eighth Air Force Group. After the Kiel raid there was serious talk of sending home all flying men who had completed fifteen missions. However their experience was considered vital and they remained on active service.

On 16 May all available Liberators at Shipdham and Hardwick were secretly flown to Davidstowe Moor in the West Country. At 09.00 hours the following day Colonel Johnson, General Hodges, and the crew of the

Bill Cameron poses in front of his new B-24, Buzzin' Bear.
Cameron

Shoot Luke *being prepared for another mission. Note the flame dampers on the rear turret guns and the white/red bomb release warning light mounting underneath. The white light came on when the bomb doors were fully opened and the red during the bomb release period.* USAF

revamped *Suzy Q* led twenty-one B-24s of the 44th to the port of Bordeaux. Bill Cameron was flying his new B-24 called *Buzzin' Bear*. This was a compromise between Golden Bear (after the State of California) and Buzzin' because the Eightballs were to train for low-level or 'buzzing'.

The Eightballs formed up over Land's End at 2,500 feet and rendezvoused with eighteen Liberators of the 93rd. Together they flew a 700 mile arc over the Atlantic to minimize the chances of enemy detection. Four of the Liberators were forced to abort with mechanical troubles. Despite her four new Twin Wasps, *Suzy Q* began to lose speed and the formation lagged behind schedule. *Suzy Q* had one engine stopped when the formation started climbing to bombing altitude. To counteract the fall behind in schedule, Ed Mikolowski, the lead navigator, skilfully prepared a new course bypassing the original curved route.

Mikolowski's alternative course brought the Liberator formation to the Bay of Biscay almost on schedule and over Bordeaux at 12.28 hours. The city had hitherto been left untouched by the Eighth Air Force and those manning the German defences had become complacent. Only thirty to forty barrage balloons had been positioned over the concrete U-boat pens on the tideless Gironde Estuary to prevent a low-level attack. But these did not deter the two Liberator Groups who, operating independently of the B-17s, bombed from 22,000 feet. This time it was the Fortresses who were acting as decoys

and they attacked Lorient. The flak over Bordeaux was light and the fighter opposition ineffectual. Only one German pilot was reported to have pressed home his attack and he went down trailing smoke after several gunners opened up on him from 300 yards.

'Gentleman' Jim DeVinney, the lead bombardier, toggled his bomb release and the other bombardiers followed suit. Hits were observed on the lock gates at Basin Number One, which collapsed and was flooded by a deluge of water from a near-by river. Direct hits were observed on the Matford aero-engine factory and the railway yards and chemical works were also hit. Six hours later a photo-reconnaissance aircraft brought back pictures of the raid revealing that the 480-yard-long pier and two U-boats, which had been in the port during the attack, had vanished. The Liberator crews were jubilant, attributing much of their success to the fact that they had not had to fly behind the slower Fortresses. Spirits ran high and the effective use of the Liberators as a separate bombing force did not go unnoticed.

The Americans could even lapse their jamming of German-controlled radio. The only casualties during the attack were two crewmen slightly wounded and a waist gunner who was sucked out of an open window after his parachute had accidentally opened. He was thrown against the tailplane and pitched into the sea with his parachute in shreds. One Liberator was forced to seek neutral territory after developing engine trouble shortly before the attack.

Crew of Shoot Luke *dress for a three day pass.* Left to right: *Floyd Mabee, Mahlon Cressey, Adam Hastak, William Mercer, James Cowan, George Foster and 'Luke' the dog. Note the spartan living quarters and the ubiquitous pot-bellied stove.*

Mabee

Wing Liberators had suffered so drastically that because of this and the 93rd's 329th Squadron's experience in blind bombing, the Hardwick outfit was selected for night operations. The 93rd was withdrawn from daylight operations during May and its B-24s modified for a night-flying role. Exhaust dampers had to be fitted to the B-24s when it was discovered the exhaust flames were visible at night, but these only restricted the bombers' speed. This and further modifications meant that the Liberators could not be flown equally by day and by night because their retarded performance made them particularly vulnerable during daylight hours. This transfer to night operations meant that the Eighth had temporarily reversed the policy of daylight bombing, as the R.A.F. had predicted it would. Albeit this was a token measure for the B-17s continued to fly daylight operations. However the lesson had been learned: the

Americans could not flaunt themselves over Europe without adequate fighter escort — on their own the bombers were no match for the Luftwaffe.

The 93rd's abandonment of daylight bombing left the 44th as the only remaining Liberator unit in the Eighth Air Force, but the latter's disastrous mission to Kiel resulted in some 93rd Liberators returning to their daylight role to replace those lost from the 44th after their night-flying equipment had been removed.

The Eightballs and the Travelling Circus flew one more mission, on 29 May, to the U-boat pens at La Pallice, before being taken off operations. They were not, as the Fortress boys thought, being stood down permanently, but were being switched to low-level training flights. They were soon joined by a third B-24 Group which had only been formed five months previously.

Chapter Three

Ploesti – Prelude and Aftermath

The 389th Heavy Bombardment Group, the third B-24 Group to join the Second Bombardment Division, was activated at Davis-Monthan Field, Arizona, on Christmas Eve 1942. It was originally designated the 385th on 30 November and placed under the command of Major (later Colonel) David B. Lancaster jun. However it became the 389th on 1 February 1943 when the Group began receiving a cadre at Biggs Field, Texas. Final training was carried out at Lowery Field, Colorado, between mid April and early June that year and on the 13th the ground echelon began departing for Camp Kilmer, New Jersey. It embarked on the *Queen Elizabeth* and on 1 July sailed for Gourock, Scotland. Meanwhile, the air echelon, comprising crews of the 564th, 565th, 566th, and 567th Bombardment Squadrons, on 13 June 1943 began flying the Northern Ferry route via Dow Field, Maine, Gander, and Iceland. It was led by Colonel Jack W. Wood who had assumed command of the 389th on 16 May of that year.

The air echelon flew into its base at Hethel, near Norwich, between 11 and 25 June. It was not until 6 July that the ground echelon arrived at Station 114 and meanwhile the 44th and 93rd had to provide a temporary ground echelon because the 389th was urgently required to become operational for the forthcoming raid on Ploesti. This Romanian city was the centre of an important strategic oilfield producing 60 per cent of all Germany's needs. By increasing the Liberators' fuel capacity to 3,100 gallons they could just make it to the target from North Africa. The 389th, therefore, was under extreme pressure to accompany the 44th and 93rd on this momentous raid. At Hethel, Hardwick, and Shipdham there was intense activity as the ground crews sweated to remove the Norden bomb-sights and replace them with low-level sights. Heavier nose armament and additional fuel tanks in the bomb bays gave the men clues as to their new role. Rumour and speculation gained momentum with the news that the three Groups were to fly low-level practice missions over East Anglia at less than 150 feet *en route* to their target range over the Wash after a five-day orientation course.

At Hardwick Colonel Addison Baker led his Liberators flying wing tip to wing tip at 150 feet over the hangar line on the base which was used as a target. On some days the 93rd was joined by the 44th and 389th in flights over the base in waves of three aircraft.

The 44th, 93rd, and 389th crews had been trained in America in the art of high-altitude precision bombing and were quite unused to low-level flying. It led, on 25 June, to a mid-air collision involving two 389th machines. Earl Zimmerman was flying aboard Lieutenant James's aircraft: 'We were flying about 1,500 feet in a three-plane formation and executed a left turn. Lieutenant Fowble's

B-24 slid across the top of our Liberator taking off numbers one and two propellers. Fowble's aircraft suffered damage just behind the camera hatch but we did not sever his control cables. Our engines ran away and James was forced to make an emergency landing. I was ordered to get all the crew into the rear of the ship. We were too low for a bale-out. James lined up for a landing on a runway [Seething]. But construction men were pouring cement on to the runway so James elected to make a belly-landing to the left of it. Our collision and descent had happened so fast that a bombardier, Lieutenant Charles B. Quantrell and the navigator, Lieutenant Cecil D. Stout did not have time to get out of the nose. The plane dug in so low that the pilots were able to step out of their seats straight on to the ground. Quantrell was killed and Stout was badly injured. The top turret fell on me and split my right shinbone. The number three engine caught fire and I was only saved by my engineer T/Sergeant Thompson who took a hand-extinguisher and jumped on to the wing and put out the fire. Stout spent many months in hospital. Fowble's Liberator made it back to Hethel.'

The 389th, the 'Sky Scorpions' as they became known were the youngest and most inexperienced of the three 201st (Provisional) Wing Groups. When they departed for North Africa at the end of the month they had only completed two weeks' training in Norfolk.

By 25 June forty-one Liberators were available at Shipdham for the Ploesti mission, code-named 'Operation Statesman'. Five days later the three 201st (Provisional) Wing Groups began taxiing out on to the runways at their bases at Hethel, Hardwick, and Shipdham for the flight to the staging-post at Portreath in Cornwall. Forty-two Liberators took off from Hardwick and thirty more left the runways at Hethel. However a few 389th aircraft remained behind in Norfolk for training and Air-Sea Rescue duties. For the 93rd the long oversea flight to North Africa meant a return to the African desert they had forsaken in February 1943.

The 124 Liberators flew to Libya where they came under the control of the United States Ninth Air Force. Relationships between the two commands were never good. The Ninth accused the Eighth of being undisciplined and given to gross exaggeration over 'kills' while the Eighth complained that the Ninth's cooks withheld rations. But the Eighth steadfastly entered the African campaign which began with missions in support of the Allied invasion of Sicily. On 5 July the 93rd took off on the first of ten missions in support of the Italian campaign. Most of these missions were flown without escort and soon losses began to assume the proportions sustained at the height of the raids on the U-boat pens.

The 93rd and 389th resided at bases near Benghazi while the Eightballs were based at Benina Main, one of

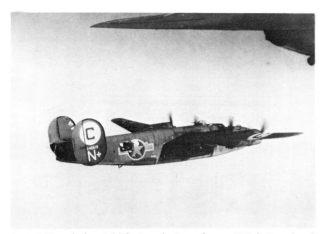

A B-24D of the 566th Bomb Squadron, 389th Bombardment Group.   USAF

Mussolini's former airfields, fifteen miles from Benghazi. Hundreds of wrecked Axis aircraft still littered the area for miles around and on the walls of the hangars the words 'Believe, Obey, Fight' were inscribed. One afternoon crews at Benina Main were hastily summoned to report to the briefing-room. Bill Cameron learned that his crew were to join that of Colonel Posey and another crew in a low-level sortie over Benghazi. Apparently the natives were demonstrating in the town, putting pressure on the British for more local control. *Buzzin' Bear*, living up to its name, and the other two aircraft, buzzed the city in a show of 'gunboat diplomacy'. A few days later missions began in earnest with a raid on the airfield at Lecce in Italy.

On the afternoon of the 16th the 44th was briefed for a raid on Naples. Next day the Eightballs took off from 'Locust Lodge', as they called it, after a paltry breakfast of thick pancakes (cold and still doughy in the middle), cold apple butter, and coffee. As the formation neared Naples crews became aware that this was to be no 'milk run'. Thick flak greeted the Eightballs and Axis fighters waded into the attack. Lieutenant Gentry was flying under the box of six B-24s and it was his aircraft that came in for the heaviest punishment. The gunners aboard *Buzzin' Bear* accounted for five aircraft, including three Macci 202s. Word later came through that Lieutenant Joe Potter, a member of Lieutenant Gentry's crew, had been killed by Italian farmers after he had baled out.

Buzzin' Bear flew past Mount Etna and out across the Aegean Sea pursued by the fighters and with a gaping hole in number three engine cowling. Bill Cameron finally

The 389th camp near Benghazi. Conditions were described as 'rugged'. This was Captain Ben Walsh's crew's sleeping quarters for their first two weeks in Africa.   Hayes

had to shut down the engine when he felt that he was reasonably safe from further fighter attack because the fuel-supply was getting short. A vast quantity had been consumed in trying to maintain formation and still more in keeping the carburettor mixture richer than normal in a desperate effort to keep the engines cool. After a hurried consultation the crew decided to head for Malta.

Sighting land Bill Cameron put down on what was thought to be Malta. But the British officer who drove up in a jeep soon after the B-24 landed insisted that it was Comiso airfield in Sicily and that the Germans were expected to bomb it that night! Comiso was only a few miles from the enemy lines. It was 16.00 hours and the gasoline in the tanks so low that Bill Cameron doubted whether there was more than fifteen minutes' flying time left. However, some six gallon cans of gasoline were rounded up from all over the airfield, on one side of which stood a shot-down Stuka. The crew had that day attempted to land unaware that the airfield had been captured by the Allies and their bodies were still in the aircraft. After about a hundred trips *Buzzin' Bear* was replenished with some 600 gallons of fuel.

After stocking up with Italian wine, of which the crew drank more than was wise in the circumstances, they left Comiso at about 23.00 hours. At the last moment a Lieutenant-Colonel attached to General Patton's army also clambered aboard. He wanted to fly in the tail turret and with him safely ensconced *Buzzin' Bear* took off, in diminishing light, for Malta. It was a hot trip and the wine flowed freely among those members of the crew not immediately involved in flying the aircraft. Bill Cameron became worried as the gunners fired tracers into the night and the prospect of flying over Malta without getting fired upon seemed rather remote. He decided to drop down to 1,500 feet, turn on his landing-lights and circle a couple of times to aid ground control in identifying him before he crossed the coastline. Amid universal relief a British voice came over the radio with landing instructions. Accommodation was not immediately forthcoming so the crew decided to sleep aboard *Buzzin' Bear*. Although not too comfortable at least the oxygen-masks would help to remove the inevitable splitting headaches the following morning!

By now the crew were all in. Indeed, Sparks had fallen out of the B-24 during the night and had remained asleep where he fell. Tom Clifford, the navigator, was constantly blaming himself for landing the crew in Sicily and as for Bill Dabney, the co-pilot, the strain and fatigue had brought on an attack of asthma. Only Jim DeVinney, the bombardier, remained his happy-go-lucky self. Dabney was treated in hospital while the others attended an interrogation. After rather incoherent questioning the crew made their way to a club-room where they fell into a deep sleep which lasted from 02.00 to 05.00 hours. Breakfast consisted merely of a cup of tea and a thin piece of toast and it must be remembered that nobody had eaten a proper meal since taking off from Benina Main. Bill Cameron agreed there was no point in inviting starvation by extending their stay and by 06.00 hours the crew were on their way back to Benghazi.

Until their return to base no one had any idea of what had happened to the crew of *Buzzin' Bear* and it had been assumed that they had gone down in the Mediterranean. Bill Cameron decided that before he

Nose art of Lemon Drop *before conversion to the 44th's assembly ship.*   USAF

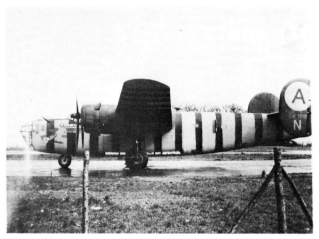

The yellow and black striped B-24D assembly ship of the 44th which was formerly Ploesti veteran Lemon Drop.
USAF

reported to Major Howard Moore he was going to get something to eat. The 44th shared rations with the Ninth's 345th Bomb Squadron of the 98th Group, which had been formed from the 44th in March 1942. However there was little *esprit de corps* prevailing as Bill Cameron was to discover: 'After some argument I was able to convince the mess sergeant that he should provide some food for us. We finally got canned fruit and a bowl of macaroni which appeared to be burnt. It was dark in the mess-room and I wanted to see if the macaroni was really burnt. I took it outside and the black bits turned out to be not charred macaroni but bugs! I went and complained to Major Howard Moore whose characteristic reply was a classic "Where have you been?", Moore took the matter up with Colonel Johnson who in turn took it up with Colonel 'Killer' Kane of the 98th. However no more food was forthcoming and things did not improve during their stay in Benina Main. Bill Cameron later discovered that the cooks, all from the 98th, had devised a scheme to improve their rations. While both Groups were there the 98th received double rations. By using up the less desirable items and withholding the best foodstuffs, only the choicest rations would remain for the 98th when the 44th returned to England.

On 19 July the Liberators made the first attack on Rome when they visited the city's Littoria yards. Although Rome had been declared an open city its railway yards had nevertheless remained the chief centre of supply for the Axis forces in Italy. Because of its cultural and religious significance, the briefing for the raid was the most detailed and concise the combat crews had ever received. Lieutenant-Colonel Jim Posey concluded the briefing with: 'And for God's sake if you don't see the target, bring back your bombs.' He need not have worried. Captain Cameron led the Eightballs to the city and all the Group's bombs cascaded down at precisely 12.04 hours right on target. It was an unprecedented success and only one bomb, from another Group, had 'got away' and slightly damaged a basilica. It was precision bombing at its best but the conditions had been kind. The only excitement Bill Cameron endured was when Jackson Hall's B-24 shut down an engine on the home flight. It transpired that he had nudged the number four engine off-switch with his knee!

The Liberators were later withdrawn from the campaign in Sicily and training for the Ploesti raid commenced. Practice bomb runs were made against a mock-up target and crews were fully briefed with film shows and lectures. It is not proposed here to dwell on the mission, which has been adequately chronicled in other books, save to mention the part played by the 201st Provisional Combat Wing Groups.

On the morning of Sunday, 1 August, 175 Liberators took off from landing-strips in the Benghazi area on the ten-hour round trip to Ploesti. The Ninth Air Force's

Ball of Fire, *the 93rd's first assembly ship. It crashed in July 1944.*   Noble

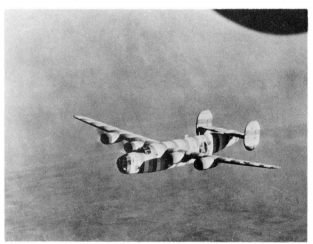

Ball of Fire *in flight. It was painted in black, white and yellow stripes.*   USAF

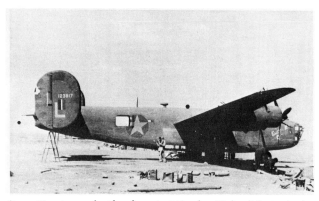

Suzy Q *reposes in the desert at Benina Main, Libya, during the Eightballs first African campaign. Colonel Johnson led the 44th to Ploesti on 1 August 1943 in the* Suzy Q. *Note the rudder which was damaged on that raid.*   Cameron

376th Group led the formation, followed by the 93rd with the Ninth's 98th Group, and the 44th and 389th bringing up the rear. The 93rd, led by Lieutenant-Colonel Addison Baker, crossed heavily defended air space and when only a few miles from the target his B-24 *Hell's Wench* was hit and caught fire. Baker jettisoned his bombs but he and his co-pilot, Major John Jerstad, decided to continue to the target. At Ploesti *Hell's Wench* was enveloped in flames and crashed with no survivors. Both pilots were awarded posthumous Medals of Honor for their sacrifice.

Captain Walter Stewart, the deputy leader in *Utah Man*, took over and despite severe damage to the bomber he managed to land again in Libya fourteen hours later

Little Gramper, *one of the first B-24s to complete fifty missions (note the horizontal bomb symbol denoting her participation in the Ploesti mission) and the ground crew which travelled to Africa as a skeleton crew. The two men (third and fourth, top row) are Art Marsh and Marcus DeCamp, members of her combat crew. (Art Marsh was awarded the Soldiers' Medal and an Officer rating in the field for his modification of the radio-room of the B-24 while in England). Sergeant Latta, a 566th Bomb Squadron Engineering Officer (far right, top row), and members of the ground and combat crews picked up a B-24 engine from a Tunisian scrapyard and installed it in* Little Gramper, *replacing one that had blown up. The engine had no available pedigree but got the crew home to Hethel. A new engine was fitted in England. All members of the crew, except those mentioned, were killed in a plane crash near Hethel en route home to the U.S.A.*   Hayes

although K. D. McFarland, flying *Liberty Lad* on two engines, was the last home by another two hours. Nine other 93rd Liberators, including two which collided in cloud, did not return.

Colonel Johnson's intention to lead the 44th in *Suzy Q* was placed in jeopardy the night before Ploesti. During engine-testing a broken spark plug was diagnosed in number two engine. After an anxious night of maintenance and repair the sick patient was pronounced well enough to fly. After all what better Liberator was there to lead the Eightballs than the *Suzy Q* by now symbolic of the 44th's determination and persistence in the continuing face of adversity.

Suzy Q with Colonel Johnson in command taxied through the desert dust to the take-off point followed by thirty-nine Liberators of the 44th. At 07.15 hours precisely *Suzy Q* lifted off on the long hop to the Danube and the others followed at regular intervals.

The Eightballs arrived at Ploesti at 15.15 hours, immediately plunging into a hail of flak and ripping tracers, smoke, fire, and explosives. Several parts of the extensive plant were already ablaze and to reach its specified target, the 44th flew directly over this fiery and bursting cauldron of oil and through a veritable forest of anti-aircraft guns. Modest barns and harmless-appearing haystacks now revealed themselves as emplacements and from everywhere, including the handcars on the sidings, flew a barrage of steel.

Colonel Johnson headed for the target followed by the Group in perfect order. The Ploesti plant was a sprawling panorama of buildings stretching over several acres of land. Because a concentrated attack on one specific target by the entire force employed would do but a minimum of damage, each Group had been given a separate area on which to concentrate its strength. That had been the real purpose of a low-level attack. The idea was to get in fast, drop the bombs, and get out fast again. But fate had ruled that it would not be so, for as Colonel Johnson's Group made its approach it was observed that through an error another Group had already bombed the target assigned to the 44th. What was there to do? Fly straight on and set for home, thereby nullifying months of preparedness, or seek an alternative target and possible doom? In a split second, Colonel Johnson chose the latter. Altering his course, and heading straight and low through smoke and flames and floundering B-24s, he made with his Group for a plant as yet untouched. Bombers went down on all sides and one, caught in the blast of an exploding bomb, pointed its nose upward and it soared about a hundred feet before falling on to its helpless back.

The greatest success, however, went to the 389th bringing up the rear of the formation and striking for its target at Campina. Each of the Sky Scorpions carried 5,000 pounds of delayed-action bombs and was the only Group that day to destroy its assigned target. Headquarters was surprised, but the success had not been achieved without cost. Four 389th B-24s were shot down on the raid and another nine landed at airfields in Turkey and Cyprus, with seventeen returning to North Africa. The Liberators flew so low over the oilfields that enemy fighters hit the ground when they failed to pull out of the dives after making their attacks on the bombers. The bravery and determination of the men of the 389th was shown in the courage displayed by Lieutenant Lloyd D. Hughes. He was given the supreme

The jubilant crew of Little Gramper *taken the day they completed their final mission in February 1944.* Top row, left to right: *Russ Hayes, Ball turret-gunner; Leonard Boisclair, Waist-gunner; Ben Walsh, Pilot; Marcus DeCamp, Engineer; Charles Cavage, Waist-gunner.* Bottom row, left to right: *Tom Campbell, Navigator; unknown replacement for wounded bombardier; Robert Hyde, Ernest 'Jack' Cox, Tail-gunner; Arthur Marsh, Radio-operator. (The co-pilot that day was a command pilot. Original co-pilot Sam Blessing, formed his own crew.) Soon after this photograph was taken Captain Tom Campbell was killed in a plane crash in Sweden. It was he who had originally called the reptiles in the African desert 'grampers', from which the ship got its name.* Little Gramper *was retired in the summer of 1944 for conversion to an assembly ship. The new all-silver* Gramper Jnr *crashed at Hethel, ploughing through a radio shack near No. 2 Hangar. A third* Little Gramper *was christened shortly after.*

Hayes

American award, the Medal of Honor, for refusing to turn back after shells had ruptured his fuel tanks. Despite fuel streaming over the fuselage, he piloted his Liberator low over the blazing target. Heat engulfed the bomber and flames licked at its fuselage as the fuel ignited. Hughes struggled to complete the bomb run but after 'bombs away' his starboard wing dipped and ploughed into the ground. Only two gunners survived.

All three of the Eighth Air Force Groups received the Distinguished Unit Citation. It was the second such award for the 44th. For the survivors, life on their bases in Norfolk would never be the same again. Colonel Johnson of the 44th and the 98th's 'Killer' Kane received Medals of Honor for their leadership on the raid.

At Benghazi, the 93rd's base in the Libyan desert, new crews arrived to replace those lost at Ploesti and those who had returned home after completing their tour of twenty-five missions. Colonel Leland C. Fiegal, who was formerly with the Group during its training days in the States, arrived from America to take command. He

succeeded Lieutenant-Colonel George S. Brown on 9 August 1943, who had been the acting Commanding Officer since the death of Lieutenant-Colonel Addison Baker. In the bitter aftermath of Ploesti crews were sent to Cairo for a well-earned leave. Then followed further raids on Axis targets in Austria and Italy.

On 13 August the Liberators journeyed to Wiener Neustadt in Austria, and three days later the B-24s' target was Foggia in Italy. This raid was considered to be a 'milk run' but the Liberators were badly mauled; the 44th losing eight bombers. *Southern Comfort* was one of the Liberators shot down by enemy fighters with eight of her crew, including Joe Warth, taken prisoner.

Joe Warth recalls: 'We had been told that the raid would be a "milk run" as we had been there a few days earlier and had encountered very little flak and only a few fighters. But conditions change rapidly in a combat zone and the German High Command getting word we were returning laid a little trap for us. *Southern Comfort* took an uncountable number of direct hits from the

Hethel airfield taken in April 1946 with Hethel Wood (centre) and Stanfield Hall (top left below bomb dump). Paths through Hethel Wood led to naturally concealed billets (right).   DoE

German fighters, which came at us from every direction. I know we shot down at least three of them when we heard the bale-out klaxon sound; three of our engines were shut off and on fire and the bomb bay was a blazing inferno. In the rear of the aircraft we were completely cut off from the rest of the crew. I made it to the camera hatch, turning round to see the door to the bomb bay vaporize in the flames. The four of us in the rear wasted no time in getting out, two going out of the waist windows.

'When I was on my way down I looked about and saw that the sky for many miles around was a mass of burning and still fighting aircraft and a patch of white parachutes. *Southern Comfort* was a mass of flame as she spun down, crashing into an Italian hillside. There was a final blast of flame and noise as if she had but one desire left — to return to the earth as the ore from which she came. Lieutenants Singer and Finder never reached the ground alive. Both their bodies were later found by the Germans who reported that their parachutes were bullet-ridden and had failed to work properly. The rest of us were captured by the Germans and sent to prisoner of war camps.'

Three aircraft from the 67th Squadron were lost, including *Buzzin' Bear* and the seemingly indestructible *Suzy Q*. Captain Cameron and 'Pappy' Moore again escaped disaster, Cameron having been promoted to Squadron Commander and Moore having completed his tour on an earlier mission to Naples. After the bombing of Cancello on 21 August the Liberators exchanged the pinkish desert of Libya for the golden wheatfields of Norfolk, returning home during the last week of the month. The Eightballs flew home soberly reflecting upon their losses during the short campaign — the highest of the three Groups.

The ground crews left behind at Hethel solemnly counted in the returning Liberators, looking in amazement at the gaping holes in their drab-olive framework, now stained an oily black. An intensive maintenance programme was immediately begun. In addition, B-24Js, with power-operated nose turrets and radar modifications, began arriving on the base. For those men who had been to North Africa it meant learning new techniques. To fly the B-24Js crews earmarked for B-17 Groups were reallocated to the 389th. Word quickly spread among the North African veterans that a fourth Liberator Group, the 392nd, had joined the Second Bombardment Wing at the beginning of August.

Chapter Four

Wings Over the Waveney

The 392nd Heavy Bombardment Group had been activated on 26 January 1943 at Davis-Monthan Field, Arizona, and placed under the command of Colonel Irvine R. Rendle. On 18 July, its training completed, the ground echelon sailed from New York, its port of embarkation. It was on 1 August while other Liberator Groups from England were attacking the Ploesti oilfields that the ground echelon began arriving at Station 118, Wendling, which was situated some eight miles northeast of Swaffham, Norfolk, and lay near the main A47 highway.

However it was not until 15 August that the air echelon began flying into the Norfolk airfield and shattering the peace of the tranquil countryside. But these were no ordinary Liberators, as any boy in the vicinity who considered himself a keen aircraft-spotter would have realized. These were the latest B-24Hs and B-24Js whose most noticeable characteristic was the installation of a power-operated gun turret in the nose which replaced the Perspex-domed nose that had been a feature of the now obsolescent B-24Ds. However their installation posed an immediate problem for the ground crews because the Group had begun receiving the B-24Hs while the ground echelon was still at sea. When the ground crews were at last able to familiarize themselves with the new aircraft, the aircrews were attending mandatory lectures on R.A.F. flying control procedures, aircraft recognition, and the finer points of the Gee navigational device. The 392nd flew its first mission on 6 September when the Liberators made a diversionary sweep to aid the Fortresses attacking Stuttgart.

On the following day the 389th, now back to full strength, flew its first mission from England to Leeuwarden in the company of the 44th. However, thick cloud obscured the target and they were forced to seek 'targets of opportunity'.

Four days later the 202nd Combat Bombardment Wing (Provisional) was redesignated the 14th Combat Bombardment Wing with all the four B-24 Groups under its control. Its headquarters was located at Shipdham and Leon Johnson moved from the 44th to command it. Lieutenant-Colonel James L. Posey was promoted to command the Eightballs with Major Beam as his Deputy Commander. The new Wing hierarchy heralded a new era for the Liberators. Johnson addressed the many new arrivals, telling them they were joining B-24 Groups which would be further increased and their squadrons strengthened. This was in sharp contrast to the early days when the Liberators were thought to be unsuitable for the E.T.O.

More diversionary missions followed and late in the afternoon of 15 September the Sky Scorpions took off from Hethel for a raid on the airfield at Chartres as part of the 'Starkey' deception raids on airfields in northern France which had begun on 9 September. Their return to Norfolk was made in darkness and all landing-pattern disciplines were abandoned by the crews, inexperienced in night landings, in their haste to get down quickly. Next morning, crews at Hardwick, Hethel, and Shipdham were stunned by the announcement that they would be returning to North Africa this time to support the seriously threatened Salerno landings. However when the groups arrived in the Tunis and Massicault areas news came through that the beach-head had been established and the Groups were switched to other targets in Italy.

With the departure of the three Liberator Groups, the 392nd was forced to go it alone. Training was stepped up and the Wendling outfit flew more diversionary flights over the North Sea to aid the Fortresses. On 4 October the Group flew its fourth such diversion, making a feint towards Bremen to try and draw Luftwaffe fighters away from the stream of Fortresses attacking Regensburg and Schweinfurt. Captain (later Colonel) Myron H. Keilman, Operations Officer of the 579th Bombardment Squadron, flew deputy group lead in a force comprising two formations of eighteen Liberators each. Previously the Luftwaffe had refused to be drawn by the diversionary feints. This time, however, the astute German controllers were convinced of the Americans' destination. The Liberators were bounced by over thirty German fighters and a terrific battle ensued. At one time it reached a peak with approximately 150 enemy fighters involved. When it was all over four Liberators of the 579th Squadron had been shot down. Among them was one with the Squadron Commander, Major Donald Apport, aboard.

Many other bombers badly damaged in the attack, limped back' to Wendling. Eleven crew members were wounded. Captain Keilman, who was assigned Squadron Commander that evening, recalls the mission: 'We sure surprised those ME-109s and FW-190s with our forward fire-power. Those Groups before the 392nd really had it tough with only flexible mounted 0.50 calibres in the nose of their B-24Ds and B-24Es. Head-on passes were really scary. On later missions, the Luftwaffe sometimes only struck the leading Group. It seemed strange that, with a few exceptions, they made their most persistent strikes as the formations were "out-bound".'

Despite the improved fire-power forward the heavy nose turrets reduced the Liberators' speed. They also made the bomber a very cold aircraft to fly in at altitude because icy draughts entered the aircraft through a gap between the nose section and the turret. However, comfort had been sacrificed because the Luftwaffe had specialized in frontal attacks on the B-24Ds.

A B-24H of the 578th Bomb Squadron, 392nd Bombardment Group being refuelled at Wendling on 9 September 1943.

USAF

Meanwhile the other Liberator Groups began arriving from North Africa. Crews had not been sorry to forsake the inhospitable climate and once again the Eightballs had suffered unmercifully at the guns of the Axis forces. On 1 October the Liberators had visited Wiener Neustadt and discovered to their cost that the defences had been tightened up since their last visit.

Sure Shot of the 44th, piloted by Richard J. Comey, was damaged by flak and enemy aircraft. Albert D. Franklin, the flight engineer/top turret gunner wrote: 'A 20 mm shell exploded in the oil tank of number two engine, causing terrible smoke when oil hit the supercharger. A small piece of flak came through the turret hitting the butt of gun beside my head. Fighters coming in at twelve o'clock high, planes going down on all sides, waist gunner wounded.

'Pilot starts evasive action, turning (almost too far) into dead engine. Still flying on three engines, hydraulic system shot up, portions of right wing tip and tail section missing, not enough fuel to return to base. Could not keep up with what was left of formation. Headed for Spitfire base inside friendly lines. Came in for landing, main wheels down, but would not lock. Pilot circled field, tilted plane from side to side, locked main wheels. Prised nose wheel down with bar from survival kit. Landed, no flaps, no brakes, ran off end of runway, through a field and a fence before coming to stop.

'American General in B-25 took wounded man back to North Africa. British on base, congratulated pilot and crew, took us in and fed us. We counted 638 holes in plane, too damaged to fly. We spent one night there, could hear big guns in the direction of Naples, abandoned equipment and weapons everywhere, tanks still smoking, rifles sticking in ground by bayonets, we started walking. American airbase our destination. Had to stay on roads and on beaten paths, due to mines, slept in bombed-out building, almost run over by an American convoy during blackout, could not make them recognize us. Without rations and very little sleep, we reached our destination in forty-eight hours.

'Catching a C-47 loaded with Axis prisoners of war to Bizerta and after they had fed and taken care of the prisoners, we finally convinced the American artillerymen there that we were American flyers. Staying there one night, we borrowed a G.I. truck and headed for Tunis. Upon arriving at what was left of our base, we found that the remainder of our Group had returned to England and our gear was piled up in the desert tagged M.I.A. We then caught a C-47 back to Marrakesh, from there a C-54 to Prestwick, Scotland, then a train to England. After eight days in all, we arrived back at our base at Shipdham. The Squadron Commander was glad to see us. Needless to say, we were glad to be back.'

In all, eight B-24s were brought down and a further eight were written off in crash-landings in Africa on the Wiener Neustadt mission. Soon after, the main part of the 44th returned to England but was stood down for the mission to Vegasack on 8 October in order to lick its wounds. These hardly had time to heal when on the following day the Eightballs joined in the raid on Gydnia on the Baltic coast. German smoke-screens proved so effective that they completely missed the target. During the latter part of October insurmountable cloud barriers blunted long-range operations over the Continent.

Throughout the remainder of 1943 the Liberator force, even with the introduction of four new Groups, was still not strong enough to mount deep penetration raids without fighter escort. Two of these new Groups, the 445th and 446th, arrived in Norfolk during the first week of November. The 445th had been activated at Gowen Field, Idaho and the 446th at Davis-Monthan Field, Arizona. Lieutenant-Colonel Robert E. Terrill, a West Pointer, was named Commanding Officer of the 445th and training began at Orlando, Florida, nicknamed 'Snafu U' by the freshman outfit, for combat initiation. During early June 1943 the 445th, now 1,800 strong, moved to the salt-flats at Wendover Field, Utah.

It was during the first week of July 1943, when the 445th moved to Sioux City, Iowa, that one of Hollywood's greatest stars joined the Group. James

Wendling airfield in March 1946 showing the living sites to the left and the bomb dump stretching away into Honeypot Wood (right). Top left is the village of Beeston.   DoE

Stewart had relinquished his £3,260 a month as a film actor in order to become a private soldier, but he had been rejected by the Army who declared that he was ten pounds underweight. Stewart gradually built himself up and applied to the U.S.A.A.F. He joined the 445th as Operations Officer of the 703rd Bombardment Squadron. Stewart was completely dedicated to his new role, to such an extent that in August he was promoted to Commanding Officer of the Squadron.

From August until early September 1943 three crashes occurred during training flights killing twenty-seven airmen of the 445th. Crews became unsettled, resigning themselves to being part of a jinxed outfit. However there were no further accidents. In early September new B-24Hs began arriving at Sioux City and the 700th, 701st, and 702nd Squadrons were moved with their bombers to neighbouring fields. Meanwhile, on 6 June 1943, the 446th Heavy Bombardment Group had moved to Alamagordo, New Mexico, but was almost immediately moved again to Lowery, Colorado, to complete training.

On 18—19 October the 446th ground echelon departed for Camp Shanks, New York, and was joined by the 445th ground echelon, which had begun leaving Sioux City on 20 October. They both sailed for England aboard the *Queen Mary* on 27 October. The great ship docked at Clydeside on 22 November but the men were confined to the ship until the following day when they boarded a troop train which carried them down the eastern side of Britain to Norfolk. The 445th detrained at Tivetshall Station near Tibenham, in the early hours of 4 November when it was still dark and the men could not see what their new base was like. Waiting to meet them at Station 124 was an advance party that had left for England a few days previously to prepare for the Group's arrival.

Meanwhile, on 18 October the 445th air echelon was inspected by the P.O.M.s. Sixty-two crews were now ready for the flight on the Southern Ferry route to England and they left Sioux City in late October 1943. Simultaneously, the 446th, which had departed for Lincoln, Nebraska, on 20—26 October, travelled by the same route. One 445th Liberator was lost between Puerto Rico and Brazil and a 446th B-24 veered off course over France and was shot down. It was under this sobering cloud that the 446th touched down at Station 125, Bungay, Flixton on 4 November 1943.

Flixton had been the home of the 93rd's 329th Squadron until March 1943, when the unit began returning to Hardwick. The airfield lay on a part of Flixton Manor near the Suffolk market-town of Bungay, seventeen miles south of Norwich and deep in the valley of the River Waveney. This flexuose river forms the border between Norfolk and Suffolk and was the original division separating the North Folk from the

One of the first 392nd B-24Hs of the 578th Bomb Squadron to arrive at Wendling in August 1943. This Liberator — B-24H-1-FO — was the fourteenth built by Ford. It featured an Emerson electrically operated nose turret.   USAF

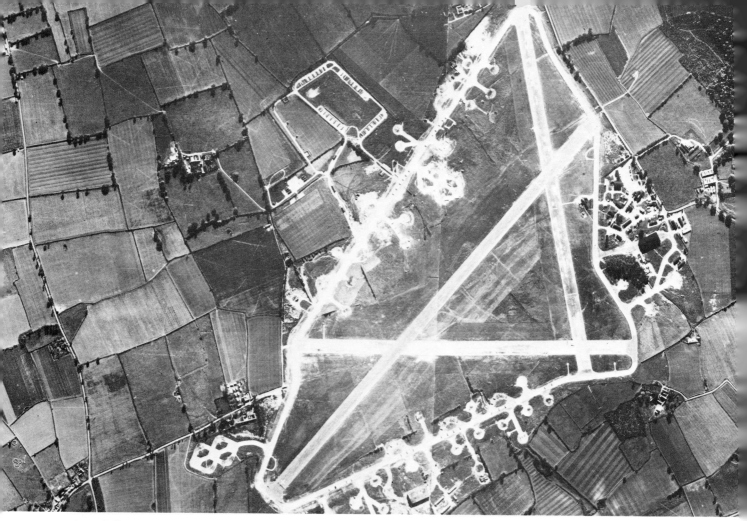

Bungay (Flixton) airfield in October 1945.

DoE

South Folk. To those of the 20th Wing who lived in its vicinity this river was later to become a familiar landmark. Flixton airbase was bare and inhospitable, partly constructed and short of facilities when the Americans arrived. The Air Ministry had started work in June 1942 on a triangular pattern of three runways. Mess-halls, billets, and an administration centre were built beyond the outer perimeter track, while the station headquarters building was complete with gas-proof doors it was without windows. Inside was the message centre and operations-room, heavily guarded like the Liberators themselves. By April 1944 when construction was completed, there were 2,826 men at the base, including 363 officers.

Early days at the base were consumed by mandatory E.T.O. lectures. The first crews to arrive in England were inexperienced in the use of oxygen at high altitude and unused to formation flying. Some could not even send and receive Morse. Particular attention, therefore, was paid to these subjects.

Tibenham offered the same hardships as Flixton. Until the 445th was deemed operational, the men would have to endure the cold and rain while they were confined to base, but the atmosphere quickly changed with the arrival of Colonel Terrill and the air echelon. Eight crews who were without aircraft and who had to travel with the ground echelon were doubly pleased to see them. On 6 November the 445th assumed complete administrative control of Tibenham from the R.A.F. and officers from Wing Headquarters at near-by Hethel constantly checked on the Group's progress. Changes in personnel were made and modifications were applied to the Liberators in the field.

During early November while the 445th and 446th were settling in, cloudy conditions prevented the operational Groups from extending the success achieved at Wilhelmshaven on 3 November by the few radar-equipped B-24s. Crews from the 44th bombed on smoke-markers released from P.F.F.-equipped aircraft without effect. However on 15 November, a few days after the first great Allied 1,000-bomber raid, operational B-24 Groups were told to make ready for a special mission to Norway where visual bombing could be used to advantage. Myron Keilman recalls the raid: 'Enthusiasm generated by this intriguing mission was paramount. That night the Division Field Order specified that the target was the secret German heavy water plant situated near the little town of Rjuken. It was a small target located in the mountains, about seventy-five miles west of Oslo, and was difficult to identify. Bomb loads had to be reduced because the distance involved a round trip of about 1,200 miles. Only ten 500-pounders were carried in each aircraft, which were to bomb from an altitude of only 12,000 feet.'

On the morning of 16 November twenty B-24s took off from Wendling at 07.00 hours and completed assembly in the dark. Their route took them north-east over the North Sea for 280 miles and then through the Skagerrak for a further 160 miles. Landfall was made at Lanngesund Fiord where Luftwaffe fighters could be expected from Denmark. The formation flew past the city of Skien and north-west to the target. Expert teamwork by the lead crew overcame navigational problems caused by scattered to broken cloud which blotted out the landscape and the 392nd reached the I.P. on schedule.

The bombing run was made on Automatic Flight Control Equipment which, linked with the Norden bomb-sight, enabled the bombardier to control lateral movement of the aircraft while on run-up to the target.

Tibenham airfield in April 1946 showing the villages of Tibenham (top left) and Tivetshall (bottom right). The main living sites are in the parish of Aslacton (top right).   DoE

Bombardier 'Doc' Welland and the formation dropped its bombs simultaneously on the nuclear energy development facility. The 389th, however, encountered opposition, albeit weak, about 100 miles from the target. Three JU-88s flew alongside the formation at three o'clock and each made three passes. But the Sky Scorpions suffered no lasting damage and continued to the target. Only 40 mm cannon-fire greeted them as the Group left the target at about 15,000 feet. The probable reason for such small-calibre guns was that the diminutive square rocks could not take larger gun emplacements. All twenty Liberators of the 392nd returned safely to base.

The Worry Bird. *Left to right front row:* Hinman, Shore, Jacobson, Hart. *Rear row, left to right:* Livingston, Skidmore, Shea, Lydic, Huxley, Tanner. *Shore's wife painted on the 'emblem' at Denver.*   Livingston

Three B-24Hs of the 392nd Bombardment Group en route to their target. Ship in foreground is Our Gal.   USAF

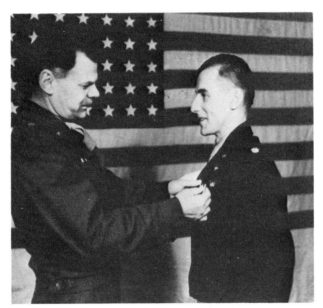

Myron Keilman (right) of the 392nd Bombardment Group receives the Distinguished Flying Cross from Leon Johnson, Commanding Officer, 14th Combat Bombardment Wing.

Keilman

Two days later the Liberator Groups received a 'frag' order for another mission to Norway. This time Division wanted to attack the JU-88 assembly plant at Oslo-Kjeller Airport. This involved another long oversea flight without oxygen and again take-off was before dawn. At about 06.00 hours twenty-four Liberators took off from Wendling, completed assembly, and slotted into their formation positions. The lead and deputy-lead ships fired off red-yellow identification flares as they headed north-east in the darkness, but three 392nd machines aborted soon after with malfunctions.

Nevertheless twenty-one Liberators continued to the target and gunners test-fired their 0.50 calibre guns, anxiously scanning the horizon for fighters. They had anticipated Luftwaffe fighters taking off from their bases in Denmark but none appeared. Nearing landfall the clouds, which had until now hidden the ice-cold waters of the North Sea, diminished. Crews could quite easily distinguish the city of Oslo when the B-24s turned at the I.P.

At 12,000 feet the 392nd shaped for the bomb run. The skilled navigator-bombardier team of Swangren and Good systematically checked off course heading, landmarks, true airspeed, wind drift, and minutes to 'bombs away'. Myron Keilman, flying deputy lead, saw the target 'standing out in the late morning sun' and thought that 'it would be a shame to miss it'.

'Bombardier Joe Whittaker was following through with every essential detail of a bombing run. Should anything have happened to the lead airplane and it had suddenly aborted the bomb run, Joe had his bomb-sight cross-hairs on the aiming point of the assembly plant. If he had been given the command "take over", he could have successfully delivered the bombs.' Lieutenant McGregor, in the lead aircraft, held his ship precisely on altitude and airspeed and he and the twenty bombers following released the 210 500-pounders on to the target simultaneously.

On the return leg the same scattered to broken clouds lay across the Skagerrak beneath the formation. Suddenly, the gunners spotted German fighters skimming across the cloud tops opposite to the B-24s' line of flight. A dozen-plus JU-88s climbed, to make fast diving passes as they circled in behind the bombers. Liberator 'outriders' moved into a tight formation providing the mutual protection of concentrated fire-power. The German twin-engined fighters, diving in pairs, lobbed rockets and 20 mm explosive shells into the 392nd. Tail and top turrets responded with bursts of machine-gun fire and the ball-turret gunners opened up below as the fighters broke off the attack.

Sergeant T. E. Johnson, flying with Lieutenant Everhart, shot up one fighter so badly that it burst into flames and was last seen in an uncontrollable dive. Two Liberators were hit and began to lose power. They could not keep up with the rest of the formation and as they fell behind the JU-88s concentrated their fire on them. The B-24 pilots dived for cover and sheltered in the clouds. For a time they played 'hide and seek' as the fighters circled. Eventually the bombers were lost from view.

Wave after wave of enemy fighters pressed home their attacks but Sergeant Forrest Clark, one of the waist gunners aboard Lieutenant Griffith's ship from the 44th, succeeded in shooting down one of the twin-engined fighters. As suddenly as it had begun, the attack broke off and the remaining bombers staggered home. Lieutenant Houle's aircraft, which was severely damaged, tottered gallantly to within fifty miles of the English coast with safety in sight. But by now his fuel indicators were reading zero and he was forced to ditch in the sea. The aircraft seemed to break in two and four minute figures were seen to slip into the icy waters of the North Sea. First Lieutenant Griffith, himself flying on three faltering engines, circled over the scene while his radio-operator called Air-Sea Rescue. With his own fuel-supply running low Griffith dipped his wing in salute to his fallen comrades and turned towards his base. Air-Sea Rescue were unable to trace any of the crew or the aircraft. Griffith made it back to Shipdham where he bellied in after most of the crew had baled out.

Three Liberators, one each from the 44th, 93rd, and 392nd, had been forced to land in Sweden. *War Baby* from the 93rd landed at Orebro, as did one from the 392nd. A 44th ship circled the airfield at Trollhattan firing signal-flares to inform the Swedes that they were about to land. Policy at that time called for the burning of any aircraft that landed in neutral territory and the 44th crew set fire to their Liberator shortly after landing. Meanwhile, the other 392nd Liberators were bucking a headwind which reduced their true airspeed to almost 100 m.p.h. The Group took an hour to clear the Skagerrak and thus place itself beyond the range of the enemy fighters. Ten hours after take-off, Deputy Goup Commander Lorin Johnson peeled off the formation and landed at Wendling.

Altogether six B-24s were lost. Some of these were forced to ditch in the North Sea through lack of fuel. Air-Sea Rescue B-17s equipped with lifeboats went to their aid. A few survivors were spotted in the water and lifeboats were dropped to aid them but the sea cruelly tossed them over and away out of their grasp.

At the end of November 1943 the 448th Heavy Bombardment Group flew into Norfolk to join the 446th and the 20th Wing. The 448th had been activated on 1 May 1942 and placed under the command of the

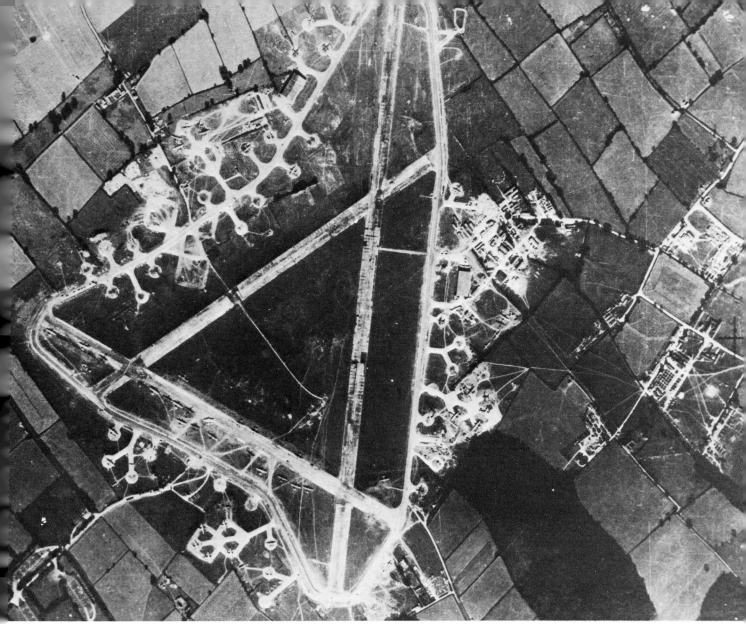

Wartime aerial view of Seething.

via Dugger

inveterate Colonel James McK Thompson. Initial training was completed at Gowen Field, Idaho. By early
September 1943 the Group was completing its final
training at Sioux City, Iowa. In late November the
ground echelon left for Camp Shanks in New York and
on 23 November 1943 sailed on the *Queen Elizabeth*,
arriving off Clydeside one week later. Meanwhile, on
3 November, the air echelon had moved to Harrington
Field, Kansas, After final processing the B-24s began
leaving for England on the Southern Ferry route in
pursuit of the ground echelon *en route* for Station 146
at Seething in Norfolk.

One of the pilots of the air echelon who made the
South Atlantic crossing was Second Lieutenant Tom A.
Allen: 'It was a bright sunny day and the radio was
playing "The Lady is a Tramp". Loaded the way we
were, I was wondering if it were possible the wings
could break off. One minute we were climbing at 4,000
feet a minute and the next we would be flying at minus
3,000 feet a minute! Aboard our aircraft was Colonel
Thompson. We left the Florida coastline through high
cumulus cloud and flew on through a storm cloud over
Puerto Rico to Trinidad and Belem, landing at Natal in
Brazil on 17 November. Next day we took off for North
Africa.'

One Liberator had been lost at Belem, and worse was
to follow. The 448th landed at Dakar and then flew on
to Marrakesh where First Lieutenant 'Stumpy' Pearce

and his crew were killed when their Liberator took off
and hit a mountain-peak, just fifteen feet from the
summit. Their navigator had preferred to start on course
at altitude over the field of departure so that he could
obtain an exact airspeed drift and navigational check. A
third B-24 was lost when on reaching England it crashed
and burned.

Another 448th member on the flight to England was
armourer-gunner Sergeant Francis X. Sheehan. He and
most of his crew on the *Harmful Lil'Armful* had formed
the nucleus of the 715th Squadron at Orlando, Florida,
and recalled, 'As we approached the coast of England
we were given an unusual greeting. We later found out
that this was routine. Out of nowhere I spotted two
beautiful Spitfires on each wing which escorted us to
the nearest airstrip. Only after they were on each wing
did I observe them; not saying much for my alertness.
This was my first introduction to the fine English
hospitality and only after some combat experience did I
appreciate this action and very necessary precaution. As
we came across the coast of England it looked very
beautiful. On many an occasion it looked even more so,
especially when two or four engines were spluttering
and the ship was full of holes. It was home to us. The
expression "home" was used every day on every intercom
system in our aircraft. We flew into Plymouth on
22 November but had to wait for bad weather to clear
before flying on to Seething three days later.'

Classic shot of ground personnel 'sweating out' a mission at Flixton, Bungay, home of the 446th Bombardment Group.

Tootell

Seething was a very small village located about ten miles south-east of Norwich, offering little for exploration, as Staff Sergeant Gene Gaskins remembers: 'There was one pub, one small store, a church, and maybe six houses; not very large but very picturesque. The pub became a very popular gathering place for many of the air and ground crews — plain but clean and dimly lit like most English pubs. The Americans took to the English beer very well. Since it was all they could get it was either adjust or do without. Since I didn't see many of them doing without, it must have been easy for them to adjust. Numerous farms were scattered around the "field" making it easier to camouflage. They were typically English — right out of the history book. The barns were built adjoining the houses for convenience in tending the animals and many of the buildings still used thatched roofs and stone walls. Much of the farming equipment was outdated: some farms were manned by the Women's Land Army who kept them productive while the men were away in the Services.'

Over at Tibenham the 445th was still not quite operational when on 13 December 1943 it was ordered to prepare for its first mission. Less than one month after landing in Norfolk fifteen aircraft took off from Tibenham and joined with the Division for a raid on Kiel. Despite heavy flak the 445th returned without loss and all twelve crews hit the target. It was a quite remarkable effort. Three days later the 446th also flew its first mission of the war when it joined in an attack on Bremen.

On 1 December, the 448th's ground echelon had arrived in Norfolk, but it was not until the 22nd that the Group was ready for its first operational mission,

when it joined with Groups of the Division for a raid on Osnabruck, Germany. It was the Group's first taste of combat and for Sergeant Sheehan 'the most exciting and eventful mission apart from the Hamm raid on 22 April 1944'.

'Osnabruck turned out to be heavily defended. Although flak was minimal the fighters were there in abundance as we found out. My first encounter with combat commenced with black puffs of flak dotting the sky around us. It was something we never did get accustomed to. The effectiveness of this was shown when part of a ship began trailing smoke and parachutes. As we approached the target the aircraft to our immediate right began dropping bombs. At the moment it occurred I could not believe my eyes. I thought it could not be happening at all. The aircraft leading this box formation dropped its entire bomb load on the left wing of one of its wing men's aircraft that had drifted down and under him. Stunned I watched the damaged aircraft fade left and over on its back. I prayed for 'chutes to appear, but none did. I was brought back to reality by the call over the intercom, "Fighters!" At this point everything seemed unreal and I guess I was doing things purely automatically and practically as I had been taught.

'Twin-engined enemy aircraft were lobbing rockets into a formation of bombers to my right. At first they seemed oblivious to our presence. I commenced firing at one of the fighters, which began trailing smoke and fire and went down through the clouds. I was later given credit for this. (To receive credit for downing an enemy ship it must be confirmed by the aircraft directly behind you.)'

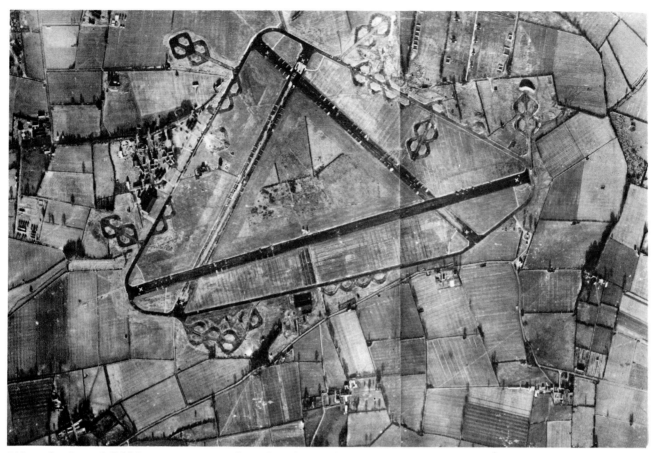

Old Buckenham airfield in January 1947 when obstacles blocked the runway and taxi-ways. Top left is the mess site with the sick quarters to its right. Below that is the Group Headquarters site and bottom left of that is the Communal site. DoE

The Division lost thirteen Liberators that day. Two of these came from the 446th and two more came from the 448th. The Osnabruck mission was the 445th's fourth and hitherto its luck had held, with no losses. However two of its bombers also failed to return from this raid in which a navigator was killed and several airmen were wounded. In another incident a bombardier and navigator had baled out over enemy territory thinking their aircraft doomed. The pilot had given the order to bale out after the Liberator had rapidly lost height and was about to enter into a spin. He succeeded in pulling the bomber out of the spin but too late to rescind the bale-out order. The 445th gunners were credited with two 'kills' and one 'probable'.

That same day, the 453rd began flying into Station 144 at Old Buckenham in Norfolk to form the 2nd Combat Bombardment Wing's third Group in England. This Group had been activated at Wendover Field, Utah on 1 June 1943 and Colonel Joseph Miller had assumed command soon after. The Group continued its training at Pocatello, Idaho, moving to March Field, California on 30 September. Early in December that year the ground echelon travelled to Camp Kilmer in New Jersey and then to New York to sail to Scotland. Colonel Miller led the air echelon to England on the Southern Ferry route.

Meanwhile, for the operational groups, short-haul missions to the 'no ball' sites were the order of the day, as Myron Keilman recalls. 'Two days before Christmas 1943, maintenance crews were working hard on the Group's thirty aircraft. The Group was on stand down after flying some tough missions over the last ten days.

445th B-24H of the 703rd Bomb Squadron. USAF

Colonel Joe Miller, 453rd Commanding Officer. Kotapish

With one engine on fire this 392nd Bombardment Group Liberator, a victim of enemy action, banks away from the formation.   USAF

But at 10.00 hours the Squadron Commanders and the officers of eight lead crews were ordered to report to the Group briefing-room.

'The Intelligence Officer gave us a thorough briefing on the V.1 and the launching sites in the Pas de Calais. He made it quite clear that Intelligence estimates indicated that not only was London highly vulnerable, but that the invasion might also be delayed. He concluded with, "If these sites are not destroyed within the next three months, London will be totally devastated."

'After the briefing these lead crews adjourned to the target-study room where a special sand-table mock-up of a typical V.1 launching site was displayed. Then there were the bombardiers' target folders to study — with maps and aerial photographs for each assigned target. There was a more than usual degree of excitement over this mission. It was different and its urgency was more closely felt. The bombing was to be from 12,000 feet and executed by four six-ship squadron formations. Spare airplanes were to accompany the force all the way. Visual bombing was a must. It was thought the mission would only take from four to five hours and friendly fighters would cover the entire route. Little or no flak was expected. In fact a "milk run".

'The "frag" order on the night of 23 December called for a maximum effort. The 392nd was able to have ready twenty-eight Liberators, each carrying twelve

500 lb bombs. Take-off was at 11.00 hours and the weather was very good. Assembly was easily completed and we joined the Wing and Divisional bomber stream on schedule. At the I.P. we turned on to our respective targets, the scattered cloud providing no obstacle to our highly skilled bombardiers: they quickly picked out checkpoints and identified the target area. Peering through bomb-sight optics they smoothly placed the cross-hairs on the V.1. launching sites. They literally took control of the aircraft: synchronizing the bomb-sight controls, the airspeed and the altitude, "killing" the airplanes' drift, and giving running commentaries to anxious pilots and crews. When indices crossed the bomb release lights flickered and the Liberators bounced. Pilots then took over, rolled up their bomb doors, and steered to the rendezvous heading. The mission had proved ideal for Captain "Doc" Weiling, Lieutenant "Big Joe" Joachem, Lieutenant "Pud" Good, and Lieutenant Moss, who had their excellent and accurate bombing verified later by photographic reconnaissance.'

The New Year began with the famous General Jimmy Doolittle taking over command of the Eighth Air Force on 1 January 1944. His directive was simple: 'Win the air war and isolate the battlefield!' In other words: 'Destroy the Luftwaffe and cut off the Normandy beaches for the Invasion.' At Squadron and Group level the men under his command were impressed. They all

The 446th's all-yellow assembly ship Fearless Freddie *flies under the port wing of the 448th's assembly ship.* Fearless Freddie *was a B-24D named after Fred Sayre of the 446th. It operated from January 1944 until its replacement by a similarly marked B-24 carrying the same nickname.* USAF

felt they knew the famous American aviator, not only from his aeroplane racing days but from his leading the famous B-25 raid on Tokyo.

The Eighth continued its pathfinder missions into January 1944 when German ports and industrial conurbations were the main targets. Then snow began to fall and cold set in throughout the region. At Old Buckenham first mud caused problems and then frost cracked the tarmac on the runways causing the surfacing to lift and pot-hole. Runways were in a constant state of disrepair throughout the year but in the winter of 1943—44 they were particularly bad. British firms delivered asphalt for repair work and one of these delivery drivers, Mr Ernie Powell, vividly remembers one particular visit to Old Buckenham. Powell and the driver of another truck passed a guard hut at the lower end of the airfield where an American G.I. waved them past. 'It was only when we had turned on to the taxi-strip and had gone quite a few

yards that I noticed in my rear mirror that a Liberator was following us. There was another behind that and then another. In all eight Liberators were following us. We had got in front of a bombing raid take-off!' Then another line of Liberators appeared at the end of the

93rd Bombardment Group Liberator Wham Bam *(41-23738) before conversion to the 453rd's assembly ship.* Noble

445th assembly ship B-24D (41-24215) with orange and black bands encircling the fuselage, top surface of wing and empennage. Letter 'F' six feet high in white lights both sides of fuselage. Lower surfaces natural metal finish. USAF

Wham Bam *in the livery of the 453rd's assembly ship colours of six-foot yellow and olive-drab checks and two large 'Js' forward of the waist windows in amber-coloured lights.* via Olds

Two 453rd crewmen recount their mission experiences to an avid audience of British schoolchildren at Old Buckenham in February 1944.
USAF

taxi-strip. Powell was unable to drive his truck off the taxi-strip without becoming bogged down in thick mud. He decided to stop. 'The Liberators pulled up too and a couple of Snowdrops [Military Police] on motor-cycles roared up brandishing revolvers. I tried to reverse the truck but I ran it off the strip and into the mud and bogged it. They called up a half-track to haul me out and badly damaged my truck in the process.' The Liberators, delayed by the incident, were by now running behind schedule and still not properly lined up. The first aircraft in the line ran off the edge and also became bogged in the mud. 'We were taken to the police headquarters and held there for more than two hours until they found out that the guard who let us through had not been told of the take-off time.'

Despite the bad weather conditions, which continued unabated, the mission to Kiel scheduled for 4 January went ahead. Next day the Liberators returned to the German port. A poor assembly robbed the 448th of a tight formation and reduced the Group to between twelve and fifteen aircraft. They came downwind over the target at about 300 degrees, almost due north, and at 25,000 feet. The B-24 carrying Major K. D. Squires took a direct hit just behind the wing, and hurtled down minus its tail. Leaving·the target area Tom Allen's Liberator joined several others in formation. With an increase in the speed the formation became strung out. It was then that the yellow-nosed Focke-Wulfs waded in,

attacking from underneath the formation, firing as they climbed. On one of their first passes they raked Tom Allen's aircraft, knocking out one turret, killing the bombardier instantly, and badly wounding the radio-operator. First the cockpit filled with flames and then the entire aircraft began to smoke and ignite. The order was given to bale out but only Tom Allen and his navigator, Dick Wheelock succeeded in doing so. The rest of the crew perished. Incidentally, the two survivors were the only ones in the aircraft wearing back-pack parachutes at the time of the attack. Both men were later interned at Stalag Luft I.

The bad weather continued on the following day when it caused Division to be stood down. However, on 7 January, the Liberators again struck at German targets. The 445th went to Mannheim, losing their third B-24 in four days and the 20th Wing struck at Ludwigshaven. Before any follow-up strikes could be made the weather again turned bad. It was not until 11 January that the Liberators could resume operations, with an attack on Brunswick. By the end of the month, the restrictions imposed by the weather were reflected in the total number of missions flown — ten by the 446th and seven by the 448th for instance.

After less than two months on operations rumours about the 448th's poor performance were spreading. On 23 January, Major Newton L. McLaughlin, the Special Services Officer at Attlebridge, was called to Second

Bombardment Division Headquarters at Ketteringham Hall, near Hethel, by Colonel Foote. McLaughlin was asked if he would volunteer to transfer to the 448th to help correct a bad morale problem with the proviso, 'that if the job got too hot, he would be relieved upon request'. McLaughlin agreed and arrived at Seething to find that 'Casualties had been high and morale was zero. The law of the jungle seemed to have taken over. Men refused the liberty runs, claiming that it was far too dangerous riding behind a drunken driver speeding without lights along the narrow winding roads. There was a severe shortage of coal and the PX offered poor merchandise and of limited quantity. The Quartermaster said he could not stock regulation quantities because of the rat problem.' There were many other manifestations of neglect, including 'salt used for de-icing the runways stored in the squash court' and 'the turning of the gym into a warehouse'. McLaughlin set to work almost immediately but only time could transform the situation.

Meanwhile, at Tibenham the 445th was presented with a different problem. On 24 January, soon after a visit by General Hodges and top-ranking officers from the Second Bombardment Division, the 445th was informed that it would be required to form a fifth Squadron from existing ground personnel. The 445th would then eventually lose one of the five Squadrons which would be allocated to a new Group whose ground echelon by a similar procedure was being formed from three other Second Bombardment Division Groups. All five Squadrons had to be of equal strength so that when Headquarters selected one Squadron, four Squadrons of the same strength would remain. To have concentrated the best personnel in one squadron and then have transferred it would have proved both imprudent and embarrassing. (It was decided that on 14 April 1944 the 445th's 700th Squadron would be transferred to the embryonic 491st Bombardment Group.)

On 30 January 1944 East Anglia witnessed the largest American bomber formation hitherto dispatched from England when 778 bombers went to Brunswick. The 392nd and the 44th, making up the 14th Wing, became separated from the bomber stream but chanced upon a break in the clouds and forty B-24s bombed the German synthetic rubber plants at Hanover without loss.

Missions in February followed the pattern set in January, with pathfinder missions to German cities and raids on the 'no ball' sites. Just under half of all missions flown by the Eighth in February 1944 were against Germany's 'wonder weapons'. But by 8 February 1944 the Germans had moved in rail-mounted heavy anti-aircraft weapons to defend the V.1 sites. On this day the 392nd flew its seventh 'no ball' and crews were greeted with heavy and accurate flak and bombing results were 'poor'. The 'milk-run' days came to an end and the bombing altitude was increased to 20,000 feet.

On the night of 15 February 1944 Flixton offered sanctuary to the crew of R.A.F. Halifax, *Pubwash* in difficulties after a fire raid on Berlin. For the Americans it was an opportunity to compare their B-24s with an R.A.F. machine and for Flight Sergeant Ted Grimwood and his crew a chance to sample some American hospitality. The R.A.F. men stayed overnight and at breakfast-time Ted Grimwood and his crew were presented with a plate of bacon topped with seven eggs. One of them began sharing it out among the other six,

when a G.I. quickly pointed out that it was his ration and that the others would soon follow! Later at the PX each man was presented with 200 cigarettes and a free shaving kit.

The camera carried by the Halifax had been unloaded and the film together with the debriefing report were sent on to Croft. A replacement engine and a ground crew arrived from Yorkshire and twenty-four hours later *Pubwash* was on the way home. Although rations on American bases exceeded those of R.A.F. bases, much was the same for the two air forces. Where American crews consisted of men of every ancestry and from every State, the R.A.F. crews were of the same stock but from almost every country in the Commonwealth. *Pubwash*'s crew were French Canadian, part of R.A.F. No. 6 (Canadian) Group. They too had crossed the Atlantic to fight the common enemy.

Meanwhile General Doolittle and his Staff were waiting for a week of good weather in which to mount an all-out air offensive against the German aircraft factories. In late February the weather-forecasters gave the General the news that the week of 20—25 February would probably be suitable for the Eighth to complete its task. It became known as 'Big Week' and one of those airmen who participated was Myron Keilman: 'I remember that the weather had been so bad that the 392nd had flown only sixteen missions since 1 January. But by 20 February we had been both alerted and briefed, and had taxied for take-off nearly every morning since General Doolittle took command. We waited for hours in the dense fog before the red flare fired from the control tower signalled "mission cancelled". Then back to the airplanes' dispersal pads; back to the dank Nissen huts; and back to the damp, ice-cold cots for needed sleep and tomorrow's alert. "Damn the foggy weather, damn the war, and damn General Doolittle too." After those early-hour breakfasts the Mess Sergeant had to pick up the General's portrait from a face-downward position in the middle of the floor and rehang it in its respected place. Disrespect, yes, but who wants to be rousted out at 03.00 hours day in day out just to sit in the fog? We couldn't win the war doing this and you didn't have to be a General to see that the weather was unfit to fly a bombing mission.'

However, on Sunday, 20 February, aircraft of the Second Bombardment Division taxied out and this time all was well and they took to the air. The Liberators formed part of a 1000-bomber force raiding the aircraft factories and aircraft component plants from Tutow, Rostock, and Stralsund on the Baltic coast to those in central and eastern Germany.

The Liberators struck at Brunswick and Magdeburg but cloud cover forced the 392nd to switch to a target of opportunity at Helmstedt. Results were described as 'fair' and the Group lost one Liberator. Over Brunswick the 445th braved the powerful German defences and lost three Liberators to flak. The Group's gunners claimed six kills, two possibles, and two damaged. Although the Eighth suffered badly during the raid it had inflicted major damage on the city's aircraft industry.

Next day the Division was again allotted Brunswick but again cloud obscured the primary target despite the good weather predicted for the area. Some 14th Wing crews bombed the secondary target at Diepholz where losses were light. The 392nd lost another ship in bombing the fighter airfield at Vorden, north-east of Arnhem.

A formation of B-24Js from the 446th Bombardment Group en route *to the Me.110 assembly plant at Gotha in Germany. Nearest aircraft belongs to the 706th Bomb Squadron.*
USAF

On 22 February overcast hampered the Liberators' assembly over East Anglia and eventually conditions became so bad that the Second Bombardment Division had to be recalled while flying a scattered formation over the Low Countries. Twenty-seven B-24s had taken off from Tibenham for Gotha and for twenty-five of them the recall was merely a stay of execution for the tragic return to the German city on the 24th. Two aircraft, which did not receive the recall, went on to Gotha and bombed the target. Some Groups did strike at targets of opportunity in Holland and western Germany. The Italy-based Fifteenth Air Force bombed Regensburg and on 23 February followed this with the bombing of Wiener Neustadt while their contemporaries in eastern England were again grounded by bad weather. The Eighth was not idle, however, during this lull in operations. Repairs and maintenance were carried out for the next raid on Gotha.

The target for the Eighth's Liberator Groups was the city's aircraft works, 420 miles due east of the White

Jim McGregor's 392nd lead crew which led the 14th Wing over Gotha on 24 February 1944. Standing, left to right: *Myron Keilman (579th Squadron C.O.), Good, Swangren, McGregor,* Kneeling: *Galloway, Putnam, Long, Padden and Housteau.*
Keilman

Cliffs of Dover. This was to be a lone Second Bombardment Division effort with eight Groups crossing the target and a ninth, the newly operational 458th, flying a diversionary sweep over the North Sea. Twenty-eight B-24s from the 445th joined with the 389th and 453rd to form the leading 2nd Wing. The 14th Wing's 44th and 392nd Groups flew behind the 2nd Wing while the 20th Wing brought up the rear.

Briefing for crews at Wendling took place at 06.30 hours and the briefing officer related the importance of the large plant to Germany's ability to carry on the air war. He also told crews that, 'it was heavily defended by large 88 mm and 110 mm anti-aircraft batteries'. These 392nd pilots had already experienced this type of heavy artillery over Bremen, Kiel, and Wilhelmshaven. On this, the 392nd's fortieth mission, the Liberators were almost certain to encounter heavy fighter opposition over enemy territory — 400 miles there and 400 miles back.

At 08.10 hours the 392nd Liberators started up their engines and five minutes later the lead ship taxied to take-off position. At 08.30 hours the green flare from the control tower was fired to signal 'take-off'. Jim McGregor, the lead crew pilot, revved his engines, checked his instruments, released his brakes, and rolled along the runway. Thirty-one Liberators followed behind at thirty-second intervals. At 12,000 feet, firing red-yellow identification flares into the clear sky, the Group formed up over Radio Beacon 21 into three Squadrons and flew the Wing triangular assembly pattern to King's Lynn.

The 392nd led the 14th Wing, falling into number two position of the Second Bombardment Division over Great Yarmouth. Gunners test-fired their guns as the DAL headed east over the Channel, climbing to 18,000 feet. At 11.31 hours the force of 235 Liberators, each maintaining a speed of about 135 m.p.h., crossed the Dutch coast just north of Amsterdam and flew on over the Zuider Zee. Streaming vapour trails signalled the bombers' presence and their intent. By 11.99 hours the leading 2nd Wing was flying ahead of schedule due to increased wind velocity and an unforeseen change in direction.

Flak was heavy over Lingen and the Liberators encountered persistent attacks by the Luftwaffe. Even the arrival of three Thunderbolt Groups just after 12.00 hours was unable to prevent five Liberators from the 445th being shot down in the space of six minutes. Over 150 enemy fighters ferociously attacked the formation all the way to the target despite close attention from escorting fighters. The Division beat off incessant attacks as it flew on over the Dummer Lake where it veered south-eastwards to Osnabruck and the bombed-out airfields near Hanover. Three more 445th B-24s were shot down before the formation turned south near Gottingen at 12.53 hours. Nine minutes later a 445th B-24 belonging to the 703rd Squadron was shot down.

To the right, flying parallel to the Liberators' course, were the Fortress formations of the First Bombardment Division heading for the ball-bearing plants at Schweinfurt. Out over the North Sea B-17s of the Third Bombardment Division were *en route* to their Baltic coast targets. P-47 Thunderbolts had escorted the Liberators to the vicinity of Hanover and then the twin-boomed P-38 Lightnings and P-51 Mustangs orbited the formation as it proceeded to Gotha. Undaunted, FW-190s, ME-110s, ME-210s and JU-88s raked the American formations with cannon and rocket-fire. Using the Liberators' thick vapour trails to excellent advantage, they often struck at any lagging bomber from below and behind. The Luftwaffe even attempted to disrupt the large and unwieldy combat wings.

At 13.09 hours the Division changed course to the south-east with a feint towards Meinegen. Some confusion arose at the I.P. when the navigator in the 389th lead ship suffered oxygen failure and veered off course. The bombardier slumped over his sight and accidentally tripped the bombs. Altogether twenty-five Liberators bombed the secondary target at Eisenach. Before the small 445th formation reached the target its tenth and eleventh victims fell to the German guns. By now the 445th consisted of only fourteen Liberators, three having aborted before entering Germany. Another 445th machine was shot down just after leaving Eisenach.

The thirteen remaining 445th B-24s, realizing that they had veered off course, continued alone. They arrived

over the target at 13.25 hours and executed an eight-minute bomb run. Some 180 500-pounders dropped from 12,200 feet inflicted considerable damage on the Gotha plant. Other Second Bombardment Division Groups, totalling 171 Liberators dropped another 468 tons of assorted bombs from varying altitudes and directions. The 445th's thirteenth B-24 fell victim to the German defences, minutes after bombs away.

Myron Keilman was flying deputy lead to Lieutenant-Colonel Lorin J. Johnson: 'The weather was very clear as we turned to the target. Red flares from the lead ship signalled "bomb bay doors open". The bombardier removed the heated cover blanket from the bomb-sight (they had heated blankets before the people did!). He checked his gyroscope's stabilization and all bombing switches "on". Our high and low squadrons fell in trail and all seemed great. Then pilotage navigator Kennedy, in the nose turret, observed the lead wing formations veering away from the target heading. A fast and anxious cross-check with lead crew navigator Swangren and a recheck of compass heading and reference points assured command pilot Lorin Johnson that the target was dead ahead. Within minutes Good, the lead bombardier' called over the intercom "I've got the target!" Lead pilot McGregor checked his flight instruments for precise 18,000 feet altitude and 160 m.p.h. indicated airspeed and carefully levelled the aircraft on auto-pilot. He then called back, "On airspeed, on altitude. You've got the aircraft." Making a final level of his bomb-sight, Good took over control of steering the aircraft with the bomb-sight.

'At 18,000 feet it was 40 degrees below zero but the bombardier never felt the cold as his fingers delicately operated the azmith and range controls. He cross-checked all the bomb and camera switches to the "on" position, especially the radio bomb-release signal switch which simultaneously releases all the bombs of the other aircraft in the formation.

'Maintaining perfect formation the 392nd fought its way through the German flak defences and bombed the Gotha works with pinpoint accuracy. After Lieutenant Good had dropped the bomb load the camera recorded the impact of the bombs. Lieutenant McGregor took over and swung the formation to the outbound heading and the rallying point.

'Despite the now accurate flak the second and third squadron bombardiers Lieutenant Ziccarrilli and

 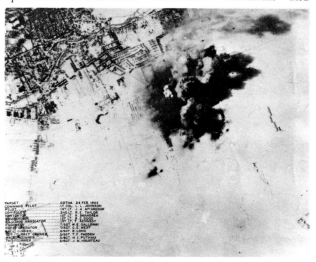

Gotha on 24 February 1944. Before and after. Some 98 per cent of the 392nd's bombs fell within 2,000 feet of the aiming-point.
Keilman

Neatly stacked formation of 392nd Liberators, one with its ball turret lowered, head for their target.   USAF

Lieutenant Jackson, steered their Squadrons to the precise bomb delivery points too. Of the thirty-two B-24s which took off that morning, twenty-nine of them each delivered their twelve 500-pounders precisely on target as briefed.'

The 44th had also achieved a highly accurate bomb run. Intelligence later estimated that six to seven weeks' production of the ME-110 was lost but the 392nd paid dearly for its accuracy. Strung out in trail and with some B-24s slowed down because of flak damage, the three Squadrons became vulnerable to vicious fighter attacks. For an hour after bombing the 392nd was subjected to head-on passes and tail attacks from singles and gaggles of Luftwaffe fighters. When the Group returned to Wendling at 15.30 hours, seven hours after take-off, seven B-24s were missing and another thirteen landed with varying degrees of damage. Sixteen enemy fighters were confirmed destroyed by 392nd gunners.

The thirteen surviving 445th Liberators, nine of them suffering from varying degrees of battle damage, limped into Tibenham at about 15.45 hours. Altogether they had lost 122 men on the bloody mission, including Major Evans, the 792nd Commanding Officer, and most of the Operations Staff. Captain Waldher, Operations Officer of the 700th Squadron, was also lost. The Group's gunners were credited with the destruction of twenty-one enemy fighters plus two probables and two damaged.

Six 389th Liberators were shot down in quick succession during the raid while the survivors received further punishment on the homeward journey.

The 392nd was extremely accurate, dropping 98 per cent of its bombs within 2,000 feet of the aiming-point. The average percentage of bombs dropped by the Second Bombardment Division which fell within 2,000 feet on visual missions under good to fair visibility in February 1944 was only 49 per cent. (In comparison the First Fortress Division achieved 76 per cent and the Third 77 per cent.) American Intelligence described Gotha as 'the most valuable single target in the enemy twin-engine fighter complex'. Its destruction was well received by the Eighth Bomber Command who later awarded the 392nd and the 445th Presidential Unit Citations for their part in the raid.

The very next day — Friday, 25 February — marked the culmination of 'Big Week', with 800 American bombers being dispatched to German aircraft production centres. Second Bombardment Division Liberators were allocated Furth, near Nürnburg. The 14th Wing, with the 392nd's two Squadrons of twenty-two Liberators, bombed the plant with 'excellent' results. Despite nine hours of flying deep into Germany no losses were incurred by the Wendling outfit. On the same day Fortresses successfully attacked aircraft plants at Regensburg, Augsburg, and Stuttgart, after which the weather again closed in. General Doolittle had gone a long way towards achieving his aim of isolating the battlefield, Within a couple of months, through persistent bombing of airfields and railway marshalling yards in France, Belgium, and western Germany, the battlefield of Normandy was isolated and ready for invasion.

Chapter Five

The 96th Combat Wing

On the assumption that 'Big Week' had dealt a severe blow to German fighter production, it was decided to increase the pressure on the Luftwaffe with a series of raids aimed at luring the enemy fighters into conflict. Doolittle now had a much stonger force of Liberators at his disposal to help achieve this objective.

With the addition of three new Groups of the 96th Wing, the Second Bombardment Division had grown to eleven Groups strong by March 1944. The first of these, the 458th, began arriving at Horsham St Faith at the end of January. It was followed by the 466th who flew into Attlebridge a month later. The third Group, the 467th, joined the Wing during the middle of March and went to Rackheath, some five miles north-east of Norwich.

The airfield at Horsham St Faith had been built during the period of R.A.F. expansion, from 1935 to 1939. Towards the end of 1939 it had accommodated Bristol Blenheim light bombers. During 1942 the base was completely rebuilt and in September of that year some Martin Marauders and personnel of the 319th Medium Bombardment Group used the base as a satellite to Shipdham. Attlebridge also accommodated other elements of the 319th until it left England to take part in Operation Torch in North Africa at the end of November 1942. On 30 November the U.S.A.A.F. Second Bombardment Wing assumed control of Horsham St Faith. However, it was not until 5 April 1943 that the 56th Fighter Group flew in from Kings Cliffe in Northamptonshire. Equipped with P-47 Thunderbolts,

Horsham St Faith airfield in April 1946. R.A.F. Mosquitos and Mustangs can be seen. During the Americans' sojourn it was used first by P-47s then by the 458th's Liberators. Note the pre-war R.A.F. facilities including five hangars which can be seen at the foot of the picture.   DoE

Attlebridge airfield in April 1946 with the village of Weston Longville (top right) *and Greensgate* (top, centre). DoE

this unit had only arrived in Britain three months previously. The blunt shape of its fighter's fuselage earned it the nickname 'the Flying Milk Bottle'.

The 56th only remained at Horsham St Faith until early July 1943 when on the 8th it began to move to its new base at Halesworth in Suffolk. By the end of the war the 56th could show an impressive list of achievements. It was unique in being the only Fighter Group to use Thunderbolts throughout the period of hostilities.

Colonel Arthur J. Pierce, Commanding Officer of the 466th (extreme right) *arrives at Attlebridge and is greeted by Lieutenant-Colonel Steadman, Deputy Commanding Officer of the 466th* (second from right) *and other personnel. John O'Cockey* (third from left) *was killed in the Group's fourth mid-air collision.* Woolnough

The Group's decision to always fly Thunderbolts was vindicated when it finished the war as the top-scoring Fighter Group in the Eighth Air Force for 'kills' in the air. Not surprisingly it collected more fighter aces than any other Group, Francis G. 'Gabby' Gabreski and Robert Johnson scoring an unbeatable twenty-eight 'kills' apiece.

Meanwhile, on 12 April 1943, administrative control of Horsham St Faith had passed from the R.A.F. to Substitution Unit Headquarters, Second Bombardment Wing. The Wing retained its umbilical link with the airfield until 14 September 1943 when the Headquarters was transferred to Hethel.

The 458th, with brand-new B-24H and B-24J Liberators, was originally activated on 1 July 1943 at Wendover Field, Utah, and had begun assembly on 28 July 1943 at Gowen Field, Idaho. Successively based in Florida, Utah, and Nevada the Group's training activities came to a close. On New Year's Day 1944 the ground echelon departed by rail from Tenopah, Nevada, for New York, where it embarked on the U.S.S. *Florence Nightingale.* The air echelon travelled to Hamilton Field, California, where its new Liberators were waiting to be flown to England. *En route* to the E.T.O. the Liberators took in Brazil and Africa on the Southern Ferry route. Crews were reunited with the ground echelon at Horsham St Faith on 18 February 1944. With the advance guard had travelled Colonel James H. Ibsell, who had taken over command of the Group from Lieutenant-Colonel Robert Hardy in December 1943.

First Lieutenant (later Lieutenant-General) James M. Keck recalls his arrival in England: 'I was with the original Group to arrive at Horsham St Faith in January 1944.

Extricating a wounded gunner from Liberty Lib *(41-29393) of the 752nd Bomb Squadron, 458th Bombardment Group, at Horsham St Faith after a raid.*   USAF

'Horsham St Faith was a good base — permanent and close to town. We attended church across the street from the Club, got fresh eggs for fighter claims (our crew claimed three destroyed, two probables and four damaged — totally unofficial, but it did get us eggs). We hunted birds and rabbits on the airfield and took turns driving the game on bicycles — and had game dinners in our crew mess — courtesy of Dusty Rhodes, our Mess Sergeant.

Captain Keck returned Stateside in late 1944, returning to Squadron Operations as a Major. He is currently Vice-Commander in Chief Strategic Air Command.

On 11 January 1944 Brigadier-General Walter H. Peck and his Staff had commandeered part of Horsham St Faith for use as the Headquarters of 96th Wing. It displaced the 93rd Wing (part of the Third Bombardment Division) which in turn moved its Headquarters to Elveden Hall, near Thetford, Norfolk. The 96th Combat Wing's second Group, the 466th, was to take over the airfield at Attlebridge, eight miles north-west of Norwich. The base, located in the parish of Weston Longville, had been built in 1941. In the July of that year the station opened as a satellite to near-by Swanton Morley for No. 2 Group, R.A.F. Bomber Command.

During August Bristol Blenheims flew into the partially completed airfield and remained there until September when R.A.F. Attlebridge was closed for further runway construction. Part of this work was undertaken by an Engineering Detachment of United States Training Command from Colorado. Although work commenced on 2 August it was not fully completed until two years later when the number of men at the base totalled almost 3,000. In March 1942 Attlebridge received some B-25 Mitchells crewed by Dutchmen and they used the base until August 1943 when they were superseded by rocket-firing Typhoons. Continuing its diversity of roles, Attlebridge also became the home for some war-weary PBY-4 Liberators of the United States Navy which had accumulated thousands of hours flying over the south coast sea-lanes searching for U-boats.

Towards the end of 1943 plans were made for Attlebridge to receive the 466th Heavy Bombardment Group, and to this end the 61st Station Complement

Squadron arrived to administer the base. One of these early arrivals was Newton L. McLaughlin, the Special Services Officer. Too old for flying at forty-three, McLaughlin was to be responsible for morale and in the course of his duties he became involved in organizing many kinds of social activity. Much of his work was routine and unglamorous but a more rewarding side involved the entertaining of British children at the base.

The hospitality of the Americans was boundless and at Attlebridge Christmas 1943 was dedicated to the children. Second Lieutenant (later Major) Newton L. McLaughlin and his Staff laid on several parties and on Christmas Eve they entertained orphans from Dr Barnardo's Home resident at near-by Honingham Hall. Visits were also made to hospitals in the region and here the Americans' generous pooling of rations ensured that the old folk, too did not suffer the austerities of a wartime Christmas.

Throughout the festive season preparations went ahead to greet the arrival on the base of the 466th

Winter scene at Attlebridge airfield. When missions began 466th crews tried to spin the sails of a windmill in the vicinity with their B-24s' prop wash and bets were placed on who could fly the nearest to its sails.   Woolnough

Wartime view of Rackheath airfield with Salhouse station (centre right) and railway line to the right of the airfield.

Healy

467th assembly ship Pete the POM Inspector. *Painted black overall with yellow discs outlined in red. Later replaced with a similarly marked B-24E.*   Healy

main ground and air echelons. The 466th flew in after completing periods of training in New Mexico, Utah, and Kansas. Much of its training had involved flying monotonous patrols in obsolescent B-24Ds. Then in February 1944 they were ordered to England flying improved B-24Hs. The ground echelon sailed for the United Kingdom in March. Waiting to greet them was the staff of the 61st Station Complement Squadron, together with a small R.A.F. liaison team. At this period American losses were running as high as 25 per cent for each mission flown and the 466th, like any other fledgling group, was soon to find that the realities of combat flying in the E.T.O. bore little resemblance to the training flights undertaken back home in much kinder conditions.

The third star in the 96th Wing nebula was the 467th. Orders from Air Force Headquarters in Washington dated 1 August 1943 directed that the Group should become operational and about a month later these orders were put into effect. Colonel Fred Glantzburg became the Group's first Commanding Officer and held that office until 25 October 1943, when he was posted

Natural woodland and the general agricultural features helped camouflage Rackheath airfield from the air. Sir Edward Stracey's residence is in the foreground (right).

Healy

Aerial shot of the 467th on the march at Rackheath. Colonel Shower ordered parades every Saturday morning when possible. In the background is the technical site. Healy

to the South West Pacific. His successor was Colonel Albert J. Shower who took command at thirty-four years of age. During 1942–43 the Colonel had gained valuable experience in the South West Pacific as a Provisional Group Commanding Officer in the Second Air Force. Upon his return to America in August 1943 he became the Group's Air Executive with the rank of Lieutenant-Colonel. He joined the 467th in Orlando, Florida, in mid September 1943.

The 467th started its training at the Army Air Force School of Applied Tactics at Orlando. Further periods of training at bases at Mountain Home, Idaho, in Kearns and Wendover Field in Utah, put the Group on a war footing. It was at Mountain Home on 22 September 1943 that Lieutenant-Colonel Ion Walker took up his duties as Group Executive Officer. The 467th had left for Wendover Field on 31 October 1943 where its training continued for a further three months. On 27 February 1944 the ground echelon sailed for New York on board U.S.A.T. *Frederick Lykes* and arrived in Scotland ten days later. Meanwhile, after serious deliberations by the P.O.M. inspectors, thirty-six aircraft had taken off from Morrison Field at Palm Beach in Florida at midnight on the 28th. One hour's flying time from Palm Beach and the pilots opened their sealed orders. Their destination was not the Pacific, or Italy, or even Norway as some had thought it would be, but Station

145, Rackheath, Norfolk — the English station lying nearest to the enemy.

While flying the Southern Ferry route, the 467th suffered its first casualties. A B-24 of the 790th Bombardment Squadron crashed in the Atlas Mountains in North Africa killing the crew of ten. Then a second B-24 crashed on take-off at Dakar, injuring two members of the crew. Leaving North Africa the Liberators flew to Valley and Mawgen in Wales and on to Prestwick in Scotland. Crews, ever watchful for enemy aircraft, kept their guns at the ready as the bombers skirted Spain and Portugal. Their careful watch was maintained until long after passing the Brest Peninsula.

Bad weather prevented many of the crews from flying straight to Rackheath. With an improvement in the weather, the first of the B-24s to leave America flew on to Station 145. By coincidence it circled and landed just as a train filled with the ground echelon steamed into Salhouse Station. Both parties had arrived on 11 March 1944.

Norwich was now surrounded by Liberator airfields: a constellation of blue and white stars spread throughout Norfolk. To the west lay the 14th Wing airfields while to the south lay Hethel, Hardwick, and Old Buckenham and farther afield Tibenham, Seething, and Bungay. The men on these bases soon discovered there was little entertainment to be had outside Norwich, the nearest 'liberty town'. Norwich was like a huge octopus and like tentacles the city's eight major roads reached out into the countryside and along these ventured countless G.I.s in their 'Liberty trucks'.

The men of the 458th at Horsham St Faith had an obvious advantage over other Groups as their base was the nearest to the city centre. Among other things this meant they could get to the Red Cross Club at the Bishop's Palace in the Cathedral grounds and enjoy a hot shower long before the men from the outlying bases were anywhere near the city. In the evening the most usual form of entertainment was either a 'pubbing mission' or a visit to one of the city's dance-halls. Probably the most popular was the Samson and Hercules on Tombland, which was affectionately known as the 'Muscle Palace', though no one seems certain whether it derived this nickname from the two legendary stone figures at the entrance or from the fights that went on inside. At Blackfriars Hall the men could attend the weekly basketball sessions and boxing bouts, while

Witchcraft (right) undergoes an engine change at Rackheath. Despite the often bad weather maintenance standards remained high. One ground crew did a thirty-hour engine change in eight and a half hours one cold October day! Healy

The 466th (ex-44th B-24D 41-24109) assembly ship painted in red zigzags. It was also used for picking up downed aircrews and once towed a magnesium flare to France after assembly had been prevented over Norfolk. Archer

Norwich was the nearest 'liberty town' for most of the Second Air Division bases in the region.   Krause

occasional games of baseball were played at Carrow Road, the home ground of Norwich City Football Club.

Carrow Road was even the setting for a Wild West Show which was staged on 5 August 1944. It was jointly sponsored by the Special Services section in conjunction

Arthur Colbourn from Hardwick asks a Norwich 'Bobby' directions in The Walk.   Colbourn

with the Norfolk War Charities Fund and attracted a crowd of over 15,000 most of whom were unaware that only hours before many of the 'cowboys' had been flying over Germany. One of the stars of the show was Lonnie Harvard, a Texan cowpuncher. He was a waist gunner with the 453rd and had flown his nineteenth mission that day with a visit to Brunswick. The ringmaster was Captain Jack Maher, while Corporal Guy Rennie, a former Hollywood showman, was master of ceremonies to help to make it an occasion to remember.

Meanwhile, in March, the 467th at Rackheath was also finding it difficult to adjust to its new way of life and for the first thirty days personnel were restricted to base. However, life was not entirely devoid of pleasure, and even on the first night some British beer and cider found its way on to the base. It was during this settling-in period that the men of the 467th experienced their first air-raid warnings. At first this caused a certain amount of disruption but the Tannoy warnings soon ceased to have much effect.

The Air Ministry had chosen a good site in Rackheath. Work had started on 7 September 1942 and the base

Colonel Albert J. Shower poses on the wing of the 467th monitor ship, the P-47 Little Pete II. *Shower brought the 467th to England and remained in command throughout the war — the only Eighth Air Force Commanding Officer to do so.*   USAF

Colonel Shower, as depicted in a contemporary cartoon.

was built on a natural plateau near Sir Edward Stracey's estate. The plentiful woodland and the general agricultural features were deliberately preserved and helped to camouflage the base. The building work, however, was not without its problems and not least to the local children who had to walk past the Sole and Heel Public House and along Green Lane to their school at Stone Hill. The road split the base, putting the technical site on one side and Sir Edward's estate on the other.

Mr Jack Bunkell, Clerk of the Rackheath Parish Council at that time, remembers that the children were in danger from the build-up of military traffic that used the road and the way in which this particular problem was solved: 'I explained the problem to Colonel Shower and he kindly allocated two lorries to the job of carrying the children safely to school. However the American school bus service only lasted two weeks because when the Norfolk Education Committee heard about it they asked the Americans to stop it. So to bypass all the red tape, Colonel Shower requisitioned the road and put it under military control. Picket-posts were erected and the 467th lorries continued the daily run until Norfolk Education Committee finally provided a bus.' Making provision for local school-children seems, in retrospect, a very small problem compared to the principal activity of making war on Germany but, in its small way, it was

not untypical of the problems associated with 'settling-in' at a new airfield.

Rackheath, like many other airfields, had its own Red Cross Club on the base. Dances were held once a month and a band called the 'Airliners' was formed from base personnel. Films were also shown at the base theatre while live shows were often produced in the canteen. Noël Coward's *Blithe Spirit* and Madame Osina's Children's Dancing Troupe (from Norwich) were always great favourites with the men. On a smaller scale, pianists John Gile and Dick Gray entertained at the Officers' Club and Gile even composed a song called 'Pete the Pom Inspector'. Sport was also popular and at Rackheath the men were fortunate in that they could play tennis on Sir Edward's court.

In many ways Rackheath was a remarkable base and in Colonel Shower the 467th had a remarkable leader. He in turn was supported by a fine back-up team of Staff officers on the base like Lieutenant-Colonel Ion Walker and Lieutenant-Colonel Walter Smith. Smith was the Operations Officer and in Colonel Shower's opinion 'he was outstanding'. 'He came to the Group through the good offices of Colonel Thomas Power — later S.A.C. Commander-in-Chief. Power had visited me at Wendover Field during the early stages of our training and asked me if he could do anything to help the Group. I told him there was a certain Operations Officer at Dyersberg, Tennessee, training B-17 crews. Three days later Colonel Smith joined us at Wendover.'

When the 467th was finally to leave England in June 1945 Colonel Shower was to be the only Eighth Air Force Commander to have brought his unit to England and to retain command of it throughout hostilities. He drove his men hard but got results. The fact that the 467th's bombing accuracy was unsurpassed throughout the Eighth Air Force speaks for itself.

While the 467th was finding its feet at Rackheath a new Group farther to the north-west of Norwich was about to encounter some of the same problems.

'The Golden Gates', entrance to Sir Edward Stracey's estate at Rackheath.   Healy

The famous 'nose-art' of Double Trouble.

Chapter Six

The Hamm Incident

The triangle of American airfields in the Swaffham—Dereham area was completed in March 1944 with the newly constructed base at North Pickenham, four miles south-west of Swaffham. The 14th Wing now had in juxtaposition the three airfields of North Pickenham, Shipdham (44th), and Wendling (392nd). North Pickenham had originally been scheduled for the 491st Bombardment Group then undergoing training in America. In the event another Group, the 492nd, considered to be almost operational, was the one selected to join the 14th Wing in April 1944.

Meanwhile, the 458th, which had flown a diversionary mission on 24 February, made its operational début on 2 March when a small formation was dispatched to Frankfurt, Germany. P.F.F. equipment was used, flak was moderate, and only four FW-190s were sighted. One Liberator limped home and crashed at 9 Pinewood Close, Hellesdon, which lay on the flight path to Horsham St Faith. It partly destroyed the house, killing seven of the crew and seriously injuring three others. The three occupants of the house were trapped in the rubble for a time. Next day the 458th set out *en route* for Berlin only to be recalled. A few Liberators continued on their way and bombed targets of opportunity. One Liberator of the 755th Squadron was lost.

On 4 March the Berlin mission was again cancelled and on the 5th the mission to Bordeaux was aborted. One returning 458th Liberator crashed at the Crown Public House near Hellesdon Golf Course in the vicinity of Horsham St Faith. On the 5th a small force of B-17s had managed to overcome the bad weather conditions and bomb Berlin. Then on Monday, 6 March, the Liberators were at last able to go all the way to 'Big B' with the Fortresses on this, the first full-scale raid on the German capital. If the locals throughout East Anglia could have possibly counted them they would have discovered to their amazement that there were over 700 bombers overhead. But once again the cloud came to the Berliners' rescue and the 458th, which put up twenty-seven aircraft for the mission, was forced to bomb using P.F.F. Of the twenty Liberators dispatched from Tibenham, six aborted early and returned to base. Only nine succeeded in dropping their bombs on the capital, while another six bombed a target of opportunity at Celle.

Hello Natural from the 448th was forced to seek refuge at Bulltofta airfield in Sweden after experiencing difficulties became the first of nine Liberators from the Group which were forced to land in Sweden during the war — the highest of all the B-24 Groups. Altogether sixty-nine bombers were lost on the mission. Sixteen of them were Liberators and of these five belonged to the 458th. The losses to the Eighth were the heaviest yet for a single raid. Two days later the Second Bombardment Division returned to Berlin, this time to the city's industrial district of Erkner which came in for a heavier bombardment than the capital itself had received two days before.

At the beginning of the week-end of 11—12 March the B-24s received stand-down orders because of the bad weather prevailing throughout Europe. The adverse weather was reflected in the number of missions flown by the 446th and 448th that month — only fifteen. But the respite did not last long and on 15 March the 458th was required for the mission to Brunswick. The 446th and 448th were grounded. However the 458th, comprising twenty-six B-24s using P.P.F. equipment, bombed through thick undercast but the results were unobserved. On the following day the Group lost its ninth aircraft of the month when a 755th Squadron Liberator returning from Friedrichshaven was forced to ditch in the Channel. Air-Sea Rescue picked up three of the crew but only two survived.

The mission to Frankfurt on the 17th was abandoned but on the following day the Liberators again returned to Friedrichshaven and the city's Dornier works. The Germans seemed to be ready for them, having lost their complacency on the 16 March raid, and the 14th Wing in particular came in for some rough treatment. Heavy flak dispersed the formation to such an extent that many Liberators flew over Swiss territory on the opposite side of Lake Constance and drew fire from the Swiss guns. Because of mistiming the fighter escort failed to turn up on schedule and the 14th Wing was left to fend for itself against an estimated seventy-five single-engined enemy fighters. They attacked in line abreast, three and four at a time, and harried the Liberators for over a hundred miles. Captain Keilman remembers: 'Between flak and the many fighter attacks only fourteen of twenty-eight aircraft returned to Wendling. The lead ship had an engine shot out on the bomb run; then persistent fighter attacks worked the Group over all the way to Strasbourg. The lead navigator was blinded by a 20 mm shell. Even when P-38 Lightnings came to the rescue, the German pilots continued to press home their attacks and the 44th lost eight Liberators.

The intense flak over Friedrichshaven damaged fifteen of the nineteen aircraft dispatched by the 458th but none from that Group was shot down. But the 453rd's Commanding Officer, Colonel Joseph Miller, was. Jim Kotapish, the co-pilot aboard *Reluctant Dragon*, flying below Colonel Miller's aircraft, recalls: 'Our astute Group navigator had led the Group over the harbour and everyone was waiting for us. The first flak burst hit the bomb bay of the lead ship with Colonel Miller in it and it immediately burst into flames. All I

North Pickenham airfield in January 1946. DoE

could think of was "Please God, don't blow up right now or we'll get the whole plane in our nose." It didn't: it banked right in a slow spiral and several men baled out of the plane which was streaming flames from the bottom and the waist windows. Those men who escaped were evidently from the waist and tail.

'The second burst hit our left wing. While I heeled over to follow the deputy leader out to sea, Ray Sears, the pilot, was busying himself with number two engine which had taken the brunt of the burst. At that point Ray took over since the bank was obstructing my view of the leader and I wasn't sure that we were flying into our left wingman. I followed the flight of the plane as long as I could but it fell behind the line of vision and to my knowledge did not blow up. Much later I heard that the early parachutists were swept out across the lake and drowned before the speedboats could pick them up, while those who stayed with the plane were captured, including Colonel Miller.' Next day Colonel Ramsey D. Potts arrived to succeed him.

The month of March had proved particularly cruel to the 14th Wing, to which belonged over half of the forty-three bombers shot down on the second Friedrichshaven raid. But other Groups had also been severely tested that month. The 445th at Tibenham lost twelve bombers, as did the 458th, which, despite their preponderance over the Luftwaffe on many occasions, revealed the inexperience of the American crews. Three of the losses at Horsham St Faith that month were attributable to crashes on practice missions.

Towards the end of March the weather grew worse and grounded many bomber Groups throughout the region. It improved enough, however, on 21 March for the 458th to be dispatched to the V.1 sites at Saint-

Omer. All aircraft received varying degrees of flak damage and thick cloud again prevented accurate bombing. Next day the Liberators returned to Berlin with the 466th participating in the air war for the first time. It was customary for the Germans to 'welcome' new Groups over the Reich with a barrage befitting the occasion but this time the 466th, as if in deference to its inexperience, was fortuitously spared. Two 466th Liberators, however, collided and further losses were only averted by surprisingly light flak.

On 24th March the 466th, the 'Flying Deck' as it came to be known, lost another two Liberators, in a collision near Osterburg *en route* to their target, the German airfield at Achmer. Towards the end of the month the Liberators were dispatched against other airfields in

Crew of the Reluctant Dragon. Back row, left to right: *Ray Sears, Jim Kotapish, Gene Minor, and Leonard Phillips.* Front row, left to right: *Sergeants Burkhardt, Youtsey, Harvey, Marin, and Oppis.* Kotapish

The 389th assembly ship Green Dragon, *painted in concentric green and yellow twenty four inch stripes. Replaced later by another war-weary Liberator which used small yellow diagonal bands across the fuselage and wings.*   via Bailey

France. The 466th went to Saint-Dizier on 24 March and was then rested for two days. On 27 March, the third and final day of operations against the airfields, the 96th Wing was dispatched to the airfield at Biarritz on the Bay of Biscay coast near the Franco-Spanish border. But the spectre of collision returned when two 466th B-24s collided shortly after take-off from Attlebridge and twenty-four men plunged to their deaths in the fields at Hoe and Gressenhall, only a few miles from the base runways. This third fatal collision brought the Group's losses to six in five days. However other Groups had better luck. The 458th executed a highly accurate bomb run with twenty-four B-24s hitting the airfield at Biarritz with fragmentation bombs and destroying installations and some aircraft at dispersal. The weather, which was bad when the formation had taken off from Horsham St Faith, worsened upon the Liberators return and they were diverted to other airfields in the region.

The cloudy conditions which had dogged the late March missions persisted on April Fools' Day when the Eighth was assigned targets in the Ludwigshaven, Friedrichshaven, and Pforzheim areas. The thick cloud grounded the First Division and also forced the Third Division to relinquish the mission to the Liberators. But when the Second Division succeeded in penetrating southern Germany the conditions caused the formation to stray off course. Thick cloud filled the sky, even at 21,000 feet, and many Groups failed to locate their targets. Thirty-eight bombers from the 44th and 392nd dropped their bombs in error on the Swiss town of Schaffhausen over 120 miles from their assigned target

at Ludwigshaven. It was a mistake Goebbels was quick to exploit in an attempt to divert the public's attention from the ever-increasing number of air raids on German and German-occupied territory.

The 448th was assigned Pforzheim, near Karlsruhe, with Colonel Thompson flying as command pilot in a P.F.F.-equipped ship, leading the formation. Early reports were vague but it seems that in bad weather the lead ship lost its bearings and eventually ran low on fuel, and the order to bale out was given. Colonel Thompson's parachute failed to open properly and he was killed. This was the story given to the men at Seething some time after the raid when Captain Robert Thornton, one of the two navigators, was returned to England via the French Underground and Spain. Thompson's aircraft was one of ten Liberators lost during the day's débâcle. On 3 April 1944 Colonel Gerry Mason, an ex-fighter pilot in the C.B.I. (China, Burma, India) Theatre, assumed command of the 448th and joined the Group two weeks after Colonel Thompson's death.

The 458th was on stand-down until 5 April when it flew to a 'no-ball' site at Saint-Pol-Siracourt in France. Two more days of stand-down preceded the mission on the 8th to Brunswick-Waggum as part of a 600-strong force. Strong fighter opposition shot down a 753rd Squadron ship but thirty-six aircraft scored hits on the airfield with 'excellent' results. The 466th fared worse, losing ten Liberators to the 'Battling Bastards of Brunswick' as the crack fighter unit was dubbed. The 445th lead ship with Lieutenant-Colonel Robert Terrill aboard had two engines knocked out by flak over the target. Despite this, Terrill succeeded in bringing the bomber home on the two remaining engines and was later awarded the Distinguished Flying Cross by Colonel Ted Timberlake.

During April 1944, preparations for D-Day served to increase the threat of collisions. At Hethel a war-weary B-24D was commissioned as a forming ship but could not prevent a collision between a 389th Liberator and a 392nd machine on the 9th, Easter Sunday. It occurred at about 09.00 hours over the Foulsham area in north Norfolk. Eight men aboard the 389th ship were killed and only one man survived from the 392nd aircraft.

One of the two survivors from the 389th aircraft was Captain (later Colonel) John Driscoll, the Group Gunnery Officer with the 566th Squadron. He was in the waist position and his task that day was to take strike photographs of the target. But after taking off from Hethel in poor visibility the weather grew much worse. The Liberator first entered undercast and then disappeared into overcast at 8,000 feet on a collision course with the 392nd Liberator. The unsuspecting crews collided with such intensity that seven men in the forward fuselage section of Driscoll's Liberator were killed instantly when five 500 lb bombs and the full fuel load exploded. The forward section disintegrated and wreckage flew through the air. Three bombs, which failed to explode, fell near the bomb dump at R.A.F. Foulsham which contained some R.D.X. bombs.

Captain Driscoll and two others were trapped in the still-intact tail section which spiralled to earth like a falling leaf. The three men grabbed their chest packs and tried to escape through the hatches but the tail gunner failed to open his hatch and he was killed in the crash. Driscoll opened his hatch with some difficulty and baled out at 1,000 feet, pulling his parachute shroud as he

The tail section of Captain John Driscoll's B-24 that was involved in the collision with a 392nd B-24 on 9 April 1944.
Driscoll

Group Commanders gather at Ketteringham Hall early March 1944. Back row, left to right: *Fred Dent (44th), Milton W. Arnold (389th), Jacob Brogger (446th), Jim Isbell (458th), James Thompson (448th), killed in action 1 April 1944), Leland Fiegel (93rd), Albert Shower (467th), Irvine Rendle (392nd), Ramsey Potts (453rd).* Front row, left to right: *Jack Wood (20th C.B.W.), Ted Timberlake (2nd C.B.W.), Brigadier-General James P. Hodges (C.O. Second Bomb Division), Leon Johnson (14th C.B.W.), Jerry Mason (soon to command 448th upon the death of Colonel Thompson).*   USAF

drifted to avoid hitting the now-burning tail section. Although there was no fuel in the tail section, a combination of hydraulic fluid and oxygen from the bottles quickly started a fire. Driscoll finally landed in the back garden of the Baileys' farm near Foulsham, which housed a family with five daughters.

Over at Horsham St Faith, nineteen Liberators had defied the elements and taken off for the FW-190 airfield at Tutow, Germany. However, bad weather caught up with them over the Continent and forced the majority to seek their secondary target at the airfield at Pachion. Bombing was ineffectual and the Group lost four Liberators.

While its 96th Wing partners were flying over Germany the 467th was told to stand by for its first mission which was to be flown the following day, 10 April 1944. The Group had been at Rackheath only twenty-nine days and its state of readiness reflected the marvellous achievement of Colonel Shower and all personnel. They had knuckled down to three weeks' intensive activity and fifty-two aircraft were dispersed around the airfield's periphery. Fifty-eight Liberators had originally arrived at Rackheath but one had crashed on a training flight trying to land downwind on the shortest runway on the field. The pilot was demoted to co-pilot. 'In which ignominious state', wrote Colonel Shower, 'he flew several missions. After taking the bump in a graceful manner, I was happy to give him a crew and he turned out a very good aircraft commander.' Fortunately none of the crew had been injured in the crash. Five other Liberators had been reassigned to other Groups as replacements and now all but three Liberators were serviceable for the Group's first misson.

Tension was paramount on the base and the ground staff were keyed up and anxious that it had done a good job on the Liberators. Those air crews alerted for the

mission were also tense, their minds full of thoughts of combat and possible baling out. They thought too of escape and evasion and checked that they had photographs of themselves for use on false identity papers. Their escape kits were checked for minute compasses and maps and G.I. shoes were tied to their waists in case they had to walk to freedom across the Pyrenees. But these preparations were not yet absolute for it was discovered at briefing that the 467th had no aerial photographs of its target, the aircraft assembly plant at Bourges airfield in central France, and a false start was only just averted when they were collected from 96th Wing Headquarters at Horsham St Faith in an emergency dash.

Colonel Shower led the thirty Liberators at 06.00 hours in Lieutenant Kenneth Driscoll's B-24. The Group formation was split into two Squadrons with Major Smith leading the second element in Lieutenant Richard Campbell's Liberator. A fair assembly was completed and the 467th slipped into the 96th Wing formation which joined the other Groups in the Divisional assembly line. Altogether the Eighth dispatched 730 heavies to pound aviation targets in the Low Countries and central France. Combat crews had studied flak positions, the position of target buildings as shown on the R.A.F. night target charts, and target photographs during the pre-operational month at Rackheath. Bombardiers had paid particular attention to target photographs, from which they determined and pinpointed positions of the probable M.P.I. (mean point of impact).

The mission went well. There was no flak at all at the enemy coast and no fighters appeared. It turned out to be a 'milk run'. Good visibility over the target aided the 467th which dropped its 1,000 lb general-purpose bombs on the hangars and factory buildings. Other

James Stewart, seen here with (from left to right) Second Lieutenant Robert F. Sullivan, Captain Ray L. Sears (pilot of Spirit of Notre Dame*), and First Lieutenant Cromarty, when he was 453rd Bombardment Group Operations Officer. He is interrogating crews following a raid on Berlin.*
USAF

Crew of the Vadie Raye. *Standing, left to right: A. H. Hau, Elbert Lozes, Alvin Skaggs, Don Todt, B. F. Baer. Kneeling: George Glevanik, R. K. Lee, Frank Sheehan, Stan Filopowicz, Gene Gaskins, William Jackson.*
Sheehan

Groups, too, had bombed well and a later reconnaissance revealed that the factory had been almost completely destroyed.

The ground staff had been told of the 467th's estimated time of return and had gathered in the warm sunshine by the briefing building. The expectant ranks cheered as the aircraft flew over the airfield in tight formation and they were full of pride and relief as one by one all thirty Liberators peeled off and landed. Each one taxied along the perimeter track with the waist doors open. From inside and atop the aircraft, gunners and engineers waved to the waiting ground crews. Interrogation revealed that four aircraft had failed to bomb but the other twenty-six had dropped 149,000 pounds right on the target although one squadron was slightly west of the M.P.I.

The Group had been blooded at last and next day it raided Germany for the first time, suffering its first operational casualties in the process. The 467th was part of a 900-strong bomber force of B-17s and B-24s whose aim was to destroy aircraft factories in eastern Germany. Two men were wounded when the 467th successfully bombed Ascherleben. On 12 April the mission was recalled but on the 13th casualties continued to rise. The 467th went to Lechfeld and the first crew was taken from the Group. First Lieutenant Ernest Calvorai and Staff Sergeant Abel Williams were killed and the remaining seven members of the crew were made prisoners of war. The third man killed from the 467th was Second Lieutenant Oliver Snook. His death occurred on the Group's eighth mission to the 'no-ball' site at Siracourt, France, on 20 April 1944. The V.1 sites were always difficult to hit and on this occasion no bombs hit the target.

A mission scheduled for the following day was re-called and lead crews throughout the Division were told to stand by for a strike on the Hamm marshalling yards. Hamm had been bombed the year before by the Eighth but in the early hours of 22 April it soon became apparent that all was not going to plan. Crews at Bungay and Seething had been apprehensive from the start. They had been awakened in the middle of the night because the mission was scheduled for the usual early

morning take-off. It was later postponed for several hours because of bad weather over the Continent. After several stop-go decisions it was in the afternoon that Command finally sanctioned the mission. Crews who had been awake since 02.00 hours had their briefing updated with more recent weather information and began reassembling for take-off. It was not until between 16.15 and 16.30 hours that twenty-four B-24s, laden with men weary from waiting, took off from Seething.

The 2nd Wing led the Second Bombardment Division to Hamm — Eighth Air Force Mission 311 — with Colonel Terrill, Commanding Officer of the 445th, as command pilot. He and his crew, which included three navigators (P.F.F. Pilotage, and P.R.) used an Alconbury P.F.F.-equipped Liberator temporarily based at Hethel. The pilot, D.R., and P.F.F. navigators were all part of the P.F.F. crew from Alconbury. Terrill flew in the co-pilot's seat and he took off from Hethel and rendezvoused with twenty-four Liberators from Tibenham which had finally taken off at 16.00 hours. The 2nd Wing formed up forty-five minutes later.

The weather was still marginal and seasoned crews realized that fighter support in the target area and on the homeward flight was doubtful. There was a perceptible lack of enthusiasm about the mission and many found reasons to abort before reaching the enemy coast. Other Groups throughout eastern England had also been delayed and would have to return in failing light. The Divisional formations grew and flew south, crossing the Channel towards Holland and linking up with P-38 Lightnings, which escorted the Liberators as far as Dortmund.

The route to the target was without incident with only the occasional flak barrage and very little fighter opposition. Hamm, however, was quite well defended. In the clear conditions of late evening the bombers had little difficulty in locating their target — three and a half miles long and nearly a mile wide. Such a large target necessitated bombing in wing formation but despite the tight wing pattern adopted some bombs fell wide. When the Germans discovered the bombers' intentions, the defences opened up and a few fighters were scrambled to harass them as they left the target.

The marshalling yards at Hamm come under a heavy bombardment.

Strong headwinds and too many short zigzagging legs to the target took parts of the 2nd Wing over the Ruhr Valley, subjecting the formation to intense flak and delaying the approach to the primary target. Instead of crossing the target on a 135 degree heading as briefed they came into the target from 260 degrees. The 2nd Wing missed the I.P. and the 445th and part of the 453rd were prevented from bombing the primary target owing to other, incoming, Groups. The Liberators, therefore, continued down the Rhine where they bombed a secondary target at Koblenz. They made a bomb run from 360 to 180 degrees and bombed short of a bridge spanning the Rhine. Crews had been given strict instructions not to bomb near the Cathedral. The day's mission had been a typical 'snafu' from the outset and even worse was to follow on the homeward trip.

Captain Alvin Skaggs of the 448th was that day flying *Vadie Raye*: 'The ultimate German plan did not begin to unfold until we started back across the English Channel. It was getting dark and tail gunner Bill Jackson noticed German fighters taking off from bases along the coast. He alerted the crew and I passed the word along to the command pilot, Captain Blum. He had heard no word over the command radio but listened a while in case any of the commanders ahead of us were reporting this information to Fighter Command in England. After waiting a while he broke radio silence to report this threat and to request fighter support.'

The Liberators crossed the French coast between Nieuport and Furnes while German fighters were taking off in droves. The 448th began recrossing the English coastline at points from Orford to Southwold and other Groups were even farther north. The skies over England were fairly clear and although there was no moon the stars were out. Night flying with hundreds of aircraft in the same general area was very hazardous under the best conditions but the lack of adequate signals with which to identify themselves with British anti-aircraft forces served to increase the difficulties of the American crews. The Luftwaffe pilots soon began switching off their running lights but the Liberators kept theirs on to facilitate formation flying.

Landing procedure was for the Liberators to approach a homing beacon at low altitude near Great Yarmouth, go out to sea at about 1,500 feet and make a 180 degree turn for positive identification and return inland at this height. However, British coastal batteries began opening up, their fire not only embracing the enemy fighters but also the Liberators.

Francis Sheehan was in the waist position of the *Vadie Raye*: 'Flak was showering all around us and it hit the ship directly to our rear. It exploded in mid-air and as I watched this ball of flame fall away I was completely stunned. On board the stricken B-24 had been Lieutenant Cherry Pitts and his crew, among them our closest friends and barrack-mates, including Sergeant Arthur Angelo. It was later discovered that the anti-aircraft gunners were firing at every aircraft that had followed us back across the Channel; later identified as ME-410s [KG 51] which hit us around 1,000 feet.'

Jack Taylor, a member of the Royal Observer Corps at Beccles, was on duty that night: 'I went on duty at ten o'clock and was told that the American bombers would soon be making landfall. Then in the distance I saw them coming in low with all theirs lights on. Suddenly their mighty drone was replaced with a different engine noise. A JU-88 flew fairly low overhead, quickly followed by an ME-410. Soon tracer bullets were ripping through the bomber formation over the Beccles area. One Liberator crashed near the school at Barsham [467th] and another fell on the railway line at Worlingham [448th]. I was the first to report to our centre. "Hostile aircraft in the vicinity: sound only." They replied, "There are no hostile planes on our chart." I heard other sounds and reported the plots to the centre but received the same reply. I was very worried knowing that all these bombers were coming in and being shot at like sitting ducks. I can' only assume the German planes came in below the radar beams.'

Skaggs broke combat formation after seeing two more aircraft go down in flames and headed in trail formation back to Seething. 'Several planes from other formations had remained at altitude and we could see some of them going down in flames with the fighters shooting at them. We could see others exploding and burning on the ground. At Seething some were on fire and others were off the runways.'

Hardwick, Bungay, and Seething were illuminated by their runway and marker lamps. At just after 21.30 hours the 20th Wing split into three groups near Southwold to begin their landing patterns. By now the airfields themselves were being bombed and strafed. Some of the hardest hit were those in the Waveney Valley, home of the 20th Wing, where five Liberators were shot down within minutes. Others were prevented from landing by enemy fighters which circled like vultures waiting for bombers to make the attempt. Liberator crews panicked and many gunners fired thoughtlessly and at random. One Liberator formation dropped flares, which only succeeded in exposing a Fortress formation heading for home. Ground forces added to the confusion by opening fire on the last

John J. Driscoll of the 389th Bombardment Group being decorated by General Doolittle on 22 April 1944 for rescuing four crew members of a B-24 that had crashed at Hethel. Colonel Timberlake had watched the brave rescue from the control tower (background) General Doolittle flew down from Headquarters in a P-38 to make the award.

Driscoll

Liberator formation to cross the coast. In the chaos, *Cee Gee II*, a 453rd machine, fell to an intruder aircraft and crashed in flames near Southwold while two others, badly damaged, managed to fly on.

Vadie Raye was low on fuel but so close to home that Skaggs decided to try for a landing: 'As we approached the downwind leg with the base just off to our left, an ME-110 made a pass at us and riddled our mid section with hard-nose, soft-nose, and 0.30 calibre tracer bullets. From my vantage I barely got a glimpse of him as he came from behind and passed across to our left. I later learned that ground defences shot this one down. He had made his pass from our right rear, crossing us at about a 40 degree angle. His tracers cut some of our fuel lines and started a fire in the bomb-bay section.'

Francis Sheehan was in the mid section: 'A stream of orange tracer ripped through the belly of our bomber. There was a great yellow and orange flash in the waist position and fire broke out around us. I was struck in the leg and went down on the floor. When I came to, Sergeant Eugene Gaskins was suspended by his parachute outside the waist window. I also went to the window and baled out, pulling the ripcord as I had been taught.'

The fire swept from the rear of the bomb bay to the tail section. The rear gunner, Bob Jackson, also baled out and landed close to an M.P. station near Bungay. Alvin Skaggs remained to try to bring the blasted Liberator down safely. '*Vadie Raye* was now too low for any of the crew in the cockpit and forward section to bale out so my only alternatives were either to reach a safe altitude for baling out or try to reach the field for a landing. All too soon the engines stopped running. I glanced back at the fire in the bomb bay and could see Master Sergeant George Glevanik standing on the catwalk over the bomb-bay doors right next to the flaming fuel lines. Seconds later the two outside engines suddenly sprang to life and I was able to climb back to pattern altitude of 1,000 feet. I later learned that George was able to get some fuel to the engines by holding his bare hands very tightly over the breaks in the lines.'

Skaggs was able to bring the burning Liberator down on to the runway at Seething. While it was rolling at 70–80 m.p.h., First Lieutenant Don Todt, the navigator, and two others, went up through the top hatch and rolled out over the wing. Miraculously they all survived. Skaggs and the others scrambled from the wreckage. Glevanik, the brave engineer, was the last to extricate himself. Sheehan and Gaskins had landed safely and after some help from women at a Land Army hostel, had been returned to Seething by ambulance. Bob Jackson was later killed over Liège, on 5 September 1944, by a small piece of flak.

The burning pyre of the bomber illuminated the entire airfield. It served as a beacon for preying twin-engined German fighters who swarmed towards it like moths to a candle. They strafed the base from every direction. Ground defences, hitting back with tracer only succeeded in bringing down two of their own bombers. One intruder attempting to strafe the runway was foiled when someone extinguished the lights. Liberators making their final approach run were forced to circuit again as officers in the control tower screamed over the radio-telephone for them to remain airborne.

Crews unable to make contact with traffic control and with fuel getting low decided to land. Inexperience

Morning after the night before. Three of the wrecked Liberators (12840, 128595 and 9575) at Seething.   Sheehan

was evident as pilots bringing in their B-24s applied the brakes so strongly that they burned out from under them and crews were blinded by the flames.

Warnings were given of obstructions at the end of the runway and when landing lights were momentarily flashed on pilots were horrified to see three wrecked Liberators in their path. They feverishly cut their throttles but could not prevent their aircraft hurtling towards the wreckage. With collision unavoidable ignition switches were turned off to lessen the risk of fire. There was a terrific, sickening crash as the bombers hit. Crews scrambled frantically from the upper fuselage, their escape route from underneath thwarted because the bombers were embedded in deep mud. Then a fifth and final Liberator hurtled towards the pile and swelled the wreckage.

Meanwhile, the 467th, on their tenth mission, were also returning in gathering darkness after an accurate bombing of the marshalling yards at Hamm. Joe Ramirez, crew chief of *Witchcraft*, was waiting at dispersal for the Group to return. It was dusk and he could see smaller aircraft coming in with the formation. He believed them to be escorting P-51s.

As the first few bombers alighted on the runway the German pilots struck, firing their machine-guns and dropping bombs. The Liberators in their traffic pattern with their lights blazing were warned off. Aircraft veered in all directions and the normally tranquil Rackheath sky was suddenly turned into a tumult. Anti-aircraft batteries opened up, while some crews manned their 0.50 calibre guns and blazed away at the intruders.

A JU-88 made a pass over the airfield at fifty feet, firing tracers and dropping two bombs. A Liberator which was undergoing repairs under floodlights at the southern end of the airfield was hit and Joe Ramirez, standing only one dispersal away, saw Private Daniel F. Miney killed as he cycled across the concrete. Private Michael F. Mahoney, a ground crewman working on the B-24, was wounded in the explosion. The other burst destroyed a cottage in the vicinity.

Two B-24s were also lost. First Lieutenant Stalie C. Reid's Liberator from the 791st Squadron went down at Barsham. All the crew perished, trapped in the burning bomber. Lieutenant Roden's B-24 from the 788th Squadron crashed at Mendham.

Colonel Shower remembers that: 'One of the planes was reported hit by flak, the other by enemy fire. I wondered how they got out of the traffic pattern as we had a procedure to depart from Splasher 5 at Cromer and peel off over the base at close intervals to stay in the immediate vicinity of the base for landing. But in the dark things look different as visual reference is lost.'

Colonel Shower recalled: 'The mission had been conceived to destroy some special equipment which the Germans had brought in to repair damage in the marshalling yards. After the target the wing lead told us when over the Channel to break formation and return to base in individual streams of aircraft, due to our inexperience of night flying. We began to let down over France and some of our gunners began returning ground fire. I told them to cease firing because we could not make out the targets properly and the firing might disclose our position. As we came over the Channel I directed a manoeuvre to break out into elements and then into single aircraft from a 360 degree turn. This the Group performed. It was not a standard operation as we had never trained for night flying.

'We were very close to landing when control told us to remain airborne. Control said, "We've got an emergency here", but no further information was given. The lead aircraft, in which I was flying, was one of the last to approach the base. We made three approaches altogether. At one time we were all set to land when the runway lights were turned out and we were ordered to go around once again. Another time the lights were turned on for an approach on a different runway. Apparently the people on the ground were trying to cope with a difficult situation and this may have accounted for the lack of information given us in the air. Then one of the crew reported that someone was on our tail (this was to Campbell on the intercom). I told him to turn off even the inside lights to avoid detection. I was quite impatient at the delay in landing as it seemed every time we lined up we received a wave off or the lights would be extinguished or the runway switched. The aircraft which were shot down were those that turned on their landing lights.

Because Colonel Shower had led the mission, in Richard Campbell's aircraft, his B-24 had not consumed as much fuel as the rest of the formation. They were continually jockeying their throttles in order to maintain formation and, therefore, used more fuel than the lead ship. Colonel Shower was among the last to land and was met by a worried Chaplain, Arthur L. Duhl. It later transpired that if some of the 467th Liberators had not been diverted to other bases, they would have landed safely. The attack passed by Rackheath to be continued in the vicinity of other bases.

At near-by Horsham St Faith the 458th too had their troubles. One B-24 had already been lost over northern Holland but when the twenty-four survivors returned in the gathering dusk, German intruders intercepted them at 6,000 feet some ten miles south-east of the base. The control tower ordered the formation to fly north-east for twenty minutes before turning back. No further enemy intruders were spotted but one Liberator, piloted by Lieutenant R. T. Crouch, which crashed in the Lakenham area of Norwich a few hundred yards from the Tuckswood Public House, was thought to have been brought down by anti-aircraft batteries protecting the City.

Rick Rokicki, a gunner on *Briney Marlin* at Horsham St Faith, was not flying that day but recalls the 'utter confusion': 'I know there was much speculation about the anti-aircraft fire and some of our guys were quite bitter about it but it happened after many tiring hours in the air. Add to that the unfamiliar darkness and a flurry of fierce activity just when everyone figured that it was another mission "in the bag" — then being attacked! When it was signalled for the "code for the day" someone apparently "blew it" with the wrong or slow I.F.F. signal.'

The 2nd Wing also experienced difficulty on the return journey. Two 445th Liberators were lost on the raid. Lieutenant Sadlon's ship was lost to flak as was Second Lieutenant Frank Sneed's, which went down near Ghent on the outward trip. Sneed was captured and made a prisoner of war. Flying time was an estimated six hours so the 445th formation returned at about 20.00 hours — long after blackout time. The crews had already cleared their guns for landing when, in the gathering darkness, coastal and inland anti-aircraft batteries opened up. About fifteen JU-88s and ME-410s were in the vicinity. At 20.30 hours the twenty-two Liberators were circling Tibenham with the first B-24s making their approach when a 453rd B-24J made an emergency landing. Meanwhile over Tivetshall railway station a twin-engined intruder made a pass at a Liberator but sheered away after a red flare was fired from the B-24's waist position. None of the 445th machines was lost.

Hethel, too, had its share of trouble. Earl Zimmerman was grounded that day and was standing with a group near the radar shack about eighty feet from the control tower. 'The main runway was closed off because one plane had come in with a collapsed nose-wheel and had skidded to a halt. We had to switch round to the short runway to land the remainder of the Group. The plane came in low over the trees and the landing-strip lights were turned on momentarily so he could get lined up to land. He had his landing lights on and we thought he was a JU-88 looking for the control tower. We got ready to take off but we could see his four props turning over and knew right away that it was a B-24. This was Lieutenant Foley's plane. He had been hit by anti-aircraft fire (British) as he came across the coast. (I think the boys were ordered to turn off the I.F.F.s that night) He had received some damage and as he touched down he did not know it but his left landing wheel was flat. He pulled off the runway and headed for the control tower. But he could not cut his engines back. They were turning over at high r.p.m. He was wounded and later told me that once down he was going to stay down, it was so bad up in the air above. He missed the control tower and slammed into the radar shack killing three or four men. His crew got out alive but the aircraft caught fire and burned up.'

Next day Jack Taylor talked to American crews at Flixton: 'The first one crew knew of the enemy aircraft in their midst was as they stood near the middle of the aircraft taking some refreshment. With cups raised to their lips a hail of tracer ripped through the middle of the fuselage but luck was with them and no one was killed. They dropped the cups and rushed back to their guns.'

In all thirteen Liberators crashed or crash-landed in east Norfolk on the night of 22 April 1944. Two more were damaged on the ground. Thirty-eight men were killed and another twenty-three injured. The fires at Seething were not extinguished until the following morning at 03.30 hours.

Chapter Seven

Build-up to D-Day

While men throughout Norfolk and Suffolk cleared away the debris cluttering the airfields after the intruder attack of the night of 22 April, it was time for the Eighth to look ahead to the momentous day when the Allies would invade 'Festung Europa'. The Liberator force was further strengthened and preparations were begun immediately to get the new Group operational in time for D-Day. When that day was — no one knew for certain. But it was imminent and the Second Bombardment Division had to be prepared for a maximum effort when the fateful day finally arrived.

During April the first of three new B-24 Groups arrived to supplement the Second Bombardment Division. On 18 April North Pickenham had laid out its black carpet of runways for the Liberators of the 492nd Heavy Bombardment Group and then on 25 April there arrived at Metfield in Suffolk, the ground echelon of the 491st Heavy Bombardment Group. The latter's ground echelon had been selected from the four B-24 Groups already stationed in England. The 491st had begun life at Davis-Monthan Field, Arizona, in October 1943 but when the Group moved to Biggs Field, Texas, in early November that same year, its ground echelon was transferred to B-29 Groups. The 492nd, which was in a more advanced state of preparation for movement overseas, took the 491st's place and had sailed to England before them.

Colonel Eugene Snaveley had been posted from the 44th to command the 492nd on 26 January 1944. He and his crew flew into North Pickenham via the Southern Ferry route to be greeted with slashing rain. It had turned the runway into a skidpan and some crews experienced difficulty in landing.

At North Pickenham about this time was Bill Cameron who had transferred from the 44th in early 1944. Here he had set up a school for lead crews rejoicing in the unofficial title of 'Bill Cameron's College of Tactical Knowledge'. Bill Cameron returned to Shipdham in early June 1944 after thirty days' rest and recuperation leave in America. Colonel John H. Gibson was now in command of the Eightballs having succeeded Colonel Fred Dent at the end of March 1944. According to Cameron, Gibson 'made a big impact on the Group's morale and it was reflected in its improved bombing record. Gibson's success was built on Dent's foundation and he was very popular with all personnel.'

Meanwhile, farther south, at Station 355, Metfield which had been offically handed over to the Eighth Air Force on 10 March 1942 was also awaiting another B-24 Group, the 491st. In early August 1943 the 353rd Fighter Group, commanded by Lieutenant-Colonel Joe Morris, equipped with Thunderbolts, flew into the base. The 353rd stayed at Metfield until early April 1944.

One man who still remembers the Group with affection is Mr Leslie Pye, the General Foreman of Trades during the construction of the base. He recalls: 'The pilots were all officers and gentlemen and we civilians never had the least cause for complaint.'

Early in April 1944 plans for the forthcoming invasion of Normandy involved redeployment of both Eighth and Ninth Air Force Groups. All five of the Ninth's Fighter Groups in the Colchester area were required for the operation and the airfields at Metfield and Halesworth were now needed for two new Liberator Groups, the 491st and 489th. On 12 April the 353rd, therefore, went from Metfield to Raydon, Suffolk, and on 18 April the 56th went from Halesworth to Boxted. At Metfield some 145 key ground personnel, which had left America on 11 April 1944, arrived to supplement the ground echelon.

Men stationed at the Liberator bases throughout the region who had taken forty-eight-hour passes to London returned with vivid accounts of lorries, half-tracks, and tanks jamming the English roads and lanes. They were all heading south like one huge migrating flock. Passenger trains were withdrawn and trains out of London were crammed. All this supported the belief that D-Day was not far off but none of them knew when.

Invasion fever gathered momentum as preparations went forward on the American bases. Airfield defences were tightened up and precautions were taken against possible attempts at sabotage by enemy paratroopers. The number of air crews and available aircraft were kept at peak strength while training, especially of new crews, was stepped up. Confidential papers poured into the bases each day.

Then came a bitter pill for the crews to swallow — the announcement that tours would be increased from thirty to thirty-five missions. At the same time Headquarters announced that deep penetration raids ranked equal to the short-haul missions in the table of missions per tour. It developed into a problem of morale, which became acute long after D-Day when the Groups returned to the deep penetration raids into Germany. Eventually a fair method was evolved when Air Force Headquarters recognized the greater risks involved in flying deep into Germany where the targets were more heavily defended.

On 27 April at 07.50 hours the 467th lined up for a raid on the German airfield and aircraft factory at Leipheim. Colonel Shower led thirty-six aircraft at the head of the 96th Wing, which was third in the Divisional assembly line, deep into enemy territory. Twenty-six Liberators bombed after four had aborted. Flak was light and no enemy fighters appeared. Strike results proved that the 467th and 96th Wing had completely plastered the airfield. The first bomb released hit the

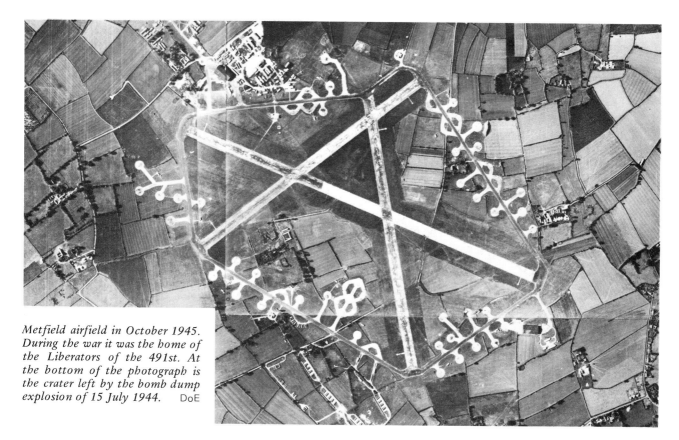

Metfield airfield in October 1945. During the war it was the home of the Liberators of the 491st. At the bottom of the photograph is the crater left by the bomb dump explosion of 15 July 1944. DoE

M.P.I. and all except nine bombs, which hung up and dropped later, hit within 2,000 feet of the M.P.I. The first Squadron destroyed the hangar and service area and the second partially hit the airfield. Colonel Shower was later awarded the Distinguished Flying Cross for his leadership of the raid.

Three days later, on 27 April, for the first time the Liberators flew two missions in one day. Eighteen Liberators took off from Horsham St Faith on the Thursday morning for Bonnières constructional works in France. All aircraft returned safely. The 445th's target was the marshalling yards at Mimoydeques and in the afternoon it flew on its second mission, to Chalons. All forty-four Liberators dispatched from Tibenham that day returned safely. These two raids were the first of eighteen invasion missions flown by the Group to France up to D-Day. Also in the afternoon of 27 April twenty-one B-24s took off again from Horsham St Faith

and split into two elements and bombed the Blainville marshalling yards. The first element fared extremely well as the Luftwaffe remained at a distance and both elements returned safely to England. The 458th was stood down the following day.

On 29 April the Eighth returned to Berlin for a disruptive raid on the German civilian population. Friedrichstrasse Bahnhof, centre of the main-line and underground railway system in Berlin, was the Liberators' target. Raids of this nature were made to undermine morale and to impede Germany's war effort by preventing people getting to their place of work. Seven hundred bombers of the three Bombardment Divisions were dispatched.

The Second, flying thirty minutes behind schedule, brought up the rear of the formation, which was met in strength by the Luftwaffe. After leaving Celle airspace the only protection afforded the Liberators was a solitary Mustang Group which was forced to retire just after the B-24s completed their bombing run. It was not until the Liberators reached the Dummer Lake on the homeward journey that American escorts reappeared, this time in the shape of P-47 Thunderbolts. German ground-controllers, however, seized upon the time lapse and directed over 100 fighters to the Hanover area to intercept.

The 467th was flying its first Berlin mission that day and Major Robert L. Salzarulo, Commanding Officer of the 788th Squadron, was shot down. Colonel Shower recalls: 'Being our first trip to Berlin I was leading a squadron effort in the 96th Wing and Bob was flying in the deputy (right wing) position. Bob was there after the target but dropped behind and went down in Holland.'

Lieutenant Salzarulo and Lieutenant William Moore's crew, with whom he was flying, were later reported prisoners of war. Lieutenant John L. Low, the Group bombardier, who was also flying with Moore, evaded

She Devil, one of the first five 491st Liberators to land at Metfield. Halbert

Halesworth (Holton) airfield taken in October 1945 during R.A.F. occupation. During the war Liberators of the 489th Bombardment Group used the base. Their stay was short — only seven months. The Group returned stateside for redeployment to the Pacific. DoE

capture for 296 days in enemy-occupied Holland and the rest of the crew were liberated a year later, on 29 April 1945. Altogether twenty-five Liberators were lost that day, including two more from the 467th, bringing its total number of men lost to thirty-two. One 458th Liberator from the 752nd Squadron was forced to land in Sweden.

It was during April that the Eighth Air Force was divorced from the Combined Bomber Offensive and was placed under the command of the Supreme Allied Commander, General Eisenhower. Operations were not affected, but by a coincidence the highest losses of aircraft during the war were recorded that month. May saw the Eighth concentrating on rail networks in France and Belgium as part of the pre-invasion build-up but bad weather cancelled many of the missions and attacks were switched to the V.1. rocket sites. These raids relied heavily on the use of H2X because of the thick cloud which obscured the targets.

The next bombing priority was the oil-refineries. The U.S.S.T.A.F. had finally agreed to attacks on German oil-production centres because it was believed that the Luftwaffe had suffered heavy losses the previous month. Before that the strategists had thought the Luftwaffe too strong for the U.S.A.A.F. to tackle. There were, however, still many officers who opposed the bombing of the refineries but they were overruled by Strategic Air Command. It was argued that without fuel the Luftwaffe would be banished from the skies. And its neutralization was a prerequisite for the invasion of Europe.

Although this vital campaign, directed against the synthetic oil production centres near the massive coal-fields of the Ruhr, and the coming invasion, meant offensive action on a grand scale, certain defensive measures had to be taken. On Monday, 8 May, a meeting was held in the War Room at Ketteringham Hall with representatives of all Groups in the Division.

General Hodges and other members of his Staff outlined precautions which were to be taken immediately to strengthen base defences against enemy attack.

That same day the Liberators attacked Brunswick. They had originally been scheduled to raid the German city four days earlier but had been recalled. For the 467th it was its second pathfinder mission and for Lieutenant Thomas Murphy it was his first mission as a first pilot. His Liberator was damaged over the target but he successfully nursed it back to Rackheath where he ordered his crew to bale out. Murphy remained at the controls and flew on to the Third Sub-Depot at Watton, where he crash-landed. It was a remarkable piece of flying for a pilot on his first mission.

'Shortly before 8 May', wrote Colonel Shower, 'General Peck, Commanding Officer of the 96th Combat

Little Lulu just after arrival at North Pickenham on 18 April 1944. Gene Snavely (un-zipping jacket) is meeting many of his ground staff officers for the first time. Halbert

Lieutenant Murphy's Liberator damaged on the Brunswick raid of 8 May 1944.   Noble

Bombardment Wing, invited me to Wing Headquarters at Horsham St Faith along with Jim Isbell of the 458th, and Art Pierce of the 466th. General Peck told us each to get out half a crown to toss. He explained that someone had to give up a squadron for a special mission. Coming up the "odd" man, I decided to give up Bob Salzarulo's 788th Squadron which he had commanded until he was shot down.'

General Peck had been ordered to transfer a B-24 squadron to the 801st Provisional Bombardment Group at Harrington, Buckinghamshire, to meet a request for further personnel and aircraft. These were needed to meet an increase in operations for the forthcoming D-Day landings. The British Prime Minister, Winston

The 489th's Commanding Officer, Colonel Ezekiel W. Napier (right) and the Deputy Commanding Officer, Lieutenant-Colonel Leon Vance at Wendover Field, Utah, in December 1943. Vance won the Medal of Honor on 5 June 1944. A flak hit killed the co-pilot and practically severed Vance's foot. Despite this he flew on and bombed the target later ditching in the Channel. Vance was drowned in late July when the C-54 evacuating him stateside was lost without trace over the Atlantic.   Freudenthal

Churchill, had decreed, 'Set Europe Ablaze'. Under the code-name 'Carpetbaggers', the 801st was helping to do just that. Royal Air Force Lysanders based at Tempsford were dropping S.O.E. 'Joes' (the Special Operations Executive's Secret Agents) into Occupied Europe. The Carpetbaggers later supplemented these clandestine operations with personnel of the O.S.S. (Office of Strategic Services) using black-painted Liberators. Originally trained and equipped at Alconbury, the 801st grew from two squadrons and moved to R.A.F. Watton in February 1944. It moved to Harrington, near Tempsford, in early April the same year.

The 788th Squadron was transferred on paper to the 801st on 10 May. Ironically, at Rackheath, the remaining three Squadrons put as many bombs on the target as other Groups did with four Squadrons. Also on 10 May the 492nd flew its fourth practice mission, to the French coast, allowing the rest of the Division to continue to the target. The next day it flew on its first mission.

During the first fortnight of May, the 489th Heavy Bombardment Group, which had been activated on 1 October 1943, began flying into Halesworth, Suffolk. The 489th, together with the 491st at near-by Metfield, were to form the 95th Wing which had been activated on 11 December 1943. This was the fifth and final Wing of the Second Bombardment Division. The 95th was to be unique in that it was the only one in the Division consisting of two Groups. The other four each had three.

The 489th ground echelon had sailed the Atlantic aboard the U.S.S. *Wakefield* on 13 April 1944 but the air crews had taken a little longer in their preparations. In March that year, they had flown a mock combat mission for the Air Force Inspector and passed the P.O.M. tests. The air echelon flew to Kansas for final processing and then on to Morrison Field, Florida for the first leg of their movement overseas.

The Liberator crews took off from Morrison Field singly and in the dead of night. They opened sealed envelopes containing their secret orders after one hour's flying time over the sea and the men heard over the intercom that they were now part of the Eighth Air Force and were England bound. The Group flew the Southern Ferry Route to England, making flights in the early morning and using celestial navigation on the longer legs. Departures from each station took place at five-minute intervals and each plane twice crossed the Equator on its flight to England.

Crews, while straining their ears for possible radio jamming, cast a wary eye over the Bay of Biscay for possible enemy fighters. Colonel Ezekiel W. Napier, who had assumed command on 20 October 1943, and Colonel Morneau, piloted the first 489th Liberator to land in England on 1 May 1944. In the same aircraft

Ex-44th Bombardment Group B-24H Lil Cookie served as the 489th's assembly ship. This photograph shows Ford's Folly (42-94842) flying above the yellow polka dotted port wing of the Judas Goat. Freudenthal

were Captain McGrath and Captain Freudenthal with Major Hoak and Major Lafferty.

At near-by Metfield, the 491st crews, who had taken off from Florida on 1 April, began flying in between 15 and 30 May. Their flight had been uneventful and crews had eaten breakfast at Land's End before flying on to Suffolk.

The 489th and 491st Liberators were sent to modification centres, returning with every pilots' clock either strayed or stolen. However, the navigators found that their blister windows had been much improved although the pilots were dismayed at the extra weight the introduction of armour-plate entailed. Long practice flights at altitude were made daily when the weather permitted. Colonel Napier preached tight formations and gradually the lead crews who made mistakes profited by them. One inexperienced navigator got his aircraft hopelessly lost and landed just south of London.

From 16 to 18 May 1944 the weather worsened, cancelling all missions. On Friday, the 19th, despite some mist the weather sufficiently improved to enable 331 Liberators to set out for the marshalling yards at Brunswick, an old acquaintance of the B-24s. The mission

began badly and, after delays and aborts, 291 B-24s finally headed out towards Holland.

Over the Zuider Zee a change in wind direction placed the Liberators ahead of schedule enabling the Luftwaffe ground-controllers to vector 160 fighters against the American formation. Despite valiant efforts by three escorting Fighter Groups, the Liberators were overwhelmed and four 492nd ships were shot down. A fifth continued to the target but exploded before 'bombs away'.

The 14th Wing arrived over the target behind schedule after turning late at the I.P. The 20th Wing, flying in front of the 14th Wing, made three turns over the target. The 14th Wing bombed at the first attempt and headed for home after almost colliding with the 96th Wing. The 492nd lost three more B-24s coming off the rallying-point, bringing their total losses to eight — double that of all the other Groups combined.

Second Lieutenant Wyman Bridges brought *Lucky Lass* home after a collision with an ME-109. His ship had only two engines and had lost half the starboard wing. His miraculous feat earned him the Distinguished Flying Cross. The 492nd was stood down the next day.

Liberators of the 844th Bomb Squadron, 489th Bombardment Group at dispersal at Halesworth in July 1944. Freudenthal

Salvage crews from the 3rd S.A.D. look over a crashed 392nd B-24 (41-29433) on 31 May 1944. Note the freshly painted wing codes over the old circle 'D'.
Noble

The 446th and the 448th also took a break in missions, being stood down from 13 to 20 May. But on 21 May, they joined the vast aerial armada which blasted targets from the French coast to deep into Germany. The emphasis now was on tactical rather than strategical missions. Good fortune prevailed and the Liberators flew their mission with little interference from the Luftwaffe. One Group, the 467th, flew five missions without loss during the early part of the month.

However, the weather remained unkind and was partly responsible for two collisions. On 23 May, during assembly for the mission to Bourges, a 458th B-24 collided with a Fortress over Eye, Suffolk, killing six crewmen. Four days later two Liberators, belonging to the Group's 755th Squadron, collided north of Cromer in undercast. One ship went into a spin and only one crewman, who left by the waist window, was seen to escape. Two men baled out of the other B-24 but those who remained with the aircraft managed to bring it home safely.

On 23 May the day the B-17 collided with the B-24, a new navigator, First Lieutenant John R. 'Bob' Shaffer, flew his first mission with the 93rd. The target was the airfield at Orléans-Bricy, France. Light flak and the non-appearance of the Luftwaffe allowed the Group to destroy the hangars and administrative buildings almost at will. Five days later Bob Shaffer doubled up as a bombardier aboard *Naughty Nan* when the Liberators went to the synthetic-oil refinery at Meresburg, the

second largest of its type in Germany. Flames reaching to 2,000 feet was proof enough that the Liberators had found their mark. Even 200 miles from the target, crews could still see the pall of smoke, which rose 12,000 feet into the air.

Second Lieutenant Ben C. Isgrig, was flying his first mission as a bombardier with the 448th that day and for him it was almost his last: 'Our particular target was the ammonia section of the plant. We were carrying forty-eight 100 lb G.P. bombs and were in the first section over the target. This was our first mission and I guess we were all pretty scared and nervous. Nothing eventful happened during the trip to the target: we saw no fighters (except ours) and very little flak. All over the area adjacent to our target were huge fires from the oil which had been set afire by preceding Groups. There was quite a bit of flak in the target area as we were approaching but it stopped before we reached the range of fire.

'I watched the lead planes' bombs begin to drop and started to toggle ours out, but instead of falling clear, seven bombs in the right rear rack hung up. This was caused by the bottom station's failure to release the three bombs in the lower rack, and four bombs from above jamming up on top of them. Two of the four were sticking between the wall of the bomb bay and the three bombs in the lower station. This effectively crammed the bombs and made it impossible to salvo them. I went back into the bomb bay and was scared to

San Diego-built B-24J Royal Flush *(44-40291) of 753rd Azon Bomb Squadron, 458th Bombardment Group, reached England on the Southern Ferry Route after suffering many malfunctions and a complete engine change. Her engine continued to plague her and on 31 May 1944 Lieutenant McCarthy and a skeleton crew gave her a shakedown flight. It lost an engine on take-off and ploughed in at Horsham St Faith, never having dropped bombs in anger.*
Noble

see that the propellers on the fuses of three of the bombs were turning rapidly, which meant they were probably fused and liable to go off at the slightest jolt.

'I got Kovalchick, a gunner, to help me and we were able to get them out by lifting them up one at a time and dropping them out. It was a wonder that one or both of us didn't fall out of the bomb bay. It is no joke to stand on a foot-wide catwalk with no parachute at 22,000 feet in a 20 degrees below zero breeze and no support, and throw out bombs one at a time. Kovalchick was using our one walk-around oxygen-bottle; I had none. As we turned to leave the bomb bay after dropping out the last bomb, I stumbled and nearly fell from the plane, but Kovalchick caught me and pulled me through the door and to the nearest oxygen outlet. The trip on home was uneventful.'

On 29 May, the Liberators visited the Junkers JU-88 assembly plant at Tutow and the Politz oil-refinery. Ben Isgrig and the 448th went to Tutow, a small German town close to the Baltic coast and wrote: 'We carried fifty-two 100 lb M47 incendiary bombs in the same ship we flew in yesterday. Armament assured me that they had fixed the bomb racks. Most of the trip was over the North Sea, and after crossing the coast the only flak we saw was in the vicinity of Hamburg. We were the last Group over the target. The Groups ahead of us were carrying G.P.Bombs. We were supposed to burn the wreckage that was left after the other boys went by. We didn't see any fighters so the ride to the target was uneventful.

'We reached the target and the bombs hung up again. We had an easier time as the bombs were not fused and I wore my oxygen-mask back in the bomb bay so there was no danger of passing out from anoxia and nearly falling out as I had yesterday. We got the eleven bombs out pretty fast. I have yet to see my bombs hit a target. Someday, I hope I can just sit in my nose turret and watch the fireworks. The results were good, on both days, we heard. The trip back was mostly over the Baltic and North Sea so we saw very little flak and no fighters.'

Returning from Politz, a 492nd Liberator piloted by First Lieutenant William V. Prewitte, got into difficulties over the North Sea. An R.A.F. Air-Sea Rescue launch, already *en route* to another ditching, received the May-Day signal from Prewitte's ship, which was directly overhead. Charles Halliday, on board the launch, looked up, saw the B-24 and informed his skipper. Within seconds the crew of the B-24 started to bale out. Only nine made it. Second Lieutenant Henry Muller, the bombardier, drowned after his parachute had failed to open. Halliday watched Second Lieutenant Elmer W. Clarey, the co-pilot, descending. On hitting the sea he failed to release his parachute and it began dragging him under. Charles Halliday bravely dived into the sea to find Clarey already trying to sever his shrouds with a dagger.

'He was in a pool of blood', recalls Halliday. 'He had been stabbing himself in his haste to get his 'chute free. I told him that I would rescue him and he was to throw away his dagger. He threw it away and allowed me to grab him. By this time he was all in and glassy eyed. When we got him aboard, he and the others were given hot drinks. We fitted them out in civilian clothing which turned out to be far too small for their large frames. One remarked that he looked like Al Capone in his small English suit which only reached half-way up his arms and legs.'

After an hour-long systematic search for the tenth man had proved fruitless the Air-Sea Rescue launch returned to Gorleston and the survivors were put ashore. Clarey was not with Lieutenant Prewitte and two others from the 29 May incident when, on 16 August 1944, they were killed, while flying a 467th practice mission.

On 29 May the 489th flew a practice mission over Major-General Hodges's Second Bombardment Division Headquarters in tight formation. Colonel Morneau told crews: 'Colonel Napier wants you to go to bed now. It may or may not mean something.' The following day the 489th flew its first mission. It formed part of a large force engaged in 'softening up' the invasion coast. Captain Titus, with the then Deputy Commanding Officer of the 489th, Colonel Leon Vance, and First Lieutenant John R. Probert as lead navigator, led three Squadrons from Halesworth to Oldenburg airfield in Germany. But the Group crossed the Dutch coast ten miles south of their briefed target where an accurate flak barrage enveloped them and a navigator was killed. On the homeward leg Lieutenant E. T. Clark was forced to ditch in the North Sea after running low on fuel and he and his crew were made prisoners of war.

On the same day John Shaffer *en route* for the 93rd's briefed target at Rotenburg, Germany also had problems. Five times his pilot lost touch with the formation and only Shaffer's navigational skill got them back in line before reaching the Dutch coast. The flak over Heligoland was accurate and tracked between Shaffer's ship and the one following. Although sustaining some damage, both B-24s shrugged off the stiff resistance and visually bombed the airfield.

Next day the Eighth attempted to bomb the bridges at Beaumont-sur-Oise, Melun, and Meulan in France but was unsuccessful. These attacks introduced an entirely new concept in bombing, using the revolutionary Azon glider bomb. The device could be released by an aircraft at a distance and then directed on to the target. Basically it was a conventional 1,000 lb bomb fitted with radio-controlled moveable tail fins. Visibility had to be good to enable the operator in the B-24 to keep a visual sighting on it right to the target. For this purpose a smoke canister was attached. Each bomber could carry three such bombs but had to circle the target as many times to release them, which was an obvious disadvantage.

General Spaatz revived interest in the Azon 'stand-off' bomb after German flak had increased both its area of operation and its effectiveness during the early part of the month. It fell to the 458th to evaluate the Azon bombs under combat conditions. On 30 May only four Liberators were used and because of the secrecy involved they were escorted by a large force of fighters. The raid, flown at 10,000 feet, was a failure with none of the bombs hitting the target. Experimental raids continued into June with at most fifteen Liberators on any one mission. But the results did not improve and prompted General Doolittle, the Eighth Air Force Commanding General, to abandon the project.

Meanwhile, the last of the 491st Liberators had flown into Metfield and combat personnel were immediately put through a rigorous induction course of detailed lectures. Often starting at 08.00 hours, these lectures would sometimes continue late into the evening. At the same time training schedules were being continuously interrupted by air-raid warnings. Battle stations were allocated and the combat crews, now on their first

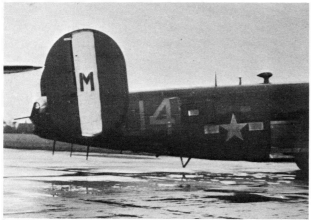

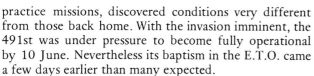

Azon masts on a B-24 of the 753rd Bomb Squadron at Horsham St Faith. The first mission using Azon bombs was flown on 23 May 1944 against a bridge spanning the Loire River.   Krause

Assembly unit of the Azon bomb. Later versions of this radio-guided bomb included the Razon and the 12,000 lb Tarzon used by B-29s in Korea.   Krause

practice missions, discovered conditions very different from those back home. With the invasion imminent, the 491st was under pressure to become fully operational by 10 June. Nevertheless its baptism in the E.T.O. came a few days earlier than many expected.

A practice mission had been scheduled for midday on 2 June, but crews were later told that the 491st would join with the 489th for a raid on Bretigny airfield near Paris — the first full 95th Wing mission. Thirty-six Liberators, led by the Deputy Commanding Officer, Lieutenant-Colonel Jack Merrell, took off from Metfield to rendezvous with forty-one Liberators from the 489th. The 95th Wing reached the C.P. on schedule but the lead aircraft from the 489th decided to ignore the briefed dog-leg route which avoided flak on the southern side of Paris and instead fly straight to the French capital. The formation rolled up their bomb bays, opened up their throttles, and at 19,000 feet headed for the primary target. One 491st ship was shot down before 'bombs away'.

The main force, led by the 489th, continued over the centre of Paris to Creil airfield while fourteen others bombed Villeneuve airfield in mistake for Bretigny. Heading for home again the 489th forsook the briefed route and four Liberators were lost to flak over northern France while fifty-nine sustained varying degrees of

damage. Thirty-five 491st Liberators approached Metfied in gathering darkness and all did well to land safely. At Halesworth, though, three Liberators crashed and had to be written off.

The 448th, meanwhile, struck at a 'no-ball' target five miles south of Fervert, France. Ben Isgrig wrote: 'There was a 10/10 overcast over Europe so we did our bombing by P.F.F. As I didn't see the ground from the time we left England, I don't know where the bombs hit. The mission was strictly a "milk run", no flak, no fighters, nothing. We were only over enemy territory about thirty minutes. I could use about twenty-six more just like this one.'

Missions continued to France and on 4 June *Sack Rat*, piloted by Second Lieutenant Clifford R. Galley of the 491st, developed a high-speed stall while forming up and crashed near Sizewell in Suffolk, killing everyone on board. Next day, on Monday, 5 June, the Division was briefed to attack French coastal defences between the Cherbourg Peninsula and the Pas de Calais. The 96th Wing struck at Stella-Plage near Bolougne. The 93rd bombed large gun emplacements in the Pas de Calais. Other Wings too had French targets and the conclusions were that the morrow's missions would be something very different from those which had gone before.

The 458th's assembly ship First Sergeant, *formerly ex-93rd Ploesti veteran* Thar 'she Blows, *burns after an accidental discharge of flares on the flight deck at Horsham St Faith in May 1944.*   Krause

Chapter Eight

D-Day and beyond

East Anglia on Monday, 5 June presented a scene of great activity. At Flixton top brass from both Divisional and Wing Headquarters descended on the base and senior officers stepped from their cars and quickly disappeared behind locked doors for a hastily convened conference. Field Order No. 328 came in over the teletape machines throughout the Division and at Flixton flying control was the first to receive the news. To almost everyone's surprise and delight, the 446th had been chosen to lead the entire Eighth Air Force over the invasion coast of France on D-Day. The 446th was advised that six Liberator elements would take off at ten-minute intervals. Squadron operations were notified that the mission was to be a maximum effort so that ground crews would have to pull out all the stops. Orders for bomb-loading and fuelling were issued earlier than usual and no one was permitted to leave the base.

All the air crews were summoned to their briefings over the Tannoy system. The main briefing was scheduled for 22.30 hours but four others followed into the small hours of Tuesday, 6 June. The briefings, given by Captain Hurr, were the longest and most detailed the Group had ever received. Major Stahl concluded the briefing: 'You are to strike the beach defences at Point de la Percée, dropping your bombs not later than two minutes before zero hour [06.30 hours]. Landing craft and troops will be 400 yards to one mile offshore as we attack and naval ships may be shelling our targets onshore. Deadline on our primary target is zero hour minus two [06.28 hours]. After that bomb the secondary target, which is the road junction in the Forest of Cerissy, or the target of last resort, which is the choke point in the town of Vire.'

At near-by Seething the 448th crews had been called to the briefing-room at 23.00 hours and Colonel Jerry Mason said 'This is it.' Crews were very excited during the briefing but had settled down by the time they took off. Their target was a beach (they later discovered it to be 'Omaha') and the landing-parties were to be only 400 yards offshore when they struck.

The first mission was primarily concerned with the neutralizing of enemy coastal defences and front-line troops. Subsequent missions were directed against lines of communication leading to the bridgehead. The Liberators would be in good company with no less than thirty-six Squadrons of Mustangs and Thunderbolts patrolling the area. Initially they would protect the bombers but would later break off and strafe ground targets. It was evident that there could be no delay and that stragglers would be left to their fate. Any aborts were to drop out of the formation before leaving the English coast and then fly back to base at below 14,000 feet. It was a one-way aerial corridor and the traffic

flow intense. If a B-24 had to be ditched, only those ships returning to England from the beach-head would stop to pick up the crews. Finally, new instructions on prisoner-of-war procedures were given. General Doolittle, in a message read out to the men at all bases, said: 'The Eighth Air Force is currently charged with a most solemn obligation in support of the most vital operation ever undertaken by our armed forces. . . .'

Briefing over, a line of trucks was assembled to take the crews to their waiting Liberators. At 01.30 hours the slumbering Cathedral city of Norwich and the pre-dawn calm of the surrounding countryside were shattered by the roar of thousands of Twin Wasps being pre-flighted at all points of the compass. Overhead the moon shone through thick black undercast.

Meanwhile at the three 96th Wing bases at Attlebridge, Horsham St Faith, and Rackheath, crews were alerted for an early briefing. At Horsham St Faith thirty-one 458th crews were briefed for the first of three missions that day. At Rackheath thirty-four B-24s took off. Altogether the Wing put up 108 Liberators to bomb the shore installations at Colleville and Port-en-Bessin. They took off to assemble before dawn but overcast conditions dispersed the formation.

By 14.00 hours the Liberators at Flixton were formed in two lines converging at the head of the runway. This avoided the problem of anyone leaving a revetment, going off the runway, and ruining the timetable. All aircraft had their navigation lights on with the yellow-orange Judas Goat, *Fearless Freddie* completing the picturesque spectacle, taking off first at about 02.00 hours to form the Group. Colonel Brogger, flying with Lieutenant Charlie Ryan of the 704th Bomb Squadron, was next in line in *Red Ass*, renamed (for public relations purposes) *The Buckeroo*. Colonel Brogger's ship, on paper at least, would be the first Liberator over the enemy coast. Just on 14.20 hours, Captain Smith in the control tower informed the chequered caravan crew at the edge of the runway to 'Give 'em the green light.' *Red Ass* thundered down the runway, followed by B-24 after B-24. Close at hand was a 389th Group radar ship.

At Hardwick, Bob Shaffer was one of the many who had spent all night in careful preparation: 'We took off at 14.00 hours. The flak was light and the mission successful. I flew as lead bombardier in *Naughty Nan* piloted by Lieutenant Sneddon. There was a full moon and I have never seen as many ships of all descriptions as there were crossing the Channel. I saw battleships firing at gun emplacements. It was quite a sight − quite a show.'

The final cog of 20th Wing, the 448th, also joined the formation. Ben Isgrig recalls: 'It was just getting light as

Tar Hell Baby (41-129125) of the 392nd passes over a harbour on D-Day.   USAF

our formation left the English coast and the clouds broke enough for us to see the hundreds of ships in the Channel heading for France. We could plainly see the heavy warships shelling the coast, which was shrouded in smoke. Besides seeing more ships than I had ever seen before, there were also more heavy bombers in the air than I thought possible to put up in one area. The coast itself was covered in clouds. We didn't see our target at all; neither did we see flak or fighters.'

Meanwhile the 96th Wing was *en route* to its target on the French coast. It flew in elements of six aircraft. One ship in each element was equipped with H2X to locate targets if they were obscured. Their inclusion was prudent because complete overcast during the mission was to prove disastrous. Many Squadrons were joined by Liberators from other Groups who had strayed off course and only sixteen B-24s of the 467th managed to drop their bombs. Only about half of the 264 500-pounders and only about a third of the 100-pounders were released over the targets. The crews were bitterly disappointed.

There was no sleep for those left behind. A second mission was being planned and this to be followed by a third. Ground crews earned no respite and after a hasty breakfast they were out again working on the aircraft. Ironically, amid all the activity, the German radio at Calais was on the air playing a song called 'Invasion Day'.

Some crews were required to fly their second mission of the day, as was Ben Isgrig: 'Instead of being excited, as we had been in the morning, we were just tired and worn out. Again we saw the landing-craft in the Channel; again our target [Caen] was covered by clouds. We saw no flak or fighters.'

The second D-Day mission was very discouraging. A small formation joined with the 96th Wing in an attack on Villers Breage, France. The Liberators had a good tailwind all the way but apart from that the weather was against them. They ran into overcast and at about 05.50 hours thick clouds drifted over the target forcing crews to release their bombs using radar aids.

The 446th dropped its bombs unobserved through the clouds while the twelve 467th Liberators returned with their bombs still resting in their racks. Ten 458th Liberators and the 95th Wing, which had been stood down for the initial attack, also returned to base fully laden. A slight improvement was made on the third mission, flown that afternoon, when overcast still draped its cloudy curtain all the way from England to the invasion coast.

The 96th Wing's target was the bridge at Pontaubault which lay at the junction of the Cherbourg and Brest Peninsulas. Of the twenty-four Liberators dispatched from Rackheath, five failed to assemble in the overcast and one aborted with mechanical trouble. Colonel Shower led the remaining seventeen Liberators to the bridge through gradually worsening weather. Crews throughout the Division caught only fleeting glimpses of the Allied Fleet ploughing through the murky wastes of the English Channel. Bombing was again aided by H2X after the 467th formation, despite a 360 degree turn, had failed to capitalize on a break in the clouds. It was later estimated that the 215 500-pounders released by the Group fell about 2,000 feet east of the M.P.I. Eighteen 458th Liberators had their results described as 'poor'. It was no one's fault: they had been defeated by the weather, which grew steadily worse as the day progressed. However the 20th Wing, led by the 446th, managed to fit in four missions, seeking targets at Vierville-sur-Mer, Coutances (twice), and Caen.

The Liberators did succeed in disrupting communications and damaging airfields while the flow of Allied troops into the bridgehead continued unabated. It was a superb effort by both the ground and air crews. Many airmen flew more than fifteen hours and went without sleep for thirty hours. Enemy fighters and flak were rarely in evidence and only three bombers were lost that day. One Third Bombardment Division Liberator was shot down and two Fortresses collided. Ground crews worked throughout the night of 6 June and all day on the 7th to ensure that the maximum number of aircraft were available for maintaining the upsurge of missions.

On 7 June the 448th returned to France but by now the invasion had lost its sparkle, as Ben Isgrig wrote: 'We were still pretty tired from the day before and were no longer able to get excited over our part in the invasion. The Channel was clear; more ships were there than the previous day. I saw four different beaches south of Le Havre. There was no activity visible in the vicinity of Cherbourg but from our altitude [22,000 feet] it was impossible to see anything smaller than a large tank, which were very numerous at the beach-heads. Our lead navigator screwed up but we managed to drop our bombs. Again no flak or fighters: hope this keeps up.'

Next day Bob Shaffer flew his ninth mission when the 93rd headed for the airfield at Laval; the nearest airfield to the front line. But it was shielded by 10/10 cloud cover so the Group flew on to Le Havre and bombed ships in the harbour and dock installations. Two ships were sunk and fires were started on the docks. Bob Shaffer wrote: 'Went with pilot Jordak in *Ma's Worry* as bombardier. Flew in over Le Havre, all of our planes were hit by flak. Almost had it today. Missed a head-on crack with a B-17 by fifteen feet. Was socked in up to 26,000 feet. We could not even see our wing tips. We were returning to base over England. Fortunately we decided to dive and they decided to climb. Otherwise it would have been a head on.'

Ben Isgrig flew his eighth mission on 10 June and was shot down two days later on his ninth. The American public was only too aware of the mounting casualties in the E.T.O. and the acceleration of missions in June required many new crews. New crews were arriving at the bases almost daily to be immediately rushed into combat.

In early June, Sol Greenberg, a newly commissioned navigator, joined the crew of *Betty Jean*, a 453rd replacement crew, at Boise, Idaho, where they were mostly involved with gunnery and bombing practice. *Betty Jean*'s crew, led by Allen Bryson, had been together for about four months. Sol Greenberg's arrival,

Albert Gehrt, Allen Bryson, and Sol Greenberg, three of the crew of Betty Jean.   Greenberg

at a time when there was a shortage of navigators, brought the crew up to full strength. But even at Boise life could be dangerous, as Sol Greenberg remembers: 'We spent six weeks flying day and night navigation missions to work me into the crew and on one of these we went out for thirteen hours. Our B-24 landed and another crew was on the pad waiting to take over the plane. They gassed up as we unloaded our gear and it took us about twenty minutes to get down to the operation shack. The plane rolled down the runway for about eighty yards and then exploded, killing all aboard. We suspected a broken fuel line but that was never determined. The black smoke could be seen in Boise and Bryson's wife Ruth, naturally apprehensive, called the base where she contacted some acquaintance. He checked and they had not yet removed our names from the aircraft assignment so that Ruth was told that it was our crew. She fainted and over an hour later Al returned home and found her lying in a stupor.

'One night we were supposed to be flying a practice run on the radio range and noticed that other bombers from Pocatello were flying the same exercise at the same

Crew of Betty Jean *at Boise, Idaho, in May 1944. The B-24J sports an early Corvair turret.* Back row, left to right: *Allen Bryson, Pilot; Ed Watson, Co-pilot; Albert Gehrt, Bombardier; Sol Greenberg, Navigator.* Front row, left to right: *Clarence Mayronne, Waist-gunner; Joseph Grunas, Nose-gunner; Robert Atkins, Tail-gunner; George Walker, Waist-gunner; David Mitchnick, Radio-operator; Maxey Spencer, Engineer, top-turret.*   Greenberg

altitude, We then decided to leave and headed for Salt Lake City, which was situated in Bryson's home area. Naturally we told no one and when we returned the tower was very surprised to hear from us since two planes had collided into mountains while flying the range and they assumed it was a three-plane collision as we had not been in contact for four or five hours. There was one heck of a lot of explaining to do after we landed. Needless to say we lied our heads off and there was no punishment since we were so close to being sent to combat.

'The rumour mill at Harrington, Kansas, was that we would head out for Kunming, China. However after the second day we were hurriedly placed aboard a train and shipped to Camp Kilmer, New Jersey, which was a staging area for outgoing troops. We stayed perhaps forty-eight hours and were then sent to Staten Island Pier, quite late at night, and put aboard the *Brazil* which had been a cruise ship. We were jammed tight, three high, into rooms the size of a sardine can. The heat was unbelievable and most of the voyage was spent in our birthday suits, roasting in the bunks. For the enlisted men below deck in the holds it was even worse and we did what we could to make them a little more comfortable but nothing much could be done. The one laugh we did have was that the W.A.C.S. had to line up for chow twice a day along the corridor where our doors were. We would then go through the motions of doing exercises in our cramped little quarters and they would shriek at the sight of nude officers wearing only their caps. We were eventually admonished for conduct unbecoming to junior officers. However, we had our fun.

'When we arrived at Liverpool we entrained for Stafford in the Midlands. We stayed a week and were then flown in a battle-weary B-17 (*The Bad Penny II*) to Cluntoe in Northern Ireland. I recall flying over the Isle of Man. We had about ten days of escape and evasion training, one night off in Belfast at a dancing club, and then off by an old ferry to Liverpool again. The boat had originally been a Miami to Havana shuttle boat and the crew was Cuban. We were then placed on trains and after an all-night trip, we eventually arrived at Attleborough, which was the station just outside Old Buckenham airfield.'

One of those to arrive at Flixton, meanwhile, was a twenty-year-old gunner, Jim Tootell. From January to June 1944 he had trained at gunnery school in America

She Devil *(44-40123) of the 491st dropping bombs with another 852nd Squadron Liberator.*   Winston

where his brother Harry was one of his classmates. Both left for England within a few hours of each other on 18 June. Jim circumnavigated the North Atlantic via Labrador and landed at Belfast in Northern Ireland. After advanced gunnery training at Greencastle he went to Stone where he rejoined his brother. Jim Tootell was posted to the 446th. Leaving Ireland in a C-87 he landed at Flixton on 26 July. The Group was celebrating its 200th mission and General Jimmy Doolittle was among those present. Harry Tootell was posted to Attlebridge and the two brothers visited each other on bicycles. Later in the war Harry arrived at Flixton to discover that his brother had been shot down and was listed as M.I.A. In fact Jim had baled out but it was not until three days later that he arrived back at the base, just before a telegram was sent to his home.

Among the many new faces at Shipdham was First Lieutenant Pete Henry, who joined the 67th Squadron. Pete Henry's crew had arrived at Salt Lake City on 16 January 1944 and D-Day had passed with their first mission still to be flown. Extensive training in America, Northern Ireland, and the north of England meant that their first mission was not to be flown until early June 1944.

While the new arrivals settled in the established Groups were encountering the old problems. At Metfield on 8 June fog had delayed take-off and Mr Leslie Pye, the Chief Foreman of Trades witnessed two tragedies caused by the conditions: 'The bombers were revving up at dispersal, their crews waiting for the word to go. Tension was very apparent and then fog closed in over the assembly line and the Tannoy crackled out "Delay Take-off." A gunner from Lieutenant Snow's crew, who must have been highly tensed, climbed from his bomber and walked straight into a spinning propeller. He was killed instantly. This happened at about 06.00 hours.'

The second tragedy occurred at 08.15 hours when Lieutenant Sharp's *Lucky Penny* of the 853rd Squadron suffered an engine failure on take-off. Despite a brave attempt by Sharp to keep the bomber airborne, he dragged one wing and ploughed into the ground. Mr Pye recalls that Sharp had received permission to land but the aircraft 'fell straight to the ground'. Two of its four 1,000 lb bombs exploded ripping the aircraft apart with the crew trapped inside. Other Liberators in the vicinity were damaged.

Meanwhile twelve ME-109s had swooped on the 446th in a surprise attack off Jersey and had succeeded in shooting a Liberator into the sea. However the American gunners accounted for two of the fighters. (Four days later in a brief engagement near Rennes the 446th lost another Liberator to ME-109s.) This was significant because it was the Group's last confirmed shooting down of an enemy fighter of the war. It was the occasion when the 491st used their assembly ship, *Little Gramper*, for the first time for forming up, producing a dramatic improvement in technique. This yellow-painted ship with red polka dots had arrived at Metfield from Hethel.

The Liberators now experienced their period of most concentrated activity during operations from England. In the nine days from 14 to 29 June the 446th and the 448th each flew twelve missions, bringing their totals for the month to thirty-two and thirty-one respectively. The 491st flew eighteen missions in

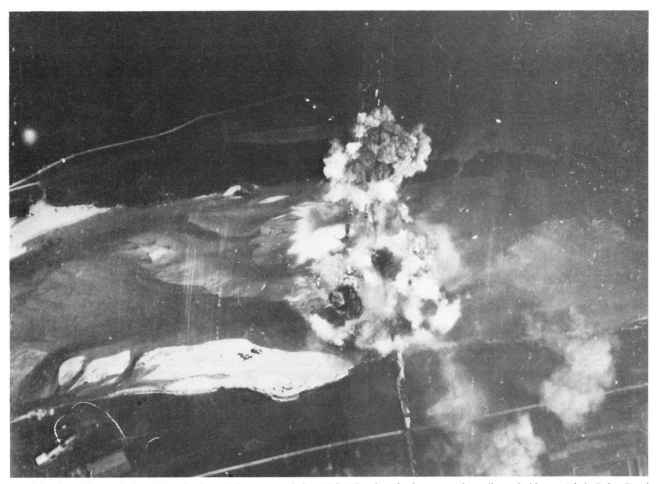

Precision bombing at its best! Bombs from Liberators of the 96th Wing hurtle down on the railway bridge at Blois-Saint-Denis in France on 11 June 1944 effectively preventing the flow of supplies to the beleaguered Germany Army in the Normandy bridgehead. This photograph was taken by Harlan Oakes of the 466th Bombardment Group at 5,500 feet while suspended half out of the camera hatch!

Oakes

eighteen days with eight raids on the 'no-ball' sites. Missions were flown by the Division each day without pause.

On 11 June, benevolent weather enabled the 96th Wing to strike at the highly important railway bridge at Blois-Saint-Denis on the Loire River, about half-way between Tours and Orleans. This mission was entirely a 96th Wing effort but other Wings were simultaneously attacking other targets in France. After the briefing the 96th Wing crews were in no doubt as to what must be the final outcome of the attack on the bridge which the Germans were using to supply troops attacking the bridgehead established by the Allies. The Field Order called for the destruction of the bridge at all costs. There was to be no minimum altitude established for the bombing, which was to be made through the clouds in three-ship elements if overcast obscured the target.

The 458th, with twelve Liberators from the special 753rd Azon Squadron, led the mission. Fifteen Liberators took off from Rackheath led by Colonel Shower flying with Lieutenant Douglas Volk's crew. The formation made up two Squadrons. Nineteen B-24s of the 466th bombed the bridge from heights ranging from 4,900 to 6,350 feet. Their run on the bridge started at about 6,000 feet following behind the 467th and 458th. It was the first low-altitude bombing ever performed by heavy bombers operating from England and the result was decisive. The bridge was completely

destroyed in the hail of bombs dropped by the three Groups.

Lieutenant-Colonel Harlan Oakes was one of those who flew with the 466th. 'I was not authorized to go on this raid, being in A-2 section and working with the MI6 section of British Intelligence (Intelligence Officers were frowned upon as crew members.) Warren K. Burt pilot of the ship I flew in agreed to say nothing of the matter. We proceeded to the hardstand after a briefing which was short, being told that we would be more fully briefed when we were airborne, as this was to be an "all-out" effort. Had I known, coward that I am, I would not have picked this mission for a "joy ride". I should have had an inkling that something was amiss as we were loading bombs at the hardstand in the darkness. One 2000 lb general-purpose bomb out of a total of three dropped on the hardstand: deathly silence, and Burt's voice roared out "What the hell are you trying to do, kill us all?"

'We were advised in the air that our rendezvous was with the 467th and were given a diversionary support unit which faked a flight towards Paris. We were also advised to bomb visually no matter how low we had to fly. Our cameras and intervalometers for photos were set for 20,000 to 25,000 feet, the normal altitude. As a former photographer for the Air National Guard, I realized that the automatic cameras were going to leave a lot of blank spot on film and the results could not be ascertained.

'I was fortunate in having a good man, Sergeant "Pop" Julian, with me in the waist of the ship. "Pop" was the oldest of the regular crew and came by the name naturally. We maintained strict radio silence until we turned on the bomb run. By this time we were down to about 6,000 feet as the cloud cover had lowered. On the actual drop the altimeter reading was approximately 5,500 feet according to Captain Burt. Our Group lead navigator, Captain Leeds, had us dead on target, and our lead bombardier, Captain Gerald Merket, had us dead on with bomb-sights. There was a lot of chatter on the intercoms during the run. Most of us were a little concerned over automatic flak at that altitude. We were certainly sitting ducks, lumbering along at about 155 m.p.h. indicated air speed.

'But the Lord takes care of fools and drunks and babies. Although no one had been drinking we certainly were thankful for his consideration of the other two categories.

'I had to open the escape hatch in the rear to get a shot of the run, and was glad when "Pop" Julian said he would hold on to my 'chute harness while I leaned out of the hatch to take the pictures.

'We had not one shot fired at us in anger although we did see a convoy of Germans off to our right after the drop. Significantly there were a couple of French farmwomen near the bridge, waving white cloths at us as we flew over. I should guess the most danger we were in on this raid was at bomb-loading time and when the lead pilot started to fly over a convoy in the Channel when we were returning to England. We bombed about 09.00 hours and made landfall about 10.00 hours in the West Country.'

Three days after the raid the 96th Wing was cited by the Second Bombardment Division in General Order No. 96. The destruction of the bridge had closed up a vital gap in the German's supply line to the front and had relieved pressure on the Allied armies pinned down on the Normandy bridgehead. Later Lieutenant-General Jimmy Doolittle, in Eighth Air Force General Order No. 466 dated 12 July 1944, cited the Wing for its 'extraordinary heroism and outstanding performance . . .'. Some other Liberators from the 96th Wing also attacked Beauvois with 'good' results.

On 12 June the 96th followed up its success with another good showing, this time against Eureux-Fauville, France. Three Squadrons comprising thirty-six Liberators from the 458th, its largest formation to date, took off from Horsham St Faith. The first Squadron carried fragmentation bombs. All but three aircraft, who had to abort, bombed the target with 'good' results. Light flak damaged only three of the 458th formation. Lieutenant Charles Grace of the 467th became the first Allied aircraft to put down on a beach-head landing-strip after two of his engines had been put out of action and the two others damaged in the attack. After eight of his crew had baled out, Grace and his co-pilot managed to land the Liberator safely. That day Pete Henry flew with the Eightballs to Illier L'Evêque, France. Then two days later the target was again in France when the 44th went to Châteaudun.

On 15 June the 44th returned to France for a raid on the railway bridge at Tours. Three JU-88s lobbed rockets into the Eightballs' formation in an attempt to break it up and managed to put a few holes in Pete Henry's ship. This did not deter the Group, however,

which went on to bomb the target. With all this, the bridge escaped destruction. Henry's crew had only been together six days when, on 18 June, they made their first trip to Germany. The airfield at Luneberg was the target the Eightballs sought but due to a miscalculation in the lead ship no bombs were dropped. On the return trip flak over Heligoland hit the helmet of Pete Henry's co-pilot, Second Lieutenant Albert M. Winter, but he escaped injury.

About this time North Pickenham witnessed the beginning of the end of 492nd Group. By 19 June 1944 it had flown twenty-one missions, losing four Liberators. That day the Group's 858th Squadron was transferred to Cheddington as a replacement Night Leaflet Squadron. This transfer was really a 'paper transaction' because the 858th crews and sixty ground personnel were distributed among the other three Squadrons. More moves followed and during June—July five crews were transferred to the 44th. Those who remained were about to face their greatest test yet.

The bad weather which had grounded some of the Groups during the early part of June cleared and on the 20th the Eighth mounted the largest force it had hitherto dispatched when 1,402 bombers attacked twelve large oil-refineries in different parts of Germany. The bombers were well protected with 700 escorting fighters. The First Bombardment Division made for Hamburg while the Third raided the Hanover and Magdeburg areas, leaving the Second to penetrate even farther into German territory. A nine and a quarter hour round trip took the Second to Politz and Ostermoor, but the Luftwaffe intercepted them while they were temporarily without fighter cover. The Steeple Morden-based 355th Fighter Group had been delayed by its new-type drop tanks, which failed to jettison, leaving the 339th Fighter Group from Fowlmere as the only Mustang Group to protect the entire Second Bombardment Division. To make matters worse, the Mustangs were forced to escort a strung-out formation. The 14th Wing in the van was six minutes behind schedule while the last Wing was two minutes behind..

Messerschmitt-110s and ME-410s ripped through the formations making one pass at the 44th which caused so much damage to Lieutenant Keller's aircraft that he was forced to make for Sweden. Flak was also heavy but it was the fighters that were to wreak havoc among the 492nd. The Luftwaffe pounced over the Baltic Sea with rockets firing and cannon blazing. Heavy casualties were inflicted on the 44th and the 492nd, the latter losing five bombers in the skirmish. There were only nineteen survivors from all five crews.

Anxious eyes scanned the skies over England when it was realized that thirty-four bombers were missing. The severest blow was felt at North Pickenham, home of the 492nd, when fourteen Liberators sadly failed to return. Lieutenant Velarde's B-24 of the 856th Squadron, which returned early with engine trouble, was the only Liberator from that unfortunate Squadron to survive the mission. Five Liberators, including *Say When*, *Sknappy*, and *Silver Witch* put down at Bulltofta airfield at Malmö in Sweden. Altogether, eighteen Liberators landed in Sweden that day. Command was extremely concerned about the losses, particularly as so many aircraft had landed in Sweden. There was some consolation in that synthetic-oil production at the Politz plant had been severely reduced.

491st B-24s of the 852nd and 853rd Bomb Squadrons head for the airfield at Romilly in France on 8 August 1944. Nearest aircraft is Heavenly Body *(42-10155) which had sustained damage on 20 June.*
Winston

Meanwhile, the 491st had flown two missions that same day and crews reported some of the worst flak they had hitherto encountered. *Heavenly Body*, piloted by First Lieutenant Dudley Friday, was hit by a shell which tore through the floor of the flight deck and ripped through the roof of the fuselage, taking the radio-operator's seat with it. Fortunately no one was injured. Another flak burst rocked Lieutenant Charles Stevens's B-24 and shot away the nose section. The bombardier and navigator were killed but Stevens nursed the bomber back to England and made a superb one-engined landing on Dover beach. Two crewmen were killed when they decided to chance jumping from the B-24. They delayed pulling their ripcords and their parachutes failed to open properly. The casualty list grew when a tail gunner in another B-24 was killed by flying shrapnel.

The following day the Liberators merged with the massive bomber stream aimed at Berlin. The raid had been planned as a joint R.A.F.-U.S.A.A.F. venture with the R.A.F. participating in retaliation for the mass 'doodle-bug' attacks on London. However, insufficient fighter support compelled the R.A.F. to withdraw. The Eighth went ahead and amassed over 1,000 fighters and 1,300 bombers, including five Groups seconded from the Ninth Air Force for the biggest raid Berliners had ever suffered.

John Hildebran, the radio-operator aboard *Ford's Folly* of the 453rd's 792nd Squadron, was one of the many who at 22.00 hours the night before had discovered that 2,700 gallons of fuel were being pumped into the Liberators' tanks. This meant one thing only — a long haul. 'And who could sleep with 2,700 gallons on his mind?' The 453rd crews had been put on the alert list the afternoon of the 21st and at about 12.45 hours they were awakened and told they were to eat between 13.15 and 14.15 hours and that briefing would follow at 14.30 hours!

When John Hildebran and his crew entered the briefing-room a large map of Europe stared at them from the front of the hut. They were unable to see the target and the routes they would have to take because a screen hung over the map, partly obscuring it, 'like a veil over an artist's masterpiece'. When the veil was removed it revealed that the target was to be 'Big B' —

Berlin! Amid groans the S-2 explained the route in and out. He was followed by the weather man who predicted 8/10 to 10/10 low cloud and contrails at 24,000 feet. The main briefing was followed by special briefings for all crew members except the gunners, who went to inspect their guns.

Pre-flight checks over, the taxiing began. One Liberator a minute took off from the runways which were illuminated by the eerie glow of the red and blue marker lamps. *Ford's Folly* was the fifth to take off, leaving the runway at 140 m.p.h. with a bounce. Altogether twenty-eight B-24s completed assembly and pierced the cloud to enter a different world of sunshine. Allen Orr, the navigator aboard *Ford's Folly*, shouted over the interphone 'We're swinging on course.' This meant that straight ahead lay the North Sea. To avoid flying over enemy territory for as long as possible, the formation headed for Denmark, later turning south-east, north of Wilhelmshaven. The thick cloud which had obliterated the features below all the way across at last began to break up. Crews identified Hamburg on their right. Dense smoke from the still-burning oil-refineries,

Crew of Ford's Folly. *Back row, left to right:* Joe Corry, *Top-gunner;* Jim Sinclair, *Waist-gunner;* John Hildebran, *Radio-operator;* Frank Gerulski, *Tail-gunner;* Jay Jeffries, *Waist-gunner;* John Schoening, *Nose-gunner. Front row, left to right:* Allen Orr, *Navigator;* Bill Baker, *Bombardier;* Rudolph Kremer, *Pilot;* Ed Anderson, *Co-pilot. Taken at Old Buckenham after the crew's first mission to Orleans.*
Hildebran

Liberators formate on the replacement 458th assembly ship, Spotted Ape *over the city of Norwich.* J4-L *is* Shack Time *and* J4-V *is* S.O.L.   USAF

bombed three days before, was rising to the Liberators' height of 28,000 feet.

Two Wings of the Third Bombardment Division led the formation with the First Division Fortresses in the middle and the Liberators forming a five-pronged formation bringing up the rear. In an effort to confuse German radar and to reduce flying time over land, the formation droned out over the North Sea. But ME-410s, probably lurking in the vicinity because of the fine weather, intercepted and attacked the First Division near Berlin even though there was practically one fighter for every bomber.

Directly south of Berlin there was no cloud at all. Flak started to burst to the left of the formation as the Liberators circled to make a run on to the target from the east. From the right the Luftwaffe started peeling off and attacked as the Group flew a straight bomb run. Flak and fighters opened up on the formation for about fifteen minutes, which to John Hildebran and his crew seemed like two hours. He opened the bomb bays amid the flak bursts and Bill Baker, the bombardier, shouted, 'Bombs away.' Five thousand pounds of bombs from each Liberator hurtled down on to the target. The formation ahead had already plastered the factory. To John Hildebran, the 453rd's bomb pattern looked like 'a bed of roses that all at once had burst into bloom'.

The Luftwaffe inflicted some damage before P-38s and P-51s had arrived during 'bombs away'. The 389th

took the brunt of the fighter attack, losing the greater part of the day's forty-four Liberators shot down. Attacks were directed at the nose and rear sections of the Liberators and it was claimed that a 'wolf in sheep's clothing' — a B-24 carrying 389th markings — was used by the Germans as a decoy.

Now the big problem was lack of fuel and some crews began throwing out excess weight. They made it to the English coast, barely distinguishable through the haze, dropping to 2,000 feet and going in below the clouds. Rudolph Kremer, the pilot of *Ford's Folly*, ordered everyone out of the nose. Alan Orr and the nose gunner, John Schoening, climbed up to the flight deck as the Liberator began to circle Old Buckenham. On the second time over, Kremer peeled off and came in to land downwind behind Lieutenant Counselman in the lead ship. So ended *Ford's Folly*'s fifteenth mission and the crew's first to Berlin.

That night the Fortresses, which had bombed and continued to Russia on their first-ever bombing shuttle, were badly mauled by the Luftwaffe at Poltava.

On 23 June Liberators began taxiing from their dispersals at Horsham St Faith at about 10.30 hours, preparatory to their attack on three 'no-ball' targets. But one bomber lost height shortly after taking off, forcing the pilot to jettison his eighteen 250-pounders. They fell in the vicinity of Gillet's Farm, Newton St Faith, a parish bordering the airfield. Mrs Gillet snatched her daughter to safety with pieces of shrapnel flying about them. The Liberator crash-landed at R.A.F. Swannington, only a few minutes' flying time away, and the crew escaped uninjured.

During June the 458th flew thirty missions in thirty days and the month was significant for almost all Groups, in that many established individual records. Many crews completed their tours and returned to America. The first to leave Rackheath, on 25 June, was Lieutenant John Steward and his crew followed him home a few days later. They departed at a time when the Eighth was taking increasing advantage of the predominantly fine weather to fly tactical missions in support of the bridgehead.

During July the Liberators returned to raiding centres of oil supply and then to Germany itself. On 7 July they were dispatched on an eight and a quarter hour round trip to the Junkers factory at Bernberg. A raid that was to provide the sternest test yet for the 492nd.

Tactics directed that all three Divisions would leave the English coast at different points with the two B-17 Divisions converging about 100 miles west of Berlin, leaving the B-24s to fly farther north and parallel with the Fortresses. It was a massive plan of deception intended to lull the German defences into believing that only Fortresses were to attack German targets. Unfortunately the B-17s arrived late and so the Luftwaffe concentrated its attacks on the luckless Liberators. Over 200 German fighters rode into battle, throwing the Second Division into confusion. The 44th was forced to veer to the right in order to avoid a collision with the four incoming Liberator Groups and the fighter escort went with them. Pete Henry noted that: 'Seventy-five ME-410s attacked the Eightballs in mass formation, getting four ships in the low squadron.'

The unfortunate 492nd had been left completely exposed and eleven of its ships were shot down in quick succession. Only the day before, *Boulder Buff* had been forced to land in Sweden but this time there was no escape for the hapless 492nd. Losses of this kind not only affected the morale of the experienced crews but also that of the replacements, as James J. Mahoney recalls: 'There were two officer crews in each Nissen hut, making eight occupants in all. Two of these crews in a hut opposite mine were lost one day. Because all the occupants were from this one hut, their possessions were locked in. This was to prevent "ghouling", which often occurred after a crew had gone down. Men who had lost money at crap games issued I.O.U.s promising items to individuals should they fail to return from a mission. A banjo was "sold" in this manner. When the owner was shot down, twenty men besieged his hut looking for their promised instrument!

'A First Sergeant had moved all the officers' eight-foot-high lockers to the end of the hut because there was no other room available. When the bright and eager replacements arrived, they asked what these were doing. I told them that it was the stuff left behind by their predecessors. This knocked the wind out of them. These two crews were later lost on the Bernberg mission. So now there were four crews' lockers in the room. When their replacements arrived, they asked whose property it was, pointing to the first set of lockers. I told them "Those are the fellows' lockers you are replacing." They then asked about the other stuff and when I told them that they belonged to the fellows they replaced, their faces really dropped!'

On 11 and 12 July Munich was attacked. Its nearness to Switzerland, only just 100 miles away, afforded a natural escape route for bombers in trouble. Lieutenant Gallup, from the 445th, was forced to avail himself of the neutral country's proximity but three other 445th ships were lost on the first of the two raids. On the 12th the 44th led the Division back to Munich, with Pete Henry flying deputy lead for the Eightballs' high squadron. Only light flak greeted the 44th and no fighters showed but the rest of the Division were not so fortunate. First Lieutenant Gordon W. McDonald, of the 491st was forced to run for Switzerland. He and his entire crew landed safely and were eventually returned to Metfield in November;

One week later the 445th returned to Gotha for the first time since the débâcle of 24 February 1944. This time the Group hit the target without loss. But then came the disturbing news that Colonel Terrill, who had commanded the Group since April 1943, was leaving Tibenham to take up an appointment as A-3 at Division Headquarters. Lieutenant-Colonel William Jones, who had been the 445th's Deputy Commanding Officer and former Operations Officer, assumed command on 25 July.

The unlucky 13 July claimed five lives of a 491st replacement crew in a B-24 which crashed on its approach to Metfield. Two days later a further tragedy occurred. There was no mission scheduled for that day and during the evening while most of the men were viewing a movie, a convoy of trucks carrying bombs was being unloaded at the 476th sub-depot at Metfield. There was an explosion and five men were killed. The 3rd S.A.D. maintenance unit was notified of the blast at 21.00 hours. An hour later a UC-64, loaded with engineering officers, landed at Metfield to survey the damage to the B-24s. However they returned to Griston because five unexploded bombs were scattered about the dispersal area. By daylight the UXBs had been removed and the engineering officers returned. They found only twenty-nine B-24s operational, seven could be repaired at the sub-depot while nine had had to be transferred to the 3rd S.A.D. for major repairs and six were salvaged at Metfield. The 3rd S.A.D. sent several maintenance parties to assist in the repairs.

Lead crew of Beaver's Baby *of the 93rd Bombardment Group at Hardwick.* Top row, left to right: *Bob Shaffer, Kilcheski, Cook, Briggs.* Bottom row, left to right: *Newbaugh, Downing, Crawford, Kirkpatrick, A.H. Cox, G.C. Cox.*
Shaffer

Lieutenant Robert Shaffer poses in front of Little Lee, *a B-24H named after the daughter of the 93rd's Commanding Officer.*   Shaffer

Mr Pye, the Chief Foreman of Trades, recalled: 'It seemed the explosion was caused by some engineers who were unloading bombs from a truck to the bomb dump. The bombs were not primed and the men were kicking them off the truck and on to the ground. While they were being unloaded in this fashion, one went off. The grass from the bomb dump to the hangar was scorched and the bottom of the hangar ripped out. Sometime later the truck's differential axle was discovered in a village about a mile from the scene of the explosion, thrown there by the blast!' The bomb dump had contained 1,200 tons of high explosive and incendiaries.

Missions from Metfield were cancelled for three days while Headquarters held an inquiry. Lieutenant-General James Doolittle, Major-General James P. Hodges, and Major-General Kepner headed the investigation, which at first suspected sabotage.

On 17 July the 93rd went to Rilly La Monteigne, south of Reims. John Shaffer, who was lead pilotage navigator of the Division that day, flew with Lieutenant Metz on his second trip in *Little Lee.* This new ship had been named after the daughter of Colonel Leland G. Fiegal, Commanding Officer of the 93rd. It had been christened on the Group's mission to Munich on 12 July. On the Rilly mission the flak was very heavy and six holes punctured the new bomber. A shell missed Shaffer by about a foot and an engine was knocked out by flak. *Little Lee* was not ready the following day so John Shaffer flew as pilotage navigator in *Beaver's Baby.* That day the Liberators were sent in with fragmentation bombs to hit enemy troop concentrations that were holding up the British advance to the plains. Only a four-gun flak battery and some 80 mm artillery fired on the formation but still left three flak holes in *Beaver's Baby.* Again Shaffer escaped injury when a shell missed him by a couple of feet.

On 24 July, 1,586 bombers were dispatched to bomb German positions at Saint-Lô which were holding up the American advance on the town. Some crews did not feel justified in releasing their bombs through thick cloud for fear of hitting their own troops. But on the following day the Liberators returned to Saint-Lô and did bomb short, hitting their own troops. Shaffer, in *Little Lee* piloted by Lieutenant De Yot, was one of those who went in with fragmentation bombs at only

9,000 feet. The German gunners traversed their dual-purpose 88 mm guns on the Liberators, shooting down one ship from the 93rd. *Little Lee* was peppered with twenty flak holes, three of which appeared at John Shaffer's feet and one beside him.

Unfortunately, the mission, which had been set up with smoke-markers, foundered when the wind changed, blowing the markers, including those released by the lead and semi-lead ships on bomb release, slowly back towards the American lines. The remaining Liberators were to have dropped on the smoke signals manually and not by bomb-sight. The bombs from the last few B-24s in the Division hurtled into American forward positions killing 102 men and wounding 380. Among the dead was General McNair.

Late that month ball turrets were removed from many Liberators to improve stability and altitude performance although some crews preferred to retain the twin-fifty retractable turret and in some cases substituted twin turret guns in the ball-turret position. More Liberators began to arrive from the Third Bombardment Division, which started re-equipping with Fortresses. It was General Doolittle's plan to make the Eighth Bomber Command an all B-17 force but the war ended before the plan could be realized.

The roughest mission yet for Bob Shaffer came on 1 August when the 93rd visited Paris. Shaffer went with Lieutenant J. P. Schmidt in *Nancy Lee* and the target they sought was a fuel dump. However, the bombardier could not pick out the target and the aircraft was forced to run the gauntlet of intense flak as the Group circled Paris for an hour and a half. Three Liberators were shot down and *Nancy Lee* had one engine shot out and received over twenty flak holes.

Next day the Liberators went out again, this time the 93rd knocked out a bridge at Montreau, France. Shaffer went with Kilcheski as lead pilotage navigator and recorded in his diary: 'This tops all missions for being rough. . . . We had eighty-four flak holes in *Little Lee* and had our hydraulic systems, oxygen system, two gas tanks, and an engine shot out. My flak suit stopped two pieces of flak on my chest. They went through my Mae West life-preserver and stopped in my clothing. Another was on my shoulder; it was stopped by my flak suit, went through my clothing and it burned me. I guess luck was with me, with all of us. Our Group lost one plane. We crashed at an R.A.F. base at Woodbridge, my first crash-landing. No one was even scratched. All in all, I just about filled my pants four or five times on this one. Our ship will be under repairs for fifteen days. I was so glad to get back, I kissed the ground.'

This was Shaffer's twenty-fifth mission but others were just starting theirs. During July there arrived at Old Buckenham a replacement crew headed by Lieutenant Don Baldwin, a former pilot instructor on B-26 Marauders. In July 1944, after a few practice flights, he and his crew flew in their new B-24 to Nutts Corner in Northern Ireland via Goose Bay, Labrador and Iceland. Just when the crew were becoming attached to their new ship it was taken away from them and a B-17 ferried them to Old Buckenham on 30 July 1944. While he and his crew were becoming operational, a target of special significance loomed for the 44th at Shipdham.

Chapter Nine

'Trucking'

On 4 August 1944 the Liberators were assigned Kiel. At Shipdham crews began taxiing out at 09.54 hours. It was still damp and humidity caused condensation to gather round the tips of the propellers forming strange patterns as the Liberators moved forward. The two 44th radar ships took off at 09.55 hours and climbed into the low ceiling approaching about 200 feet with visibility down to approximately one and a half miles. But above the thin overcast brilliant sunshine prevailed as the aircraft circled Shipdham at 11,600 feet, still climbing at 300 feet per minute, preparatory to forming up.

By 10.48 hours the large formations were having difficulty forming up, many only just avoiding colliding with B-24s from other Groups. The Eightballs had problems in finding their lead ship but were helped by the appearance at 11.15 hours of Colonel John Gibson in the P-47 monitor ship. Every few minutes calls were radioed to the formation on Channel A (VHF), giving it the lead ship's position, altitude, and heading. At 11.20 hours another Group to the left forced the lead elements to abandon their flight plan and veer to the right in order to meet the combat wing assembly line on schedule.

At 11.24 hours the leader of the combat wing reported that he was over his field and leaving on the Divisional assembly line. By now the 44th was approximately four minutes late and was not helped when another Group flew across its line of flight and circling round to its left narrowly avoided collision. By 12.00 hours Colonel Gibson in the P-47 reported that the formation was 'looking good' but the high squadron, although formed, was too far back.

At 12.23 hours the Group started to climb, having made good their leeway by closing up on one of the turns on the flight plan. Crews put on their oxygen-masks and looked about them. It was clear over the North Sea with clouds on the horizon. Nevertheless at 13.02 hours, the Friesian Islands could quite clearly be seen. However, the Division was still experiencing difficulty in maintaining formation and the leading Group and the Groups to the rear were strung out. Forty-five minutes later, when it was about to cross the enemy coast, it was still strung out. At 13.25 hours it had been joined by P-38s. By now the Liberators had reached 23,500 feet and the crews had donned their gloves.

The Liberators hit the target at 14.44 hours. Although the weather was clear the Germans had laid down a very effective smoke-screen and crews were unable to verify the results of the bombing. At Wilhelmshaven there was also a heavy smoke screen but shortly after leaving the target area the B-24 crews witnessed a squadron of B-17s wipe out a row of hangars just across Kiel Bay north of the city.

On the following day, 5 August, the Liberators, led by the 491st, attacked the six armament and aircraft factories at Brunswick. North-western Germany was clear for visual bombing and the results were 'very good'. The 453rd, with Major Van D. Dowda flying as command pilot, and Captain Homer C. Bell as lead pilot, was the B Group of the Second A Wing, flying lead, low left, and high right squadrons. All three Second Wing Groups bombed the same target — a closely knit collection of buildings situated in a wood three miles north of Brunswick. Flak was moderate and all the 453rd's ships returned safely. Bob Shaffer, of the 93rd flying in *Beaver's Baby*, almost ran out of oxygen, another five minutes' delay and he would have died.

Two days later twelve 492nd B-24s flew the Group's sixty-seventh and final mission from North Pickenham. Losses on the scale of Politz and Bernberg could not be tolerated and the 492nd officially ceased to exist. It was redesignated, on paper at least, and removed from the order of battle. Crews were later dispersed throughout the Eighth with the Night Leaflet Carpetbagger Squadron at Harrington receiving seven Liberators and the 492nd's designation. It was decided that the 491st, which had flown thirteen missions in the first fortnight of August, losing four B-24s and only ten all told during the last three months, would transfer from Metfield to join the 14th Wing. In sharp contrast to the 491st, the 492nd had lost fifty-four aircraft from May 1944 to July 1944 and four in seven missions during August.

The 93rd, meanwhile, returned to Paris on 8 August to bomb an airfield. Bob Shaffer, flying *Beaver's Baby*, was the lead ship and anti-aircraft guns quickly traced her course. The first burst exploded twenty-five feet under the bomb bay and another knocked out the oxygen system. *Beaver's Baby* was forced to abort, making her exit covered by four Mustangs. The deputy lead ship was not so lucky and was shot down.

Shaffer had to wait until 14 August to fly his twenty-eighth mission — a long haul to Dijon, France. Visibility was the finest he had experienced and crews were able to distinguish the beautiful outline of the Alps. Their target was an airfield which was being used by retreating Germans. Flak was moderate and the Liberators put the airstrip out of commission and set all the hangars ablaze. Farther south the 491st, led by Colonel Miller and in their last mission from Metfield, bombed the airfield at Lyon-Bron. Next day the 491st, the Ringmasters, transferred to North Pickenham.

On 10 August 1944 136 officers and 532 enlisted men, late of the 492nd Group's 859th Squadron and commanded by Lieutenant-Colonel James J. Mahoney, arrived at Rackheath to form the 467th Group's new 788th Squadron. Many of the newcomers were upset about losing their parent Group and did not at first take

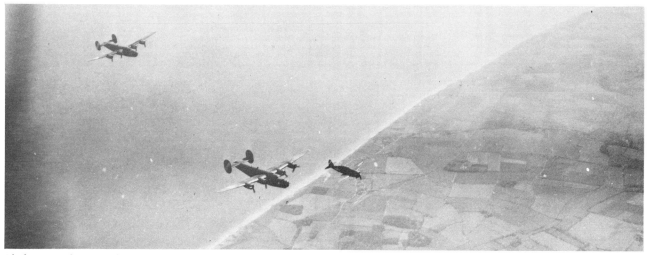

Little Pete, *the 467th's P-47 monitor ship, leads the Rackheath Aggies to Clastres on 8 August 1944.*   USAF

to Station 145, Rackheath. The Rackheath Aggies were currently completing an intensive training programme, and creating an atmosphere of strict command and efficiency. Lieutenant-Colonel Mahoney and his men were to discover that hegemony and harmony could and would be fused to produce one of the most effective Liberator Groups in the Division.

Lieutenant-Colonel Mahoney's men became operational four days later when the 788th Squadron dispatched six ships to Dole-Tavau in France. Two days later the spectre of the ill-fated 492nd still haunted the Squadron. Lieutenant Gayle Miller's crew failed to return from the Magdeburg raid and Captain John Taylor, the 788th Squadron Operations Officer, and his crew, were brought down in the North Sea while on a training mission. In October 1944, Captain Taylor, who had recently been discharged from hospital after his North Sea escape, was promoted to Major and given command of the 788th Squadron. Lieutenant-Colonel Mahoney became Group Executive Officer in place of

Lieutenant-Colonel Herztberg, who was transferred to the 96th Wing Headquarters.

The 95th Wing, which had begun with only two Groups, ceased to exist when, on 14 August, the 489th was transferred to the 20th Wing as a fourth Group. But the 467th Group enjoyed another triumph that month. On the 15th the Rackheath Aggies flew to Vechta and achieved their one hundredth mission in a Divisional record time of 140 days. During that time the Group had dispatched 2,375 sorties, losing twenty-seven Liberators and forty-six men. Forty-five men had been wounded and another 182 listed as missing. The Group was stood down the following day to celebrate the achievement and a party held on the base did much to heal the rift between the 788th and the 467th Bombardment Group.

Two days later the 466th also held its hundredth mission party. A baseball-match was played behind the Attlebridge control tower and in the evening horse-racing, albeit on a limited scale, was held on the perimeter track. Even bookmakers were in evidence and many dollars changed hands at the north hangar entrance. Both these events were eclipsed later that night by the appearance of two touring orchestras. Rudy Starita's All-Girl Orchestra and the top-billed Glenn Miller Orchestra were given a rapturous welcome from the audience gathered in the cavernous north hangar. The Miller Orchestra flew into Attlebridge just as the 'Flying Deck' was about to land on its return from a bombing mission to Woippy, France. Miller's band circled the field until all the bombers had landed. His guest appearance was the result of the 466th purchasing more War Bonds than any other Group. James Stewart was also present at the performance. Miller later gave a concert in Chapel Field Gardens, Norwich, and at a local dance-hall.

Bob Shaffer's luck held and the 24th saw him flying the thirtieth and final mission of his tour. Nine days earlier he had flown his penultimate mission, to Wilhelmshaven when *Beaver's Baby* had sustained twenty-three flak holes. Now, on 24 August, he had to endure one last trip, to the hotbed of Brunswick in *Beaver's Baby* with Lieutenant J. A. Schmidt at the controls: 'We went after an airfield to which all the Nazi fighters were retreating. Other bombers went in on the left side of the city and knocked out gas and oil storage tanks. You could see smoke up to 15,000 feet. The flak was terrifically intense. Our ship was holed twenty times

The 467th plaster the airfield at Clastres in France on 8 August 1944.   Shower

The Rackheath Aggies bombing Dole in France on 14 August 1944.

Shower

and one engine was knocked out. Some P-38s and P-51s brought us home and prevented us from getting jumped by the Luftwaffe. I prayed on this one and sweated it out more than on any other mission. Six months previously I had never thought I would make it.'

Other crews too were completing their tours and at Shipdham changes in personnel were made. On 15 August Colonel Gibson had relinquished command of the Eightballs to Colonel Eugene Snavely, late of the disbanded 492nd. Snavely was an original member of the 44th and, therefore, a well-known figure to many of the men. Bill Cameron remembers: 'When the 44th got word in the summer of 1944 that Gene Snavely would return and was bringing with him some senior 492nd officers, the 44th Staff was much displeased. It would mean that the Eightballs would be under ex-492nd management, a Group which, decimated by the Luftwaffe, had eventually to be disbanded.' The spectre of the 492nd haunted Shipdham. Gene Snavely brought with him his Deputy and his Operations Officer, Major

Turnbull. This triumvirate rejoiced in the inauspicious *noms de guerre* of 'the Stump', 'the Skull', and 'the Brain'. They were, however, all very good officers and got on well with the 44th Staff. 'Tragically Major Turnbull was lost on the last Berlin mission when the lead crew pilot became disorientated in a thunderstorm and they spun out.'

The sunny days and clear skies of August gave way to thick cloud and heavy rain during the first days of September. It was not enough to deter the Liberators from bombing Karlsruhe on the 2nd but the intense and accurate flak almost did. Thirteen 466th Liberators returned to Attlebridge with varying degrees of battle damage and four others were forced to land at alternative fields. Two crewmen were also wounded and it became obvious that any return to the city would be no 'milk run'. On the next day the 466th did return to Karlsruhe but added 3,000 to 4,000 feet to the height attained on the previous day. The weather remained the worst enemy and three crews were forced to land at alternative bases.

Urgin' Virgin of the 491st sporting black and silver 14th C.B.W. markings. Not wishing to incur the same fate that had befallen the 492nd, the 491st at first refused to paint the new colours on their empennage. However, German Intelligence soon learned of the 491st's re-designation. Winston

Enemy flak claimed *Hull's Angels,* piloted by Henry Hull of the 787th Squadron. He and his crew were captured and made prisoners of war not far from the American lines.

Attlebridge crews had managed to avoid the mid-air collisions which had dogged the 466th during its first month of combat. But in early September 1944 the spectre returned with collisions claiming more lives. On the afternoon of the 16th, the 466th was stood down and Colonel Luther J. Fairbanks, the Commanding

Major Jack Turnbull, popular Operations Officer of the 492nd, arrived at North Pickenham via the 104th Observation Squadron. He was a member of the United States Field Hockey Team that won its event at the 1936 Olympic Games held in Berlin. He received his medal from Adolph Hitler.

Mahoney

Officer, elected to send the Group aloft on a practice flight for the benefit of replacement crews who had to learn what close flying was all about. Just after a simulated bomb run on King's Lynn on a southerly heading, the Liberators turned east towards the rallying-point. It was here that B-24s of the 787th Bomb Squadron experienced turbulence created by the preceding Squadron. One Liberator dropped formation slightly to find smoother air and collided with the lead ship at about 22,000 feet. Only three airmen escaped from the first bomber which spun to earth in a ball of flame. The same happened to the lead ship. Stuart M. Pearce, flying as formation observer aboard the lead ship, piloted by Major John O. Cockey jun., was the sole survivor. He baled out and landed in a field near the air base at Bodney. Altogether seventeen officers and men, out of a total of twenty-one, were killed. This brought the total number of personnel killed in mid-air collisions within the Group to sixty-six.

Meanwhile, on 28 August the 20th Wing Groups had been converted to a transportation role in support of the Allied ground forces in France, who were in urgent need of fuel and supplies. On 29 August the 93rd, 446th, and 448th commenced 'trucking' missions, as they were called. Crew chiefs stopped painting bomb symbols on the Liberators and instead stencilled flour sacks and freight cars. They flew empty to the depot in southern England where Royal Artillerymen loaded the cavernous Liberators which stood in long rows. Lieutenant-Colonel Arthur P. Hurr and Lieutenant-Colonel William D. Kyle, Operations Officers from the 446th, worked with and supervised the small force, ensuring that the Liberators were soon *en route* to France carrying urgently needed foodstuffs and medical supplies. Over the Channel the Liberator crews looked down at the naval traffic and the beach-head, and then flew on at tree-top level to Orléans-Bricy airfield, about seventy miles south of Paris. Some crews even circled the city in order to take snapshots of the Eiffel Tower.

Orléans-Bricy had previously been bombed by the Liberators and the runway was pockmarked with craters which the American Engineers had to fill in. A shack served as the control tower and pitched tents were used by the officers directing operations. In addition, many 2,000 and 4,000 lb bombs were still cluttering the landscape. French workers unloaded the B-24s and the supplies were soon on the road to Paris. These missions continued until 9 September. But when the Allies launched Operation Market Garden, using British and American airborne divisions against Dutch towns on the Rhine in mid September, the Liberators were once again called in to supplement the troop-carriers which on their own could not carry sufficient supplies.

British troops landed at Arnhem and American forces at Eindhoven and Nijmegen in an attempt to secure a foothold on the east bank of the Rhine. It was planned to cut off the German Army in the Belgian sector and save the bridges and the port of Antwerp for the advancing ground forces. It was also hoped that the operation would draw the Germans away from Aachen. For an operation of this size, the Liberators' involvement was crucial. Fuel for the Allied armour and transport was in short supply.

The 458th began its 'trucking' operations on 12 September, delivering just over 13,000 gallons of fuel to units in France. It was then stood down until the

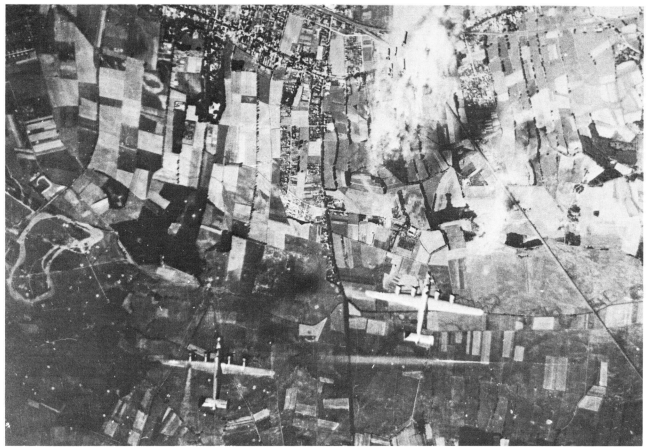

Wham Bam (left) of the 491st Bombardment Group trails smoke after being hit over Hanover on 24 August 1944. The crew baled out and Second Lieutenant Norman J. Rogers the pilot and five other crew members were murdered by German civilians.
Winston

night of the 17th. During the day Groups from the 14th and 20th Wings flew practice 'trucking' missions over Norfolk. That night motor trucks brought supplies to the bases in the region and men loaded each Liberator with about 6,000 lb of perishables and fuel supplies. Altogether 252 supply-carrying B-24s took off for France on the first full Divisional 'trucking' mission on 18 September, including six specially modified 458th Liberators, delivering over 9,000 gallons of fuel to General Patton's forces. But because of an administrative error, aircrews from the 20th Wing did not receive their pictures of the dropping zones until shortly before take-off. Individual crew briefings, addressed to the 20th Wing, had gone to the 14th Wing and vice versa, leaving crews to familiarize themselves with the correct details *en route.*

The 20th Wing Liberators, each carrying twelve supply packs stowed in the bomb bays and with trained personnel from the special 9th Troop Carrier Command to supervise the drop, took off early that afternoon. Ball turrets and turret fairings had been removed to allow the bundles to be released through metal chutes. The Liberators took off from their airfields in Norfolk and Suffolk and almost immediately things began to go wrong. Just out of Orfordness, leading elements of the 20th Wing were forced to make a 360 degree turn to port to avoid veering into a C-47 unit. This confused the Groups following and the 448th lost sight of the force completely in the sea haze and continued alone while five 93rd Liberators returned to Hardwick. The remaining Liberators began dropping from 800 to 400 feet but even at this height locating check-points over Holland proved

very difficult as the coastal area had been completely flooded by the retreating German Army. At the I.P. the 20th Wing Groups experienced additional difficulties when, because of the failure of the radio beacon, they could not receive recognition signals. But despite this and battle damage, they entered the dropping zone at Grosbeck near Nijmegen in formation.

Two Groups of escorting Thunderbolts failed to nullify the almost constant small-arms fire and seven Liberators were shot down while seventy were damaged. Among the thirty crewmen wounded was Colonel

British troops unload flour from Lieutenant-Colonel Tom Belovich's 446th Liberator at Orleans, France on 5 September 1944.
Belovich

Supplies dropped by the 491st Bombardment Group land near a Dutch village. The Liberators flew so low on the 'trucking' missions that even the smallest details such as clock faces on church towers could be seen. Here an Allied column is driving through the village street.

Winston

Pete Henry looks out of the side windows of Henry.   Henry

Brogger, who was awarded the Silver Star. The 446th and 448th each lost three Liberators and had many more damaged. These included twenty-five out of the thirty-six dispatched from Bungay. But despite some 453rd crews having to make three runs over the dropping zone and the 448th releasing the supplies some five miles short, the First Allied Airborne Army recovered 80 per cent of all supplies dropped by the 20th Wing.

The 14th Wing, meanwhile, with the 491st at its head, was *en route* for its dropping zone at Best, Holland. First Lieutenant Pete Henry flew as deputy lead of the third squadron in the 44th formation in a brand-new ship, later named *Henry* after the King Features cartoon character. Leading the 491st and the Wing was the 955th Squadron. Ted Parker, the waist gunner in a nine-man crew, flew on the left of the lead ship *F–*, which was flown by Captain Jim Hunter and carried Captain Anthony Mitchell, the Air Commander aboard. Over the dropping zone small-arms fire inflicted heavy damage. Captain Hunter's ship was shot down after the formation had dropped its bundles of supplies. Ted Parker watched her go down: 'She took one bounce and struck some haystacks, exploding in a large orange flame. Our altitude was about a hundred feet at the time. The tail gunner was the only survivor; he was hidden by some Dutch monks until liberated.'

Ted Parker's Liberator carried food and ammunition for the 101st American Airborne. He was the only waist

Liberators of the 491st Bombardment Group dropping supplies over Holland on 18 September 1944. Allied gliders can be seen littering the fields. USAF

gunner, the other position being taken by a drop-master, and together they were to do the dropping over the target. At one point the drop was in jeopardy, as Ted Parker wrote: 'The moment we took off the Quarter-master froze with fright and I got no help from him. I placed him on the forward deck and covered him up to keep him warm. He was shaking like a leaf. At the target I opened the hatch in the floor and had to work quickly because we would be passing the dropping zone fast and at low altitude. In my haste my leg became entangled in the parachute straps attached to the ammunition track and I was pulled out of the hole when the last bundle went out. I just managed to cling to the track but my legs were dangling out of the hatch. The Quartermaster ignored my calls for help. Finally the tail gunner, David Slade, heard me and came to my assistance.'

Ted Parker's Liberator flew over a small town and received small-arms fire from some Germans who could quite easily be seen in the streets. One bullet, well spent by the time it reached the B-24, hit Ted Parker in the cheek. The Liberators took countless hits from the small-arms fire and the Ringmasters lost four B-24s. Five others were forced to land at different bases in the United Kingdom.

When the 44th had released its supplies, it reverted to flying on the deck (having gone in at about 500 feet over the dropping zone). Many B-24s received hits, including Pete Henry's. His leading edge on the left wing was holed by a 0.30 calibre shell which cut the line supplying manifold pressure. It also holed the fuel tank and petrol began leaking into the bomb bays. Pete Henry got his aircraft home but one Liberator from the 44th was forced to ditch in the North Sea. Only three crewmen were seen scrambling from the stricken bomber.

The previous year, on another low-level mission, to Ploesti, the crews had to pull about thirty-five inches of manifold pressure to obtain 225 m.p.h. The weight of the Liberators had increased considerably by the time of the Best mission and crews had to apply the same settings just to obtain between 170 and 180 m.p.h.

Next day, on 19 September, the Liberators were out again. Horsham St Faith dispatched twenty-four aircraft

Jim Hunter's B-24 of the 491st Bombardment Group brought down on the supply mission of 18 September 1944. It hit the haystack (bottom right of picture) *and exploded.* USAF

The 467th fill in bomb craters at Clastres created by their bombing of the airfield on 8 August 1944.   Shower

to France carrying 38,016 gallons of fuel for the troops. Colonel Albert J. Shower's 467th was also involved in the 'trucking' operations as he recalls: 'From 19 September until 3 October 1944 the 96th Wing flew no combat missions but established a forward base at the airfield at Clastres, near Saint-Quentin in France. We ferried gasoline for Patton's tanks and motorized units.' During its fourteen days of 'trucking' the 467th delivered 646,079 gallons of 80 octane fuel to the Allied armies, first to Orléans-Bricy airfield south of Paris and later to Clastres and Saint-Dizier. Lieutenant-Colonel Allen Herzberg took a full operations staff to France including flying control, weather, and communications crews.

For Colonel Shower and others a visit to Clastres was the more interesting because on 8 August 1944 the 467th had bombed the then German-held airfield. Colonel Shower wrote: 'The French civilians were still at work, filling in the bomb craters on the runway. There was a lot of 88 mm and 20 mm ammunition all round the field. . . . I accompanied our Intelligence Officer on a trip to Paris, where he looked up a woman he had known during his service in the First World War. She was still living in the same house with her mother. The house where we were billeted in Paris for one night had just been vacated by some German officers, their trunks still lay piled up in the hallway awaiting shipment. The occupants were rather cool towards us. We felt that they were resentful because we had displaced their previous tenants!'

One enterprising communications officer, Tim Gallagher, took the opportunity to obtain a French-built Malford car. It had previously been used by the Germans

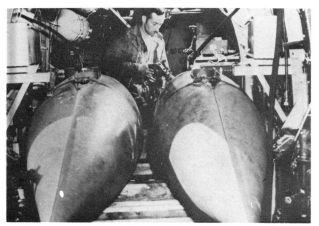

A Liberator of the 458th Bombardment Group with fighter drop tanks installed for 'trucking' petrol in September 1944.
Reynolds

as a Staff car and carried German markings. Gallagher for obvious reasons repainted it in American colours. He drove it to the Normandy beach-head only to be told by the Americans that they were not allowing any traffic to return to England. Undeterred he went on to a British post where he convinced officers that the Malford was the personal property of General Dwight D. Eisenhower and had to be returned. They shipped it home and it eventually arrived in London. Gallagher could obtain no petrol so the 467th flew some down to him. Later the initials 'S.E.F.' (Shower's Expeditionary Force) were painted on it and the leather seats refurbished with drapes made out of parachutes. At the end of the war the Malford became the personal property of a colleague's girl friend!

Everyone from Rackheath who visited France returned with stories of the wine and the lively French girls. Many Americans were able to visit Saint-Quentin where they could buy perfume, cognac, and champagne and pick up souvenirs such as pieces of wrecked German aircraft, even ammunition.

The transporting of petrol to France was stepped up and a good many war-weary Liberators were flown into Rackheath from other airfields throughout East Anglia to help in the task. The base abounded in a multitude of different-coloured fins and rudders. Local people were puzzled by the presence of so many strange aircraft on the base and the constant stream of petrol-tankers caused comment. However, security was tight and the secret was kept from the locals. Each aircraft had a crew of five and two passengers were allowed on each trip. The cargo of petrol was carried initially in cumbersome five-gallon cans and manhandled from the aircraft. To overcome the awkwardness of this method, a pumping-station was built at Clastres and bomb-bay tanks and P-47 belly tanks were installed in the Liberators. Flight crews were ordered to have skeleton crews available to taxi and guard the aircraft at all times.

Bad weather frequently prevented operations and on a number of occasions the Liberators were forced to return to base. Whenever possible crews made two trips a day but night flying was forbidden and they had to sleep on French soil — sometimes literally so. There was no accommodation on the French airfield so the only option open to them was to sleep underneath or inside their aircraft. The Liberators, never completely free of petrol fumes at the best of times, were even more inhospitable during the 'trucking' missions.

These missions sometimes proved dangerous to the English population as well as to the crews. On 20 September a 458th Liberator crashed with catastrophic

The Second Bombardment Division Wing and Group Commanders meet at Ketteringham Hall on 19 September 1944. Seated, left to right: Jack W. Wood (20th C.B.W.); Leon W. Johnson (14th C.B.W.); Walter R. Peck (96th C.B.W.); William E. Kepner (Second Bomb Division); Edward J. Timberlake; Jesse Auston (65th Fighter Wing); Milton W. Arnold (2nd C.B.W.). Standing first row, left to right: Loren L. Johnson (392nd); Eugene H. Snavely (44th); Ezekiel W. Napier (489th); Fredric H. Miller (491st); Leland G. Fiegel (93rd); Gerry L. Mason (448th); Roy B. Caviness (381st Fighter Group); Everett W. Stewart (355th Fighter Group); Claibone N. Kinnard (4th Fighter Group). Standing second row: James H. Isbell (458th); Albert J. Shower (467th); Luther J. Fairbanks (466th); Lawrence M. Thomas (453rd); Ramsay D. Potts (389th); William W. Jones (445th). USAF

results. Eleven Liberators, each carrying approximately 1,530 gallons of fuel in addition to their normal tankage, had taken off for France at about 16.30 hours. Shortly after take-off one of these modified Liberators crashed on Hastings Avenue near Horsham St Faith. In the holocaust all the crew and an occupant of one of the six houses damaged perished. During September, in thirteen days of flying 'trucking' missions, the 458th delivered 727,160 gallons of fuel to France.

Later that month Sol Greenberg and the crew of the *Betty Jean* arrived at Old Buckenham to replace Lieutenant Dean Mills and his crew who had been shot down on their tenth mission. Sol Greenberg met one of his classmates from Navigation School in the Old Buckenham mess-hall who told him that he had joined a combat crew immediately after graduation, been sent abroad without phase training, and had just completed a tour of missions. 'Apparently,' recalls Sol Greenberg, 'so many crews had rolled up big missions during the good weather prior to and after the invasion, that they sorely needed replacements, which was why I never got to Kunming.'

Betty Jean's crew were assigned to the 733rd Squadron commanded by Major Bob Coggleshall who, a week after Sol Greenberg's arrival, was replaced by Major Donald H. Heaton, late of the disbanded 492nd. On 25 September, *Betty Jean* flew her first mission, to the railway marshalling yards at Koblenz. Two days later, on 27 September, the target was the Henschel engine and vehicle assembly plants at Kassel in central Germany. The morning showed signs of rain but conditions were not bad enough to discourage the Division from putting up 315 Liberators, including thirty-seven from the 445th, which led the formation. Low cloud dogged the mission and visibility was poor. The 445th, navigating by Gee, made a miscalculation at

the I.P. and headed for Göttingen, about thirty miles to the north-east of Kassel. Major Heaton, one of the 453rd lead pilots, noticed the 445th heading off to the left in the wrong direction and he immediately checked with his lead navigator who advised him that the 453rd was on course for the target. Heaton immediately attempted to call the 445th lead pilot but the radios were not communicating clearly and the 445th was, at the time, almost out of range.

The 445th dropped its bombs through solid cloud and they fell half a mile short of Göttingen. It then swung farther to the east placing the Group well behind the main force. Major Heaton watched as they headed into an area where the Luftwaffe was forming for an attack. The 445th flew on for another ten minutes when, a few miles from Eisenach, more than a hundred

Jamaica? of the 466th which was lost on the final day of the 'trucking' operations. Woolnough

Early morning sunshine dances on the backs of three 445th B-24s en route *to enemy installations at Glinde in Germany on 6 October 1944.*
                                                                                                                                                    USAF

enemy fighters, exploiting the clouds to excellent advantage, swooped down on the Liberators in lines of three abreast. The Focke-Wulfs appeared at six o'clock followed by two Gruppen of ME-109s. The fighters, some flying ten abreast, opened fire immediately.

In a very few minutes the sky was a holocaust with twenty-five burning Liberators falling to earth. Many more received serious damage. The sky seemed to be raining parachutes. Even the intervention of the 361st Group's Mustangs was not enough to save the 445th although, in a brief battle, they did shoot down several

Paddy's Wagon (Convair B-24J-CO) of the 855th Bomb Squadron, 491st Bombardment Group.   Winston

German fighters. Two 445th Liberators crash-landed in France, a third managed to cross the Channel only to crash in Kent, while a fourth crashed near Tibenham. Only seven aircraft made it back to the airfield and they carried one dead crewman and thirteen wounded.

Sol Greenberg was oblivious to the destruction because he was engrossed in his airspeed, altitude, and compass calculations although he did get the call, 'Bandits in the area.' Al Bryson later said that he had seen flashes off to one side. Sol Greenberg recalls: 'I would assume that had the 445th not wandered into that area, the attack might have fallen upon us as we were flying directly behind, but such are the fortunes of war. When we returned to base and worked our way to the mess-hall, all the officers from the mission were huddled in one corner and no one was eating. We were quietly apprised that the 445th had been "wiped out" and that each Group was going to send over four to six planes to make up the losses so they could show their colours in combat the next day.'

In fact the initial plan to draw twenty-eight crews from other Groups in the Division was shelved before nightfall. It was decided instead that all new crews coming into the Division would be diverted to the 445th. This was probably because of the effect the day's tragic events had had on the morale of the whole

B-24H Tahellenbak *of the 445th. The Tibenham based outfit seemed to specialize in such names. Of the same genre was* Tenovus.

via Olds

Division. The grim statistics, when they became known, were as depressing as the 236 empty seats in the mess-halls at Tibenham. However, forty-five officers and thirty-six enlisted men had been made prisoners of war but not before many of them had been ordered by the Germans to collect the burnt and charred remains of their colleagues from the crashed aircraft. The very next day the 445th valiantly put up ten Liberators for a return raid on Kassel. They bombed accurately and returned to Tibenham without loss.

As the Allies swept across France and into Germany, each mission the Liberators flew became less fraught, with the skies rapidly emptying of flak, although it was still heavy and accurate over German cities. The Allies could not, however, prevent V.1s and V.2s showering down on East Anglia although Londoners gained a measured respite. At Rackheath many V.1s fell within about a mile of the airfield. Others occasionally buzzed overhead but warning of their approach was usually relayed over the Tannoy system stretching into the woods and thickets which shielded the billets from the air. British troops advancing across northern France had cut off part of the 'rocket coast' but the Germans had moved launching sites farther north and had begun launching rockets from bases in Belgium and Holland. Meanwhile the Eighth constantly bombed airfields and lines of communication east of the battle-line.

On 6 October the 491st went to the aircraft-engine plant at Hamburg where the flak was very accurate. *Paddy's Wagon* took a direct hit, cutting the left wing auxiliary fuel lines, splitting the flap pulley, and deflating the left tyre. The left wing was splattered with flak holes and all four engines were hit. There was a large hole in the cowling of number one engine and the oil lines were hit in number four. A hole appeared in the right flap and another, twenty inches across, was torn just behind the navigator's window on the right side. A fragment tore past the right leg of the navigator, Lieutenant Abe Lachterman, and smashed his table. While still on the bomb run the order to bale out was given.

Lieutenant Edgar L. Murff, the pilot, held the aircraft steady, but after 'bombs away' it began to lose height rapidly. Parachutes were donned and everyone hoped they would not have to bale out over the inferno of Hamburg, whose inhabitants were known to be, not unnaturally, extremely hostile. Murff and his co-pilot, Lieutenant Paul Fox, did a really magnificent job and managed to bring *Paddy's Wagon* home. It slewed on landing because of the flat tyre, breaking the olio strut. The radio-operator, George L. Peebles, was in hospital for six weeks from injuries received on the raid.

On 12 October 1944 the 489th took off on its ninety-first mission for the marshalling yards at Onsabruck, Germany, after British civilians had worked throughout the night to make Runway 24 usable. Captain Carl Hillstrom took off at 08.45 hours with Colonel Webb as command pilot, to lead two Squadrons to the target. Captain Wagnon flew the deputy lead position. No aircraft aborted on the mission and flak was meagre but accurate. Lieutenant Bousfield received a minor flak hit but managed to reach Halesworth.

Two days later, on 14 October, Cologne was the target of the Liberators. It was to be a maximum effort and the 489th took off at 08.45 hours led by Captain Beardslee carrying Major Harper as command pilot. Lieutenant Cunningham was in charge of the P.F.F. bombing. The flak at Cologne was heavy but inaccurate. Lieutenant McMullen, a bombardier, distinguished himself by releasing his bombs despite flak having knocked out his oxygen system four minutes previously.

The Eighth returned to Cologne twenty-four hours later, and Captain Hillstrom led the Second Bomb Division for his fourth time. Despite adverse weather conditions the 489th dropped its bombs at 13.00 hours from about four miles up. This time flak was more accurate and Lieutenant Cotton's ship received fifty holes and a punctured tyre. Sergeant Hurst was struck in the leg but remained at his post throughout the action.

The Eighth returned to Cologne on 17 October for the third time in a week. Extremely heavy flak over the target enveloped the 491st formation and during the

X+ which crashed at Charleroi, Belgium on 17 October 1944.   Winston

bomb run, Ted Parker, who was 'dropping chaff out of a 'chute near the left waist', took a piece of flak through the back of his neck. The aircraft took a burst under the nose, knocking out number four engine, which began smoking badly and had to be feathered. The aircraft began to lose height and the number two engine and supercharger were also knocked out. Despite this, and the hydraulic system being shot out, the bombs were dropped on the marshalling yards.

A number of P-47s and P-51s escorted the stricken bomber to Charleroi in Belgium, where it landed on a grass airfield that had only just been captured by the Allies. Lieutenant Murff was forced to make a sharp turn to the left to avoid the hangars. The nose wheel collapsed and the bomber skidded on its nose. With only the outboard brake pressure working, it came to a stop at an angle of 45 degrees. The navigator was slightly hurt in the landing. All the crew, except Ted Parker, returned to North Pickenham via Paris. Some medics from the ground forces attended to him and he was taken to a near-by church were he had to wait some hours before a surgeon could be found.

Ted Parker wrote what happened next: 'When the surgeon arrived my wound was cut open to be cleaned because flak had taken with it some of my scarf and there was fear of infection. I was taken to a hospital in Liège and received some further treatment. Numerous casualties arrived while I was there. My warm leather flying-jacket had been stolen and my boots mislaid; the only outer clothing I possessed was my flying-suit. I was taken to a mountain of shoes removed from German dead and I picked out a pair that fitted me. There were no outer coats so I was given a German blanket to wrap round myself. The Red Cross gave me a kit and the only

available bag to carry it in was one supplied by the Luftwaffe.

'With the walking wounded from the infantry I was put on a train for Paris. I was mistaken for a German by the men on the train until a nurse came in and asked if I was ready for my shot of penicillin. When I said I was, the boy next to me said, "He speaks perfect English!" I was quick to tell them who I was and how I happened to be dressed like a German. They told me they had intended to throw me off the train after dark! It took several days to get to Paris because of the Allied bombing of the railway system and I was able to see at first hand some of the results of our work.'

After several days in Paris, Ted Parker was flown back to England in a C-47. He was in hospital for three months where he had two operations performed on him. He returned to North Pickenham in February 1945 and flew two more missions before the war ended. He went home in June that year.

On 18 October disaster again struck the 445th when a Liberator returning from the air depot at Greencastle in Northern Ireland exploded in mid-air at Landican, outside Birkenhead in the Merseyside area. Twenty-four people were killed. It was raining at the time and it was thought that lightning had struck the B-24H causing it to explode. The aircraft had accompanied three war-weary Liberators to Greencastle and was ferrying home the three crews when the tragedy occurred.

On 26 October the Liberators struck at the Mittelland Canal. Major Schmidt, the 446th Operations Officer, led the Bungay Buckeroos flying entirely on instruments over 350 miles to a point near Minden situated on the Weser in Lower Saxony. Using P.F.F. equipment the 446th bombed through thick cloud from four miles up,

B-24J Sweat Box *of the 44th slithers in at Shipdham, 6 November 1944.*   USAF

as did twenty-nine B-24s from the 458th. The results of the bombing went unobserved but later reconnaissance revealed that a 2,000 lb bomb had scored a direct hit and breached a wall some 600 feet short of an aqueduct carrying the canal over the Weser. The Mittelland Canal was the only important waterway connecting the Western Front and the central German armament factories and its destruction made it impassable to ships, which floundered on their sides in the mud like fish on dry land.

On 29 October the 445th was taken off operations for ten days while the runways at Tibenham were under repair. When operations were resumed on 9 November bad weather was instrumental in causing eleven aircraft from bases throughout England to crash on take-off. During the same month the 44th pioneered a new development in radio-controlled bomb release. It enabled an entire squadron's bombs to be released by the lead bombardier. However, the new technique was still at the mercy of the elements.

On the 9 November mission to the fortifications at Fortifié L'Yser, near Metz in France, the Eightballs were

forced to drop their 2,000-pounders through the clouds with the aid of G.H. Results were unobserved but flak was light and the Luftwaffe failed to materialize. The 20th Wing also bombed the area and in total the Liberators' contribution was significant enough for General Patton to send the Eighth's Commanding General, Lieutenant-General Carl A. 'Tooey' Spaatz, a congratulatory letter. Despite difficult conditions, no casualties were incurred among the American ground troops.

On 16 November Colonel Ibsell, the 458th's Commanding Officer, flew with Lieutenant Dane's crew to Escweiler. They were the first of thirty-three Liberators to take off from Horsham St Faith in thick fog. The mission was successful and there were no losses, but on the return leg the weather deteriorated and the aircraft were diverted to Scotland. The Group received the congratulations of General Doolittle, who praised them for their 'extraordinary effort and dedication'.

At Seething morale had continued to slump alarmingly. Then, on 14 November 1944, Colonel Charles B. Westover, a young West Point officer and son of a

Jo *(41-94783) (left) and* Special Delivery *(42-94896) of the 489th, head for Munster sporting all yellow 20th Wing tail markings on 25 October 1944.*   Freudenthal

Beer Call at Seething.   McLaughlin

former Commanding General of the Air Corps, took command. Westover immediately set up a Staff Welfare Council and enlisted men were appointed to serve on it and to establish priorities. Their first request was for the appointment of a responsible officer to ensure safety on the liberty runs. Their second request was that dances for enlisted men should be held on the base. Their third request was that a club licensed to serve beer should be inaugurated.

During November 1944 the Jenny Lind Children's Hospital in Norwich was low on rations and news of this reached Seething. Some of the enlisted men expressed a wish to help in the matter so Colonel Westover sent a chaplain, surgeon, and the Social Services Officer to the hospital. They found conditions as represented and the Colonel approved the sending of powdered milk and

Newton McLaughlin, the Special Services Officer at Seething and the men of the 448th ensured that the children at the Jenny Lind Hospital in Norwich were not forgotten at Christmas.   McLaughlin

eggs. Some of the men also decided to forsake their candy rations, and these were placed in a box in the PX marked 'For the Children'. At Christmas the men sent a hill-billy band and also put on a party for the children.

During November the 458th had been stood down for four days following the Escweiler mission of the 16th and for three days following the Harburg mission of the 21st. But these periods empty of combat duty were not wasted and many Groups used the time to improve their formation flying. It was during one such training session that another 458th Liberator met with disaster. On 24 November 1944, Second Lieutenant Ralph Dooley was returning to Horsham St Faith after a practice mission when his B-24 *Lady Jane* broke cloud and struck the flagpole on top of the tower of St Philip's Church in Heigham Road, Norwich. Mr Francis Allen of Norwich was standing on a near-by hill and witnessed the incident: 'There was a sudden roar and my eyes went straight to the spot. The aircraft rose almost vertically as the pilot jerked on the controls, nearly stalling at the climb.' Another eyewitness heard the 'loud crack on impact' and saw the damaged aircraft crossing Dereham Road, 'at rooftop height'. The time was about 16.15 hours and it was dusk. Some women in the process of drawing their blackout curtains glimpsed the pilot battling at the controls, bravely trying to gain height and avoid hitting the rows of terraced houses below. He finally put down on waste ground near Barker Street, but he and all his crew were killed in the supreme sacrifice. Grateful residents of the Heigham Street area later subscribed to a memorial plaque in memory of the crew and it is still displayed near the site of the crash.

On 25 November the 445th went to Bingen and the 491st returned to the oil-refineries at Misburg, a target they had partially destroyed three weeks before. Thirty-one aircraft took off from North Pickenham but by the time the I.P. was reached at Wittengen three had

T8-B Ark Angel *(44-40073) one of sixteen 491st Liberators which were lost over Misburg on 26 November 1944. There were no survivors from Lieutenant Bennett's crew.*
                                                                                                        Winston

aborted. Three ME-262s observed the Group over the Dummer Lake area and charted their strength, route, and speed. Shortly afterwards between 150 and 200 German fighters were observed high above the bombers. They made no attempt to attack the B-24s but invited combat with the American fighter shield of some 245 aircraft. The American fighters engaged the Luftwaffe, leaving the bombers to continue to the target alone. Lieutenant-Colonel Charles C. Parmele, Commanding Officer of the 854th Bombardment Squadron, flying as Air Commander, led twenty-seven B-24s to the target, where they split. Without fighter escort the Group was extremely vulnerable.

The German anti-aircraft guns ceased firing and over a hundred German fighters bore in for the kill. They hit all three Squadrons in turn and downed sixteen aircraft in fifteen minutes. Only the timely arrival of eight P-51 weather scouts saved the remaining twelve B-24s. They held off the attack until reinforcements arrived. The tattered remnants reassembled into one formation and headed for home. Only three Liberators survived from the ten in the 854th Squadron while all nine of the 853rd, which had been bringing up the rear as the high squadron, were shot down. On the evening of 27 November, sixteen replacement B-24s arrived from Stansted. For its action over Misburg the 491st was awarded a Divisional Unit Citation.

Meanwhile, at the end of November 1944, the 489th returned to the United States for training on B-29s. This was the only Eighth Air Force Group to be redeployed stateside while the war was still raging in Europe. Many of its crews were reallocated to other Groups and Halesworth became first a base for weather squadron aircraft, then a mobile training unit, and finally a Catalina emergency rescue squadron. The 489th had flown its 106th and final mission from the base on 10 November 1944, bringing a premature end to a career in the E.T.O. spanning only just over five months.

Chapter Ten

The Ardennes Offensive

The campaign waged against German oil installations, which cost the Eighth more lives than any other strategic bombing campaign, was disrupted throughout November and December by cloud and fog. However, radar techniques had improved considerably and H2X continued to penetrate the solid layers of cloud obscuring the targets. Most of the equipment had arrived in August 1944 and there were now enough trained operators. The 389th had been the first unit in the Division equipped with P.F.F. but Micky sets still ranked second in accuracy to the Norden bomb-sights. Only half of the raids using H2X in the autumn and winter of 1944 were effective. Two-thirds of missions flown in October that year using radar bombing techniques recorded pocr results.

By the end of November 1944 more than forty-three oil-refineries, both crude and synthetic, had been destroyed. This systematic assault on the plants had been concentrated on centres at Hamburg, Harburg, and Misburg in north-western Germany. Although highly successful, Doolittle and his Chiefs of Staff were alarmed at the fanatical resistance being put up by small bands of German fighters. They were worried that Goering might conserve his fighters for one all-out battle with a large American formation, the results of which would be catastrophic. However, the German High Command had already decided on a bolder stroke.

East Anglia was still in the grip of a particularly bleak December and only a few missions were flown during the first few days of the month. On the 10th the 445th at last managed to chalk up its 200th mission with a raid on Bingen. Celebrations erupted on the base six days later. Elsewhere there was little to celebrate. Dreams of the war being over by Christmas were shattered with the news that Von Rundstedt on 16 December had broken through a weak point in the American front in the Ardennes. The Panzers had struck when the weather over England prevented any serious Allied aerial counter-attack.

The German advance caught almost everyone by surprise, not least the briefing officers at some of the bomber bases. At Shipdham the briefing did not allow for the Germans advancing so far into Belgium. Pete Henry was leading the second squadron, low left of the 392nd, using G.H. No fighters appeared but the formation received a rude shock when German guns opened up eight minutes earlier than expected. The barrage continued for twenty-seven minutes but the Eightballs managed to get to Ahrweiler, Germany, where they bombed communications and troop transports with 500-pounders. The results were described as 'excellent' and Pete Henry's bombardiers, Second Lieutenant Albert E. Jones and Second Lieutenant Lee,

both received citations from General Johnson for their G.H.-visual over the target.

It was not until Christmas Eve that the fog lifted sufficiently for the Eighth to mount its long-awaited strike. Traces of overcast still hung in the air as the heavies were summoned for a maximum effort aimed at relieving pressure on the troops trapped in 'the Bulge'. The Field Order was specific: 'Bomb Luftwaffe airfields in the Ardennes vicinity and eliminate fighter support for Von Rundstedt's troops and tanks.' A record 2,034 bombers, including war-weary hacks and even assembly ships, contributed to this, the largest single strike flown by the Allied air forces of the war.

At Rackheath a record sixty-one Liberators, including *Pete the P.O.M. Inspector*, were airborne in only thirty minutes. *Pete* was flown by Lieutenant Charles McMahon, a 'Happy Warrior' pilot now on the Group Operations Staff who decided to risk one last mission. He came through safely armed only with carbines in the waist positions. Only the remarkable teamwork displayed by the ground crews made the mission possible. At near-by Horsham St Faith a 458th record of fifty-nine Liberators were dispatched. Two formations of fourteen and eighteen aircraft bombed the marshalling yards at Scoecken and Wetteldorf with good results while three other formations, each consisting of nine aircraft, made satisfactory raids on other targets. Only one of their number was lost. A 752nd ship was hit in the bomb bay just after 'bombs away'. It split in two and the tail section fell away before it disappeared from view. None of the crew was seen to bale out.

Sol Greenberg remembers the Ardennes offensive: 'The missions during the Battle of the Bulge were pretty much "milk runs". However, we were extremely concerned about our ground forces and the punishment they were taking. On Christmas Eve we hit the race-track at Mayen, just west of the Rhine, which was being used as a tank assembly area. Our instructions were to strafe anything that moved. We took off in ground fog and we could see fires all over the English countryside from planes that had crashed. It was an eerie scene as the gunners kept calling out the locations of the orange glows. I believe we lost several planes ourselves during Christmas Week 1944 and the number seven kind of sticks with me.'

Accidents were many that fateful Christmas Eve and despite the weather a follow-up raid was ordered for Christmas Day. However, a number of Fortresses from the First Division were still reposing at other bases in the region after their own bases had been 'socked in' by the prevailing mists in the east Midlands. It was a much smaller force, therefore, which was dispatched from the Second and Third Division bases to continue the

'Yank hospitality' at its most prodigious. A Christmas party for 1,250 local children and London blitz orphans was held at Old Buckenham on Christmas Eve 1944. The British kids made toys to donate to 300 French children and the 453rd B-24 Liberty Run flew the 'Santa Claus Special' to the Red Cross centre at Rainbow Corner in Paris. The all-French-speaking crew was led by Major Tom O'Dwyer and Sergeant Brockway was 'Santa Claus'. The personnel of the 453rd contributed their PX rations to Santa's sack. An eleven-year-old London girl christened the B-24 with a cup of coffee. Unfortunately, the Liberator slipped off the runway but took off safely next morning. Kotapish

Eighth's over-all strategy of destroying the German lines of communication and so hinder the Panzers' advance through the Ardennes.

As the civilian population of Norwich and the surrounding villages prepared to make the best of another wartime Christmas, twenty-four Liberators took off from Horsham St Faith and headed for the railway junction at Pronsfield. The 467th, too, added weight to the bombing of communication centres but it came under attack from German fighters near St Vith. Two

Liberators were shot down in the short skirmish and a third flew on after taking hits in one engine causing it to catch fire. The crew baled out after the navigator and bombardier had put the aircraft on automatic pilot. The empty Liberator flew on to Wales where, out of fuel, it made a perfect belly-landing in a Welsh marsh!

The bad weather persisted, severely restricting operations on Boxing Day. However the 446th, 448th, and 467th were among those Groups who flew every day from Christmas to the New Year. Most bases were

Christening Liberty Run. *Christmas 1944.*   Kotapish

Christmas Party at Hardwick 1944.   Colbourn

The 458th taxi out on Christmas Eve, 1944.

fog- and snowbound and visibility was often so poor that officers in the control towers could not see the Liberators taking off or landing. All possible ground lights and magnesium flares were used to no avail and returning crews were either 'talked' down or diverted to other bases. Ground crews worked throughout the chill nights clearing snow off the tarmac and dispensing salt and sand. Even so some B-24s still had to take off on icy runways and climb through swirling snowstorms to assembly areas where at heights of about 20,000 feet the temperature was sometimes 55 degrees below zero.

Eighth Air Force Headquarters was only too aware of the problems confronting the bomber Groups but they were the only units that could offer respite to the hard-pressed ground forces battling it out in 'the Bulge'. It was decided, therefore, that the mission of 29 December must go ahead despite the conditions. At Rackheath a ground fog came in over the base at take-off time and reduced visibility to a few feet.

Lieutenant-Colonel James J. Mahoney recalled the tragic events which followed: 'Colonel Smith called up Division Headquarters and asked for permission to cancel or postpone the mission but Division refused. They said it was top priority and that the mission must be flown. Smith woke me for advice and I called Division and told them it was impossible to take off. But they told us to get airborne. I then woke Colonel Shower; the Division officer who was causing the trouble had been a classmate of his at West Point so we hoped he could influence him. But the officer was adamant that the mission should go ahead as it was in support of General Patton's forces neat Metz.

'Colonel Shower decided to let the lead and deputy lead aircraft from each Squadron go. These six planes would take off first and climb to form a skeleton formation and then fire flares. As the others came up it was hoped they would spot the flares and take up a prearranged position in the formation. Colonel Al Wallace, Commanding Officer of the 791st Squadron, who thought it suicide to take off, flew the first B-24. It would be a take-off using instruments. We figured the lead crew pilots would be experienced enough to take off on instruments but we had been having problems with faulty equipment sent by a subcontractor in the States. Wallace took off and within minutes called over the radio warning us not to let anybody else take off. They had made it but only just.

'The second B-24 — deputy lead of the first Squadron — taxied out. You couldn't see more than twenty feet. We heard him go on emergency power. The engines really whined and it was obvious he was in trouble. We heard a crack but nothing else happened and we kept waiting for explosions. The third B-24 touched a tree on take-off and landed minutes later at Attlebridge. The fourth aircraft took off and really whacked the trees. As soon as we heard this, Colonel Shower cancelled the mission. He didn't care what Division said; he wasn't going to let any more planes leave Rackheath. He told crews to turn off their engines and stay where they were. It was too foggy even to taxi and we had jeeps leading them out.'

Mahoney and Smith climbed in a jeep and set off through the murky fog in search of the crashed Liberator. They could hear explosions rupturing bullet cases and the

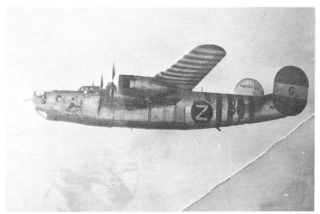

Rage in Heaven, *the ex-852nd B-24 that replaced* Little Gramper *(42-40722) as the 491st's assembly ship. Note 'WW' (war weary) on rudder. Stripes are alternating green and yellow. The aircraft was destroyed in a crash at the start of an attempted mission in support of the ground troops in 'the Bulge' on 5 January 1945.* Winston

fierce crackling of flames consuming the aircraft but the fog blacked out almost everything. Then they saw a reddish glow. The Liberator had been carrying eight 500 lb bombs and the two men heard six go off. Mahoney continues: 'We pulled over to the side of the road and climbed over the fence. Suddenly, while in the middle of a field, we heard the seventh bomb explode. We knew we were pretty close and cautiously we waited until the eighth bomb went. Then the two of us started running towards the glow but we were stopped by another explosion. Its force didn't knock us down but the air hit us. We had obviously miscounted. Then a tenth let go and it knocked us both down.'

The two men heard fire-tenders and ambulances seeking the crashed plane and failing to find it. Mahoney told Smith to drive back to the guardhouse and tell them exactly where the aircraft lay. The heat was starting to lift the fog and Mahoney was determined to get closer. He stood up but yet another bomb exploded and momentarily knocked him out. No shrapnel hit him. 'I was pretty confused. I paused but no other bombs went off. I got up and walked towards the fire. People were yelling. Coming from the direction of the airfield were two gunners who were holding each other up. One looked in pretty good shape until I saw he had a great big hole in the side of his head. You could have stuck your fist into it. Both were shocked. What puzzled me was that they were coming from the wrong direction and quite away from the blaze. There were no burn marks on their clothes.' The men told Mahoney

later that when the bomber hit the trees they were thrown out.

The second B-24 had taken off, hit the trees, and made a wheels-up belly-landing in the field. The fourth Liberator had done exactly the same and had landed right on top of the crashed aircraft. The first crew were just freeing themselves from their burning aircraft when the other had plummeted down on top of them. Fire crews found only the charred remains of their bodies. In all fifteen men were killed and four injured in this fiasco in the fog. The crew of the other Liberator baled out after heading their bomber out to sea.

On New Year's Day the 458th headed for Koblenz but forty miles from the I.P. it had to abort after headwinds, estimated at 180 m.p.h., had reduced its ground speed to about 20 m.p.h. At Tibenham tragedy struck at the 445th. One Liberator failed to come 'unstuck' and crashed at the end of the runway. Bullets began exploding almost immediately killing the bombardier and injuring several crewmen. A Military Policeman suffered severe shock when the bomb load exploded, shaking the whole base, while he was bravely attempting to carry an injured crewman to safety. He was awarded the Soldiers' Medal and was eventually repatriated to the States.

Solid undercast hampered further missions and on 8 January it was particularly bad. The 458th climbed to 24,000 feet to bomb its target at Stadkyll. On its return the aircraft were advised to descend through the cloud base west of London and fly beneath it to Horsham St Faith. Many Liberators, short of fuel, had to land in Yorkshire and ultimately only five made it home. Theirs was a doubly difficult landing as they had to cross through a Fortress landing pattern and fly through thick snow-squalls.

While missions continued to be flown weather permitting, many ground staff throughout the Division were transferred to the flagging infantry fighting in the Ardennes and disabled and injured men arrived to take their place. All at once the general 'bitching' on the bases ceased as many realized that they had been much better off than their counterparts in France. Then high-ranking pilots, with seniority over long-serving pilots, arrived and caused promotion problems.

One of the airmen who had earlier arrived at Old Buckenham was Don Baldwin. On 10 January he and his crew, flown by Lieutenant Walsh, were in difficulties on their return to base. Flak had claimed one engine over the target and shortly after crossing the Dutch coast a second engine had failed. Baldwin turned on the booster pumps to no effect: they could only glide back across

The 491st replacement assembly ship Tubarao *(44-40101) in 14th Combat Bombardment Wing markings.* Tubarao *is Portuguese for shark, hence the teeth on the nose.* Winston

the Channel at about 8,000 feet and hope that the third and fourth engines would continue to function.

They had dropped their bomb load over the target and most of the fuel was exhausted. But as a precaution the crew began throwing out excess weight such as flak suits. Don Baldwin raised Old Buckenham control tower only to be informed that the base was 'socked in' with the ceiling down to 200 feet. He also alerted the Air-Sea Rescue on the emergency Channel D (VHF) just in case they could not make landfall. They did make it to Old Buckenham at about 13.00 hours and were told to head for the south-west of England where the weather was better. But the Liberator only got as far as the Thetford area before the third engine quit with loss of fuel pressure.

Baldwin recalls: 'If it had been a clear day we could have glided down "Colorado Springs" fashion. [As an instructor at Peterson Field B-24 standardization school Baldwin had shown student pilots how to get down with no engines.] I rang the bale-out bell and everyone hit the silk. Two gunners, including the tail gunner, Sergeant Hayes, landed on the Fortress base at Knettishall while the others were scattered around the vicinity.

'I baled out at about 6,000 feet and pulled the ripcord almost immediately. I must have blacked out as I do not remember hearing the 'chute open out. The wind was very strong and was blowing me sideways right towards a fifty foot oak tree, which seemed to come at me like a freight train. I put up my arms and crashed into the crotch of the tree. My 'chute was tangled in the foliage but miraculously I was quite unharmed. Two farmers appeared bringing with them a ladder. Unfortunately it was not long enough and about fifteen minutes later they came back with another, longer one. They had also called a jeep, which came and took me to Knettishall where I was reunited with the crew. We all got back to Old Buckenham that night.'

The Liberator had crashed into a wood in the grounds of Rushford Hall, Suffolk, at 13.30 hours. One of the engineering officers later found a cylinder head a good

Ground crew of Witchcraft *of the 467th. Left to right: Joe Vetter, Walter Elliott, Joe Ramirez, George Dong and Ray Betcher. This crew was known as the 'League of Nations' crew at Rackheath.*   USAF

250 feet clear of the crashed aircraft.

Three missions later Don Baldwin and his crew had another lucky escape when their Liberator again lost three engines which were on 'tank to engine'. That is, each engine was being fed from its own tank. Sometimes engines were on 'tank to engine cross 'feed', which meant that if one engine was using more fuel than another, both tanks could be used to feed both engines. This method was used mainly during mid-flight when hydrostatic pressure became low in a particular tank.

Don Baldwin, with three faltering engines, intended heading for the emergency airfield at Manston but decided he had a better chance at Ashford in Kent — a D-Day airfield. When he levelled out for the runway, he discovered to his alarm that the temporary mesh matting had been rolled up and he had only the hard ground on which to land. Even so he brought the aircraft in on one engine, his left wing hitting a toolshed and sending a wheelbarrow spinning through the air. A piece of rolled matting struck the left landing gear and slewed the aircraft round. Fortunately no one was hurt and the small R.A.F. detachment supplied them with rail warrants for London and Old Buckenham.

Don Baldwin flew five more missions and then returned home having completed his tour of thirty-five before the end of hostilities in Europe. But for those that remained in East Anglia, base life was still far from pleasant. The harsh weather increased the need for coal and, as far as food was concerned, eggs and fresh meat were scarce. Many individuals, therefore, supplemented their meagre diet with the occasional poached rabbit or pheasant and their inadequate fuel rations with ventures into local woods where timber and fallen branches were plentiful. One base commander, worried that poaching might endanger Anglo-American relations, issued a direct order stating that the practice must cease.

At Station 145, Rackheath, it was a time of celebration. On Sunday, 14 January 1945, the 467th went to the Hallendorf steelworks in Germany. For *Witchcraft*, one of the most famous of all Liberators, it was her one hundredth mission, all without once turning back. A newspaper reporter flew in *Witchcraft* to cover the unique event. The Liberator returned safely and the crew were greeted by high-ranking officers from Headquarters, including Major William Kepner, Second Air Division Commander, Brigadier-General Walter Peck, 96th Wing Commander, Colonel Shower, and Major Ted Holdrege, Commanding Officer of the 790th Squadron to which *Witchcraft* belonged.

The ground crew, headed by Master Sergeant Joe Ramirez, were presented with honours for maintaining the bomber which had never had to abort through mechanical failure. They were nicknamed 'the League of Nations crew' because of their cosmopolitan character. Staff Sergeant George Dong was Chinese, Sergeant Raymond Betcher a Dutchman, Corporal Joseph Vetter a German, and Corporal Walter Elliott an American. They were presented with Certificates of Meritorious Service signed by General Peck. For 'meritorious achievement in the performance of outstanding services', the Mexican-American crew chief Master Sergeant Ramirez received an Oak Leaf Cluster to his Bronze Star. All these men had kept *Witchcraft* flying from the time the aircraft was delivered to the 467th at Wendover Field in Utah. Together they had 'sweated out' each mission the plane had flown and would

Lassie Come Home *crashed on 14 January 1945 killing all but one of the crew and two children playing in the garden of the crash scene. A third child had an incredible escape.* USAF

continue to do so for a further thirty missions. In 130 missions no crew members were killed or wounded and the Liberator never returned to Rackheath without first bombing its target.

By 14 January 1945, thirteen of *Witchcraft*'s engines had worn out or had been completely shot up by flak. She had been sent sixty-five times to Germany, thirty-one times to France, and four times to Belgium. *Witchcraft* first flew from England on the 467th's inaugural mission on 10 April 1944. On three missions the Liberator had been over the target with only three engines functioning. On a mission to France the pilot proceeded to the target even when an engine quit over the English Channel and he then managed to return safely.

On the same day, 14 January, at Horsham St Faith, base staff awaited the return of the twenty-eight Liberators dispatched to the Hermann Goering Works at Halle but *Lassie Come Home* from the 753rd Squadron never made the base. The pilot, flying only his third mission, was approaching on full flap and had his number one engine feathered and his landing gear down. As he banked into his dead engine he lost a second engine and the aircraft turned over and crashed upside-down in the garden of No. 14 Spynke Road, Norwich.

Three children were playing in that garden, and Richard Kemp, the sole survivor, recalls the tragedy: 'My twin sister May and our cousin Brian were playing among the raspberry-canes when I looked up to see that the sky behind my house had turned into metal, all silver-grey with black holes in it and it was coming towards us. When I opened my eyes I was in Mrs Copman's garden and before my nose lay a snake of machine-gun bullets clipped together with loops of metal. Mr Salmon from No. 68 carried me in his arms up our garden-path past a big silver tent with two large dustbins outside, a wreath of flames dancing round their tops. I was taken back through our house into a khaki-coloured ambulance.

'When I came home from hospital I remember the grown-ups talking about how Mr Spurgeon was soaked from head to toe in petrol when he looked out of his garden shed to see what was going on; how Mrs Courtney's bedroom had been snatched off the corner of her house and her Anderson shelter smashed flat by one of the engines. Later I remember the Vicar's wife calling with chocolate éclairs, which I had never seen before, and the

Americans bringing cardboard boxes full of candy, making us sweet millionaires in a ration-book society.'

Earl Zimmerman, who was stationed at Hethel, had cycled over to Spynke Road that day to visit his future wife, June Courtney: 'We were sitting round the fire at tea-time when we heard the plane coming over. Suddenly it happened – the sound of engines turning over at high r.p.m., a loud crash as the plane took off the top of our house, and a huge shadow passing by the window. I ran out of the back door and there was a lot of gas all over the place so I ran to all the neighbours telling them to put out all their fires.

'The aircraft was such a tangled mess it was difficult to know where to look to find any survivors. About the only recognizable portion was a piece of the fuselage from the waist window to the tail. It was so mangled that I could not get inside but some neighbours came running over and we eventually managed to get two boys out alive. We laid them out on the front lawn but one of them died. Some people from Horsham St Faith arrived and took the survivor away to hospital. I found out later that he recovered but never flew again.'

January 1945 was a memorable time for Dick Dugger, a top-turret gunner with the 448th. He had flown his first mission on the 13th to Worms, Germany, aboard *Roses Rivets* when it was attacked by FW-190s and flak had punctured large holes in its left side.

Three days later the 448th went to Dresden and bombed the synthetic-oil plant from 22,000 feet. Each Liberator carried 2,700 gallons of fuel for the long trip to the city, situated deep in the German hinterland on the Elbe near the Czechoslovakian border. Although temperatures hovered at about −38 °F, the ceiling was unlimited. Mustangs and Thunderbolts were also in close attendance.

On this, his second mission, Dick Dugger recalls: 'In those days we had to carry extra fuel. We were hit over the target area by flak and began to lose gasoline. The bomber had been hit in the tanks. We made it to Lille in France but could not cross the Channel. Finally, the fuel gave out and the engines quit and we had to land *Roses Rivets* in a park just outside Lille. The park was not made to land large bombers and her wheels collapsed as she settled down.' *Roses Rivets* was the only one of twenty 448th Liberators lost that day. When the crew returned to Seething they were given a new bomber, *Windy Winnie.*

Captain Dean B. Strain's B-24 (42-51481) of the 491st takes a direct hit between number three and number four engine over Harburg, Germany, on 17 January 1945. Twelve men on board were lost. Winston

During the night of Thursday, 18 January, high winds brought snow and for ten days the 445th was unable to fly a single mission. The 458th ventured to Germany on 21 January and lost two Liberators. One crash-landed near an Allied advanced airfield some eighteen miles south-east of Reims while the other limped across the Channel and 'bellied in' at Woodbridge, Suffolk. The 467th did not fly a mission that day and indeed had not flown since their visit to Harburg on the 17th.

The Rackheath Aggies were stood down until the 29th but this did not prevent the Group dispatching training missions. These flights became the pet hate of all the crews who flew them. But in retrospect many crews looked back on them as time well spent, admitting that they had benefited from them. One exception was a pilot who returned to America after flying thirty-five combat missions and thirty-four practice missions!

On the debit side, the 467th lost nineteen crewmen on practice flights between 9 November 1944 and January 1945. The last of these, on 22 January, resulted in the loss of nine men in a Liberator piloted by Flight Officer John McArthur. His B-24 crashed in Church Street, Old Catton, midway between Rackheath and Horsham St Faith airfields at 14.00 hours and caught fire. McArthur had gone to Horsham St Faith and was about to land when another Liberator began making its approach and firing red flares. It was given priority and McArthur was forced to circle the base again. Suddenly one of his engines failed and then a second on the same wing. The aircraft spun over and went straight down.

The 448th had been stood down for twelve days when, on 28 January, the weather improved enough to mount a mission. The target was an oil factory with large tanks and storage yards at Dortmund in the Ruhr Valley. Dick Dugger flew with the 448th which that day led the 20th Wing. 'It was on a Sunday at 11.59 hours when we took off and it was very cold. The heated suits and gloves did not keep out the cold air and the last time I looked, at 23,000 feet, it was 67 degrees below

zero. We were on the bomb run going straight into the target which was about forty miles away and the bombardier had the bomb-bay doors open. Everything was fine: no fighters or flak, just long contrails from the bombers.

'Suddenly all hell broke loose as the flak guns opened up. Just before the bombardier pushed the button our ship was hit and it plummeted from 23,000 feet to almost ground-level! Many of our bombs, instead of falling out of the bomb-bay doors came up front in the radio compartment and up where the pilot and co-pilot were sitting. I was in my turret spinning round above the radio-operator and the force was keeping me pinned in. We plunged downward.

'It was a mess but the pilot finally got the ship under control, although we were at tree-top level and flying round the target area with other Squadrons dropping their bombs all about us. Our navigator was knocked out and our co-pilot was hit. We had no instruments at all to fly by and no way of knowing exactly where we were. We were flying over exploding tanks and getting shot at by the German ground forces, who, incidentally, were excellent shots. Finally the pilot dropped our remaining bombs with the salvo release to lighten the load. The radio-man and myself pushed the 500 lb bombs from the compartment up front to the open bomb bay where they fell out. We also threw out all of the 0.50 calibre belts and boxes of ammunition that we had aboard. The ball-turret gunner was hung upside-down in his turret and could not get out. We finally pumped him up manually from his little cramped quarters. *Windy Winnie* flew low over a German airfield — so low that we nearly hit a flak tower. German pilots were getting in their fighters to come up after us.

'We flew on over towns, where we were hit many times, and also over countryside. *Winnie* had so many large holes in her, it was like flying outdoors. The back end was a mess; oil and gasoline was everywhere but she was still flying. The pilot was giving it red line power on all four engines when number four engine was hit and we continued on three engines. A Liberator does not fly well with three engines at tree-top level but we kept in the air by throwing out everything we could — radio equipment, supplies, and even the guns.

'We did not know if we were in Germany or wherever, but we knew we were on a westerly heading. The ground was still white and we could not see anything apart from some large power lines in front. The pilot pulled back on the stick and barely missed them and the bomber began to fall slowly to the ground. She hit it and started to bounce. Small trees were cut down and with her wheels up *Winnie* did some skating. I thought she would never stop but finally she hit a ditch and stopped. Then it was very quiet. I thought for a moment I was dead.

'For a long time nothing but large, soft snowflakes fell gracefully on the battered bomber lying in a shambles. The pilot was pinned in and we had an awful time getting him out because we had thrown all our tools out over Germany. I crawled out of the bomber on the side where it had split open and got on top to see if I could see anything. None of the ten aboard was hurt, just bruised very badly — but no blood or anything.

'Then we saw some people about a quarter of a mile away. We could not tell if they were soldiers but they just stood there in the snow. I thought they were Germans and they were going to kill us or put us in a prison camp or do something unpleasant like beating us up. We had fallen over Luxembourg! They took us to a barn where we spent the night. We were told that we had landed in a minefield and that they did not know where the mines were placed. That is why it took them so long to reach us. Later they took us to Paris and to a hotel for M.I.A. crews where we stayed for several days. The R.A.F. flew us to London and we made our way back to Seething and yet another new bomber.'

During January 1945 most of the B-24 lead crews were completing their tours after flying thirty missions. Pete Henry's crew had flown twenty-nine to date (thirty, allowing for a mistake made by a records clerk who discovered his error in September 1944). His crew had to wait until 14 February 1945 to fly their thirtieth mission. The target was the oil-refinery at Magdeburg but the 44th was forced to bomb the marshalling yards instead. Each bomber carried six 500-pounders and six M-17s. For Pete Henry's crew the eight-hour mission was agonizing, with thoughts of home always before them. But they need not have worried. The mission was uneventful and they returned to Shipdham after flying lead low element, low squadron. Celebrations began almost before the wheels touched the runway.

Then Eugene Snavely decreed that lead crews would have to complete thirty-five missions! With some pleading, Pete Henry and his crew finally reduced their deficit to two more missions. They completed these without loss. The first to Weimar on 23 February and the second to Aschaffenburg two days later. The thirty-first mission took eight and a half hours and although the Luftwaffe did not put in an appearance, bad weather forced the 44th to land in Yorkshire. With his fuel all but exhausted, Pete Henry managed to exploit a break in the clouds and put down at Carnaby.

Of the mission he flew on 25 February Pete Henry wrote: 'Nine and three quarter hours in O+. Flew number six position. Hit marshalling yards visual by squadrons —

McArthur's B-24 that came to grief over Old Catton, Norwich during a training flight on 22 January 1945.
Mahoney

three excellents — good mission but very long. Finished this time, we hope!' They had finally made it and they joyfully departed for home, leaving Southampton on 7 April 1945.

Meanwhile, other crews were participating in the final death throes of the German war machine and new Liberators were arriving to help bring the war to an end. The Second Air Division began receiving B-24Ls and B-24Ms, which were the same as earlier Liberators but fitted with lighter tail turrets in the hope that they might improve weight distribution. The B-24L sported a hand-operated turret, 300 pounds lighter than the conventional. But this was quickly supplanted by the improved B-24M which was introduced in October 1944 and reached the Liberator bases in early 1945.

Foul weather during the early part of February cancelled missions and when, on the 13th, the 458th was stood down the opportunity was taken to fly yet another training mission. Rick Rokicki, a gunner aboard *Briney Marlin* was on leave that afternoon and was cycling in the vicinity of Horsham St Faith airfield when he noticed the 458th overhead: 'It was about 14.30 hours when I observed about fifteen Liberators returning from what I later learned was a practice mission. They carried sand-filled 500-pounders. One aircraft was only about 800 feet high when I noticed he was trying to turn into two feathered engines. I said to my buddy "He'll never make the field." We cycled like mad but before we could reach the wreckage a fire-truck and other equipment were already there. A guard group prevented anyone getting close. One of the crew got out and walked towards the ambulance. Everyone tried to get to him and tell him to lie down but he kept coming. He died before they could get him into the ambulance. He died from delayed shock.' The B-24 was *It's A Dog's Life*.

Later that month the weather showed signs of improvement and this prompted the Allied air commanders to launch Operation Clarion. This was to be an all-out assault on German communication centres, many of which had hitherto been left untouched by the Eighth and Fifteenth Air Forces and by the R.A.F. The targets lay in an area of approximately 38,000 square miles. During the last few days of February and the first three days of March, the Eighth

A Dog's Life *of the 458th Bombardment Group, with the cartoon character 'Napoleon' on its nose.*   Reynolds

alone dispatched over 1,000 aircraft in support of Clarion. Despite misgivings in certain quarters, the Second Air Division flew at heights between 6,000 and 10,000 feet in an attempt to reduce civilian casualties and to achieve a higher degree of accuracy. Bombing was completed at predominantly Group level and the rate of missions flown was intensive. The 446th, for instance, flew thirty-five missions in forty-five days from 14 February to 25 March.

Other Groups returned to raiding German cities and the oil-refineries. On 3 March 1945 the Eighth went to Magdeburg. It was Sol Greenberg's second mission to the city and almost his last: 'The 453rd was after the oil-refineries and I recall it was a rather clear day above the clouds. We were crossing over the northern part of the Zuider Zee when I noticed a group of B-17s a few miles over to our left. They had apparently missed their place in the bomber stream and had flown parallel to us during the North Sea crossing and during our landfall over Holland above Bergen. Our position in the Group was high right deputy on the low left Squadron leader. Towards the approach of the eastern end of the Zuider Zee, their leader apparently decided to force his way into the main stream and began to crowd up against us. I noticed them, with their green markings on their tails, coming ever closer, squeezing us out of the line as we gave way to avoid collision. This placed us slightly south of our intended course and over the end of the East Friesian Islands.

'Suddenly all hell broke loose with the most accurate flak I had ever experienced. The guns evidently had a very good track on us. I could hear the shells bursting all around me, and when you hear that, you're in trouble. I just made the silly remark that "I have but one life to give to my country and I might as well give it now." With my head full in the left window bubble, I located the miserable battery that was tormenting us so. The thought occurred to me that I should record the position on my map so that it would be reported during mission interrogation and then the Canadians could go in and shoot it up.

'At that instant the moment of truth arrived. The entire bubble came up into my face and a piece of shell fragment, about one and a half inches wide by eight inches long, tore against my forehead. Blown down against one of the ammunition storage cans that served as seats on each side of the navigator's compartment I attempted to take stock of my situation. Obviously I could not see. I was naturally furious at having been treated to such an indignity. The metal continued on through the plane skin just under the left foot of Bryson, our pilot, and the plane rocked rather uncomfortably. Bryson recognized that this was not the usual type of peppering and asked if anyone had been hit. I replied in the affirmative and he then asked if I wanted to return to base. In true heroic fashion I bellowed down the microphone "No, no — go on with the mission, we are going in to the target." Actually I am not that much of a hero but my reactions were instinctive and had I taken a few seconds to think the situation out, I might well have elected otherwise.

'My bombardier, Al Gehrt, who had been in the bomb bay de-pinning the bombs, came up forward and proceeded to apply a bandage. The slight cut from the flak had stopped bleeding and I was beginning to see somewhat hazily through one eye as the tears washed out the plexiglass. Naturally that was the eye that Gehrt bandaged. By then I was really furious at what had occurred and ripped off the bandage, instinctively attempting to return to my navigating. After all that was my job. We had the silly sight of Al still attempting to bandage me and me fighting him off as I recorded the compass headings, altitudes, airspeed readings, and tried to pick up the next landmark to ascertain our position. It must have been five or ten minutes of insanity up

Wreckage of the B-24J A Dog's Life *which crashed at Spixworth Road on 13 February 1944 near Horsham St Faith airfield and not far from McArthur's crash of 22 January.*   Rokicki

The 467th bombing close to the Alps. Prowler *in the foreground and* T+, *a B-24L, is sporting hand-held guns in the rear turret.*
                                                                                                    via Shower

there in the nose. Finally Gehrt left me to do what I wanted although I am certain he had misgivings about leaving me in such a mental state. Instant flak happiness.

'I was glad to see him go as earlier in Boise the crew had made a pact that if anyone was badly wounded he would be shot by another crew member so as not to be doomed to life as a hopeless cripple — and blindness was one of the conditions we had mentioned. It may seem silly now but as boys we had seen the gassed and maimed derelicts of the First World War and none of us ever wanted to become that kind of a burden and live out our lives as vegetables.

'The navigation all the way into the target was extremely poor as we wandered from one major flak area to another. I kept calling them out as they appeared to be coming up on our course. Remember it was clear all the way in from Holland. As we approached the target area we could see the smoke, almost up to our altitude, as Group after Group placed their bombs into the oil-storage fields. What a beautiful sight it was and I was at least happy for a few minutes that I had chosen not to return. The flight back was just as poorly navigated and we unnecessarily took a good deal of flak.

'From the French coast on, we left the formation and went in by ourselves. Upon landing at our field we were met at the end of the runway by an ambulance and I was placed on a stretcher, my left eye giving me some sight but the right one absolutely nothing. I had been so busy that I had not pondered the possibility of blindness on a partial basis until that moment. As I was placed in

the ambulance I suddenly felt something very cold and sticky on my hands and placed my finger on my nose. No doubt about it, it was blood. It suddenly occurred to me that I must have been hit elsewhere and had not noticed it when the medic told me that they had just returned from taking a wounded gunner from another crew down to the hospital and apparently he had been badly wounded in the intestines. I must say it was at that point I had my first true fright and was relieved to find I was no worse than I had surmised.'

At 01.30 hours on Sunday, 4 March, the Luftwaffe made a surprise strafing attack on bases in Norfolk and Suffolk. The German pilots had infiltrated the stream of returning R.A.F. bombers. At Tibenham the intruders put a few holes in some buildings on the base periphery but little damage was recorded. That evening the alert sounded again and lasted for two hours. The ME-410s achieved nowhere near the damage they had wreaked in April 1944 and they sped off into the night amid clatterings of 0.50 calibre fire.

During the day, at 06.00 hours, twenty-eight B-24s had taken off from Attlebridge for Kitzingen, but again the overcast skies forced the 466th to change course. The formation left behind the snow-covered landscape and headed for France to assemble near Nancy after the weather conditions over Norfolk had made this impossible. They proceeded singly to northern France led by Lieutenant-Colonel John Jacobowitz with Colonel Ligon flying Deputy Commander in the number two aircraft. The 466th led the 96th Wing to the target after completing assembly. But thick cloud persisted over the Continent and led to the bomb run over the primary target at Kitzingen being abandoned.

The secondary target at Aschaffenburg was also clouded over so the call went out to switch to the marshalling yards at Stuttgart, about eighty miles from the Swiss border. Using H2X the 466th commenced a northerly bomb run on the Stuttgart rail yards but visibility was so poor that crews had difficulty in seeing their wingmen. Suddenly out of the murk roared a group of B-17s, also lost, sending the Liberators scattering wildly in an effort to avert mid-air collision. The mission was abandoned when twenty ships became separated.

Eight retained some semblance of formation and they formed up on the lead B-24 and turned for home. In the lead was an H2X ship which spotted a town through a hole in the clouds. The lead crew navigator identified it as Frieburg, a town lying a few miles from the Rhine and south-west of Stuttgart. Some navigators suspected that the town might be Basle in Switzerland, lying some twenty-five miles farther south. Frieburg was a target of opportunity and a bomb run was ordered. Several minutes after the bomb run, word came though from Eighth Air Force Headquarters that in fact Basle had been bombed.

The order went out for the formation to return to Attlebridge and for crews to remain in their aircraft until picked up by the base vehicles. Some crews landed not knowing that they had dropped their bombs on Swiss territory. Stringent interrogations by Eighth Air Force Intelligence officers followed in the wake of the débâcle and some crews had their return to the States blocked because of the six weeks' investigation into the incident. News filtered through that the 392nd had also violated neutral territory. It had mistaken Zürich for Frieburg and six aircraft had released their bombs on the Swiss town, forty-fives miles away. There were recriminations on the two bases and at least one lead crew was restricted to base until April 1945. General Marshall urged General Spaatz to visit Switzerland secretly and reparations involving many millions of dollars was made to the Swiss Government. The Group was stood down for two days, resuming missions again on the 7th.

Two days later another 96th Wing Group, the 458th, celebrated achieving 200 missions with a dance in No. 1 Hangar. Music was provided by the Second Air Division Band and the event was a great success. That day Colonel Isbell, who had commanded the Group since December 1943, was succeeded by Colonel Allen E. Herzberg. Next day it was business as usual and the 458th struck at the railway viaduct near Arnsberg on the Ruhr. Bombing by the twenty-eight Liberators was by P.F.F. and the results were unconfirmed.

Meanwhile, the 467th went to Berlin and two Liberators failed to return. Just under a fortnight later Rackheath received news that Lieutenant William Chapman and some members of his crew were safe in Poltava, Russia. Chapman had managed to fly forty miles to the Russian lines after his navigator and engineer had been killed over the target. Eight of the crew baled out over the Russian lines, drawing fire from both Russian and German fighters. Fortunately none of them was hit but they had difficulty in convincing Russian soldiers that they were Americans and not German paratroopers. Some were given rough treatment before their identities were established by the American military representatives in Poltava. They returned to Rackheath in a war-weary B-24 via Italy in late April.

President Roosevelt announced closer tactical liaison with the Russians and as a result the German port of Swinemunde, only sixteen miles from Marshal Zhukov's forces, was bombed on 11 March. Lieutenant-Colonel Schmidt at the head of the 446th led the Eighth over the port at noon. No enemy aircraft was sighted in the Baltic coast area and the flak was moderate. Bombing was made on instruments because of the thick cloud but later reconnaissance revealed 'good' results.

One week later, on 17 March, the 446th and 448th flew a mission to Hanover situated just to the north of the Harz Mountains. Their target was a Tiger Tank factory. Dick Dugger was one of those who flew on the raid and he recalls being greeted with a heavy flak barrage which were 'black puffs with red centres'. This was alarming because *Reddy Teddy* had taken on 2,500 gallons of fuel and had loaded up with twelve 500 lb incendiary bombs before take-off: 'We were over the target and had just dropped all our bombs when as we made our right turn to come home to England, all four engines stopped running. We thought the Germans had some new weapon but, as we fell several thousand feet, suddenly all four engines started up again. They checked over the ship many times after returning to Seething and ran several tests. Next day another crew took the bomber over Berlin and again all four engines stopped, but this time the aircraft did not recover.'

With the Allies now advancing rapidly through Germany, very few strategic targets remained. However, on 15 March the Eighth was alerted for a raid on the German High Command Headquarters at Zossen near Berlin. For Sol Greenberg it was a most memorable mission — the last of his tour: 'Although the Germans were being pressed badly on the ground their anti-aircraft guns were not yet affected and we were in fear of them. And on one's last mission one did not want to go too close to Berlin. The 453rd led the entire Eighth Air Force that day. On the way back we left the Squadron at the Dutch coast along with Lieutenant Adams who had been at Boise with us and who was also finishing his tour on this mission. We raced back to England and it was kind of a dead-heat when we landed. Believe it or not, I felt a tremendous let-down that it was all over for us.'

Crews celebrated their final mission in varying ways. One was to buzz the field. Another was to fly over the field firing flares. These antics were strictly forbidden because they endangered both aircrews and men on the ground. Flares, apart from being expensive, dropped into farmers' fields and burned crops. There were many accidents on these final mission celebrations and one of the saddest involved Captain Robert B. Grettum of the 392nd, who had previously flown with the 859th Squadron of the 492nd. Returning from his final mission to Kitzingen, on 22 March 1945, he came in over Wendling firing flares. Somebody fired a flare from a gun that was probably not locked. The flare-gun most likely spun round and the aircraft caught fire. Grettum's Liberator, a P.F.F. ship, had been only 2,000 feet off the ground and he and seven others perished.

Chapter Eleven

Nemesis

During March 1945 the Second Air Division was again called upon to drop supplies. This time to Field-Marshal Montgomery's Second Army which was crossing the Rhine at Wesel. Once again units of the Division were to supplement the troop-carriers and gliders. Those men who remembered the low-level missions over Ploesti and Arnhem regarded their part in the Rhine crossing with mounting apprehension. On 23 March a security clampdown was imposed on bases throughout the region and trucks arrived laden with weighted wicker baskets to which parachutes were attached. These were loaded into the bomb bays and ball-turret openings of the Liberators. The bulk of the supplies lay in the bomb bay with another eight to nine baskets stowed in the ball-turret and rear fuselage areas. However, this induced a tail-heavy configuration which was rectified by stowing all the ammunition forward.

On 24 March 240 Liberators, loaded with 600 tons of medical supplies, food, and weapons, followed in the wake of transports and gliders ferrying troops of the First Allied Airborne Army. The 446th, with Lieutenant-Colonel William A. Schmidt, Bungay's Air Executive, flying as 20th Wing Commander, led the 93rd and 448th with twenty-seven aircraft. Flying as low as fifty feet, the Liberators droned over the dropping zone at Wesel at 145 m.p.h. using ten to fifteen degrees of flap to aid accuracy in the drop. Grey-white smoke shrouded the battlefields and engulfed the city of Wesel. Smoke canisters which had blacked out over sixty miles of the front for over two days were still burning. The Liberators passed the German city a mile to the south and continued to the dropping zone, pockmarked with wrecked and abandoned gliders, smouldering haystacks, and dead livestock.

Eight out of the nine 20th Wing Squadrons loosed their wicker loads with attached multi-coloured parachutes in the dropping zone. They met with some spasmodic and highly accurate small-arms fire. This and heavy 20 mm cannon-fire resulted in the loss of six 20th Wing Liberators: three from the 446th and three from the 448th. Seventeen of the Bungay Buckeroos' B-24s sustained battle damage while the 448th's lead ship, with Colonel Charles B. Westover, the Commanding Officer aboard, crash-landed in England with two men wounded. The crew aboard the deputy lead, in which Lieutenant-Colonel Herbert H. Thompson was flying, was forced to bale out over England. Twenty millimetre fire pierced armour-plating and struck the formation stick of one of the 93rd Liberators but the pilot and co-pilot escaped injury in the subsequent explosion.

One of the B-24s dispatched from Shipdham was *Southern Comfort II*. In mythology the phoenix is 'a bird who can only be reborn by dying in flames'. So it was with *Southern Comfort,* which was lost over Foggia in August 1943. The ground crew returned to England and were assigned to a fresh combat crew skippered by Lieutenant Waters. Their brand-new B-24 was promptly named *Southern Comfort II.* Their luck held through twenty-five missions, the crew returning to the States to participate in a Bond-raising tour. *Southern Comfort II* passed to another flight crew, while retaining the same ground crew and identity.

Lieutenant Chandler and his crew, on their fourth mission, flew the 'phoenix' on the supply mission. When the 44th arrived at the dropping zone a fierce battle was raging. The Germans were firmly entrenched in and around the dropping zone while British soldiers attempted to wade across the Rhine at this its shallowest point. The gunners of *Southern Comfort II* strafed the German gun emplacements in an effort to help the troops who were wading across the river with their guns held above their heads. The Liberators had to drop their supplies on the opposite bank. *Southern Comfort II* was less than a hundred feet above ground-level when, hit by German small-arms fire, it lost an engine. The 'phoenix' rolled over and her belly struck the ground. She raised a cloud of dust and bounced into the air again to perhaps fifty feet and then exploded. All the crew were killed except the two waist gunners.

One of the waist gunners, Sergeant Vance, returned to Shipdham about three weeks later with both arms in plaster. He had been liberated when the British overran the German field hospital where he was being held captive. He remembered nothing of the crash but it was assumed that he had been thrown out of the B-24 either in the first bounce or in the subsequent explosion.

Approximately 6,000 aircraft, including Liberators, gliders, transports, and fighters, took part in the Wesel operation. The murderous ground-fire probably accounted for the fourteen B-24s that failed to return, including two from the 445th. The Group's Deputy Commanding Officer, Lieutenant-Colonel Fleming, was killed on this mission and twenty-five Liberators returned to Tibenham with varying degrees of battle damage. Five out of the twenty officers at 20th Wing Headquarters flew on the mission, including General Ted Timberlake, who flew in an escort aircraft. Despite intensive ground-fire the Wing hedge-hopped to friendly territory and re-formed for the return flight in the Brussels area.

One hundred and four B-24s returned to their bases with some degree of damage. Waiting to meet them were members of the Press who had sensed a big story. The audacious mission had gone well and that night General Timberlake received word through regular channels that Troop Carrier Command had expressed gratitude for the supply drop and had disclosed that 'immediate objectives

Southern Comfort, *the second 44th B-24 of that name, which was lost on the Rhine crossing mission.*   Warth

had been successfully taken'. But in the confusion five 448th machines had dropped their loads west of the river after one of their number had made an accidental release and two Squadrons of the 389th had to make a second run to drop their supplies in the right area. Later that day more Liberators were dispatched on a second mission to bomb a landing-field near Stormede. This was also successful.

German jet aircraft appeared to be on the increase during March and April 1945. It was, therefore, decided to attempt to curtail the Jagdverbande effort, not in the air where the jets were virtually unstoppable, but on the airfields. A raid had been made on the ME-262 base at Liepham on 19 March and strikes were made on five more occasions culminating in a triple raid on 24 March. The 458th sent nineteen Liberators to Nordhorn in the morning and eighteen B-24s to Kirtorf in the afternoon. Nine aircraft also bombed the airfield at Rorshain and a single machine joined with another Group in the bombing at Hormede. The day's results were described as 'good to excellent'.

Despite these intensive raids, the 458th came under attack by two ME-262s the following day when their target was the oil-storage works at Hitzacker, fifty miles south-east of Hamburg. The jets made their attack from six o'clock but were immediately driven off by escorting fighters. On 30 March the Liberators went to Wilhelmshaven and no ME-262s were sighted. However, on the mission to Brunswick the following day two jets approached the 458th at the I.P. and flew underneath the formation pursued by a lone Mustang.

On 4 April the 458th was once again attacked by an ME-262, *en route* to the airfield at Perleberg. The ME-262 made one pass and was fired on by several B-24s in the formation. It broke off the attack and disappeared. These sporadic attacks were of necessity short-lived because of fuel shortages in Germany. However, on the same day, the ME-262s successfully intercepted the 20th Wing which was heading for the jet airfield at Wesendorf near Dortmund. Three 448th Liberators were shot down while the 446th lost its Commanding Officer, Colonel Troy Crawford, in extraordinary circumstances. Paul Surbaugh, a pilot with the 446th recalls some points which were to have a bearing on the events which followed. 'After countless classroom exercises involving the identificiation of the world's aircraft from 1/100 second flashes on a movie screen, sometime in 1944 orders were received to forget all that we had learned in these exercises. From that point on the gunners were

told to shoot anything "that points its nose at the bomber formation". The Colonel was flying in a blue-painted Mosquito borrowed from the 25th Bombardment Group. Each Heavy Bomber Group employed a fighter aircraft for formation monitoring duties. With an experienced pilot aboard, this aircraft would be used to observe and advise on the state of the formation during assembly. On some short-haul missions this aircraft would accompany the formation to the target.

Paul Surbaugh recounts the events which followed. 'Someone announced over the radio the presence of an ME-262 jet and Colonel Crawford, unable to outfly it, moved in closer to the Group for mutual protection. His convergence was said to have been a textbook "pursuit curve" and with the Mosquito frontal view looking not unlike the ME-262 and considering the great rapidity of events in air combat at times plus the standing order to fire on all approaching aircraft, a hail of bullets sent the Mosquito spiralling downward.'

Colonel Crawford was captured and taken for interrogation to an airfield near Standahl. He had to endure the interrogation with the knowledge that Standahl was to be the 446th's next target. Crawford was later approached by some Germans who realized that Germany had lost the war. He and forty other Americans finally escaped to the American lines. Colonel Crawford eventually arrived back at Flixton on 25 April 1945. During his absence Lieutenant-Colonel Schmidt had assumed command, a post he continued to hold when Crawford returned to the States.

On 6 April, with a bombing raid on Halle, the 467th reached its 200th mission. Actually it was the Group's 209th mission — for those missions which had been recalled were nevertheless assigned numbers. On this mission one Liberator was involved in a collision with an enemy fighter which was suspected of deliberately trying to ram American aircraft. It tore away the starboard fin and rudder but the crew succeeded in reaching the safety of Allied territory before they baled out.

James J. Mahoney recalls the party that was held to celebrate 200 missions. 'One of Glenn Miller's bands was invited. Miller's total Army Air Force Band consisted of 120 pieces. These had been broken up to enable a number of ensembles to visit different parts of the country simultaneously. It was a tradition also that when a Group completed a hundred missions it received one day's stand-down and the officers performed the more menial tasks for the men'.

For the day's events, Mahoney telephoned the 56th and 479th Fighter Groups to ask if they could send over display teams. There was nothing the bomber boys liked better than to see their 'little friends' in action. 'The two Groups agreed to send over their display teams at 11.00 and 12.00 hours,' says Mahoney. 'Unfortunately the ceiling was only 300 feet. We had an antenna called the "clothes line" in front of the control tower. It was only fifty feet high and for a finale the P-51s flew right under it. The Mustangs went under inverted and it was then that a lone Mustang pilot flying near by, thinking it was some of his friends buzzing the base, decided to join in. The pilot, Second Lieutenant R. C. Young, was a former Liberator pilot. He came in behind the Mustangs in the inverted position but lost control over the tower and crashed behind the mess-hall.' Despite this tragedy dances were held on that Saturday night. Firework displays were put on during the dances and the locals at Rackheath were delighted to see a sight they had not witnessed for years. For the 100th and 200th mission parties, the Group was stood down on Sunday and officers and enlisted men gathered to enjoy food, beer, and music in a hangar.

On 7 April 1945 the 453rd flew its 255th mission, to the Luneburg area, about forty-five miles south-east of Hamburg. Although the war was all but over the Luftwaffe continued to put in an appearance. A few days earlier a FW-190 had rammed a lead Liberator and careered into the deputy lead, resulting in all three aircraft going down. Second Lieutenant (later Colonel) George Matecko was one of those at the 7 April briefing and wrote that 'apprehension filled the briefing room. Was the Luftwaffe resorting to kamikaze tactics?' However, Lieutenant-Colonel Jerry V. Davidson, Commanding Officer of the 734th Squadron, opined that the pilot must have either been killed or unconscious when the collision occurred. This was later proved correct at a post-war debriefing.

'The 453rd formed up over the Old Buckenham buncher and proceeded on course. At Ijmuiden eight rounds of 88 mm flak downed one B-24 but from then until south-west of Bremen the mission continued almost as briefed. Then came the warning that the Luftwaffe was in the area: 'Sergeant Harry Lee, the radio-operator, would normally have moved to a waist-gun position to allow Staff Sergeant Durwood Enderton to disperse chaff.

Visiting P-51 Mustangs of the 361st Pursuit Group based at Bottisham prepare for the 466th's 200th mission cele-brations at Attlebridge on 6–7 April 1945. Woolnough

The weather was such that chaff would not be dispersed. So instead Lee positioned himself between the pilot and co-pilot to assist in the spotting of German aircraft. Staff Sergeant Red Giblin manned the other waist gun and Staff Sergeant Lewis Manderson took the tail position. Sergeant Ralph Klien, the engineer, manned the top turret and Staff Sergeant Willard Adler the nose turret.

'Intermittent firing of the waist guns and tail position ensued. Sergeant Klien also began firing his two 50s. Staff Sergeant Adler was firing toward the one o'clock position at an ME-109. The co-pilot, Lieutenant Jesus de la Garza, undoubtedly one of the coolest and best pilots in the Group, cautioned the gunners to be certain of the identity of the aircraft before firing so as not to mistake our P-51 escort as ME-109s. Lieutenant Bruno Arcudi, the navigator, commenced looking for enemy aircraft for Staff Sergeant Adler.

'At the time Lieutenant de la Garza was cautioning the gunners, an ME-262 jet climbed between the 453rd Bomb Group and the Group ahead. I called to Staff Sergeant Adler to swing his guns to the eleven o'clock position and as he swung his turret a second ME-262 pulled up about 150 feet ahead of us. Staff Sergeant Adler fired into the ME-262 getting hits through the cockpit, left wing, and left engine. Sergeant Lee advised Staff Sergeant Adler and the other crew member that Adler had scored hits on the ME-262.

The 392nd assembly ship with possibly the weirdest paint job of all. It was standard olive drab, with silhouettes of whitish blue to represent the windows and outline of the nose and the tail turret. It was formerly Minerva *(B-24D-1-CO; 41-23689), of the 44th. Towards the twilight of its career at Wendling it was used to carry fifty-two men, each carrying 25 lb of baggage, on a ten-hour test mission on 7 April 1945.* Keilman

A heavy concentration of bombs straddles the installations at the German training centre at Lechfeld on 9 April. Note the straight line made by the smoke marker dropped from the 466th lead aircraft. USAF

B-24H 6X-S of the 491st releases its Napalm canisters over the coastal installations at Royan, France on 15 April 1945. USAF

'Sergeant Klien observed the ME-262 continue its climb, now trailing smoke, upwards another 1,000 to 1,500 feet when it fell off into a vertical dive. It was last seen burning, in the dive going straight down into a cloud at 3,500 feet. Both my crew and other crew members surmised that the ME-262 could not have pulled out of the dive at that low altitude.

'Major Erich Rudorffer, one of Germany's leading aces (222 kills) commanded Group II, Jagdverbande 7, the first true ME-262 Squadron composed of famous Luftwaffe pilots, located at Kaltenkirchen airfield near Hamburg. These ME-262s were most likely from that squadron.'

It was evident that the jets, no matter how often their airfields were bombed, would only cease to be a threat when their fuel-supplies had become exhausted or the war ended. However, strikes were maintained and on 9 April the 458th was dispatched to the jet airfield and repair and equipment centre at Lechfeld. This was an attack aimed at the jet menace's vitals but the raid was largely unsuccessful, with bombing results from the thirty-five aircraft dispatched being described as 'poor to excellent'.

One Liberator belonging to the 752nd Squadron was hit almost at bomb release and only four to five men baled out before it exploded at about 500 feet. Another

Liberator from the same Squadron received a flak hit in the tail turret over the target, killing two crewmen and wounding another. Further raids followed against airfields and oil-storage installations but on the 14th the Eighth was called upon once again to do a specialist job. Its target was a pocket of German resistance (some estimates put the force at 122,000 men) holding out and manning gun batteries in the Royan area at Point de Grave. Their resistance was denying the Allies the use of the port of Bordeaux and the Eighth was called upon to help dislodge them after all appeals to surrender had proved in vain. The Eighth's bombardment was to be the prelude of a further massive ground offensive.

Conditions were perfect and crews at briefing believed it would be a 'milk run' as the defences were negligible and the flak unlikely to reach the high-flying Liberators and Fortresses. Many had visions of carrying out the much-vaunted 'pickle-barrel' technique for the first time since their training days in America. However, almost from take-off things began to go wrong. At Horsham St Faith two Liberators crashed near the base shortly after take-off: *Hookem Cow* crashed at about 15.15 hours over the parish of Hainford which borders the airfield and the other, belonging to the 754th Squadron, crashed fifteen minutes later at Barrett's Farm, Spixworth. The 467th from near-by Rackheath fared better — twenty-four Liberators got off and arrived safely over the target and successfully dropped all their 2,000 lb bombs within 1,000 feet of the M.P.I.; half the bombs falling within 500 feet. This was a bombing pattern unsurpassed in Eighth Air Force history and was instrumental in affording the 467th the honour of leading the Victory Fly-past over the Eighth's Headquarters at High Wycombe on 13 May 1945.

Although the raid was a success the 389th lost four of its Liberators when Third Air Division B-17s, making a second run over the target, released their fragmentation bombs through the Sky Scorpions' formation. Two Liberators plummeted to the ground while two others crash-landed in France. A fifth limped back to England.

The following day the Second and Third Air Divisions returned to the area and for the first time carried Napalm; 460,000 gallons of it. The First Air Division carried 1,000 and 2,000 lb G.P. bombs while three Fighter Groups snuffed out any gun emplacements which showed signs of opening fire on the bombers. Mosquitos were also called in to sow a cloud of chaff to snow radar screens which might be used to direct the radar-controlled flak guns. These precautions were the only protection the bombers had to prevent their lethal cargoes being exploded by German gun batteries.

The 458th dispatched twenty-seven Liberators which joined up with other Second Air Division Groups and released their seventy-five- to eighty-five-gallon liquid-fire tanks, along with conventional incendiaries, on the east bank of the Gironde Estuary. One 458th B-24 left the formation after bomb release and headed inland with one engine feathered. No flak was encountered and French forces later captured the port.

The 458th flew four more missions during the last fifteen days of the month and on 25 April they joined with other Second Air Division Groups in the final Eighth Air Force mission of the war. Their targets were four rail complexes surrounding Hitler's mountain retreat at Berchtesgaden. The R.A.F. made a simultaneous attack on the retreat with six-ton bombs. The Division expected to fly another mission on the following day but by then the Germans had surrendered.

Groups flew 'trolly missions' over Western Europe so that ground crews could see at first hand the destruction their charges had wrought. When crews began leaving for the States people thronged the streets of the towns and villages as 'the Yanks' marched to waiting trucks and railway stations en route to ports of embarkation. Many people, of course, were sad to see them go. They had become a part of everyday life and their departure was greeted with great sadness.

Eleven-year-old Russell Foster, who lived in Abbey Road near the Old Buckenham airfield, had been the envy of all his friends while the 453rd had been flying on raids from the base. When Old Buckenham airfield was built by the Air Ministry, its hardstands had encroached on surrounding fields and sometimes on the gardens of neighbouring houses. One hardstand had been built near the garden of Russell Foster's home. He had walked across to inspect the B-24s of the 732nd Squadron on many an occasion and had been adopted by the Squadron as its mascot. 'They stood me on an ammo box and taught me how to strip down the fifty calibre guns. It got so I could do it with my eyes closed. I also had rides in a Liberator around the taxi way from the hangar to the hardstands', he remembers proudly. Russell was also allowed to sit in the gun turrets and

Hookem Cow *B-24H-25-FO (42-95120), one of two 458th aircraft that crashed on take-off on 14 April 1945. Pilot D. R. Totten. Five were killed and two injured. The other, B-24J-100-CO, crashed at Spixworth. Six killed, one injured. Pilot R. M. Gibson.* Reynolds.

sometimes he was permitted to rotate them.

The middle of May saw the Bombardment Groups begin leaving the east of England for America. Twenty-man crews left almost daily and ground crews worked all hours to ensure that they got away on schedule. Liberators of the 467th Bombardment Group circled Rackheath in a final farewell gesture. *Witchcraft* was flown home by Lieutenant Fred Jansen with Joe Ramirez, the crew chief, aboard.

At the same time many personnel changes took place. Colonel James Stewart, who had been the 453rd Executive Officer since March 1944, became the new Second Wing Commander.

Some Groups left monuments to their achievements. The 392nd at Wendling constructed a marble obelisk. Its

Marêchal Valin for the French Air Force presents the Croix de Guerre to Colonel Alan Herzberg at Ketteringham Hall on 3 May 1945 at the award ceremony for the bombing of Royan. Seventy men received awards for 'exceptional services rendered in the course of operations for the liberation of France'. James Stewart (far right). Shower inscription, with a few alterations, could have been dedicated to any of the Eighth Air Force Groups that flew from England: 'Dedicated to the men of the U.S. Army Air Forces Station 118, who through their efforts, devotion and duty, aided in bringing victory to the Allies in World War Two.'

Most ground crewman journeyed back to America either in the *Queen Mary* or in the *Queen Elizabeth*. Others in less-well-known ships. The aircrews flew home via Valley and the Azores. Even these trips were not without disaster — on 19 June a 446th Liberator with fifteen passengers on board disappeared over the Atlantic.

There was also a good deal of clearing up to be done. Much of the equipment was now surplus to requirements and had to be destroyed or given away to local people.

Roxy Marotta was one of the last men to leave Shipdham and he recalls: 'On 8 May 1945, the entire air base was in a happy mood, awaiting the trip home to the U.S.A. In a short time the order came. Air crew personnel *only* were to fly home in the Liberators with a 40 lb luggage allowance. Needless to say those of us left behind had a wistful look on our faces as we watched the B-24s take off into the wide blue yonder. Our 806th Chemical Company (Air Operations) was given the odious task of cleaning up the station prior to handing it over to the British.

'Since the "fly boys" had left in such a hurry, and with limited baggage, there were tons of supplies that had to be returned to different depots. The depots were not happy about this as they were also in the process of packing and leaving. We were assembled, and urged to get the job done and promised some time off. We responded with enthusiasm and worked very hard from dawn till dusk.

'After the final inspection, four American and four British airmen stood to attention at the flagpole. One lone bugler played and the American flag was lowered for the last time, and the British flag raised for the first. This seemed to me a very quiet and unpretentious ceremony to end the three years of occupation by the 44th Bomb Group of Shipdham. Three months after the end of hostilities, and several air bases later, our Chemical Company got aboard a rusty old Liberty ship at Liverpool for our trip home. It looked like a luxury liner to us.'

On 13 April Colonel Eugene Snavely had handed over command of the 44th to Colonel Vernon Smith. Snavely was later promoted to General and, together with Lieutenant-Colonel Howard Moore, formed Headquarters, Occupational Air Force, Austria. Moore and Snavely had left Verona, Italy, on 2 June 1945 to represent the United States on air matters at the Vienna Mission. They spent two weeks in the Austrian capital, during which time they attended such functions as a party at Marshal Tolbuhkin's villa where the vodka flowed freely. While in Vienna Moore learned of an American flyer who was in hospital after losing a leg in a flak burst on a raid over the city on 22 March. After visiting several hospitals he was finally traced and placed in the hands of American officials.

With the war's end American administration facilities in England remained at High Wycombe and Honington but most of the famous Combat Groups had disbanded. In 1948 an informal agreement was reached between General Spaatz, Commanding General United States Strategic Air Force in Europe and Air Marshal Tedder of the R.A.F. for the transfer of five East Anglian bases for use by B-29s, if the need arose. Events moved quickly that year and in April the Russians began the Berlin Blockade. In June the Americans mounted Operation Plainfare and the R.A.F. Operation Victuals from England, flying in vital supplies to the beleagured Berliners. On 7 August 1948 Major-General Leon W. Johnson, late of the 14th Wing of the Second Air Division, assumed command of the Third Air Force and from that date onwards the American Air Force has been an integral part of Western defence.

V-E DAY
SEETHING, ENGLAND
8 MAY 1945

A Norfolk Liberator Factory

Some of the most important but little-known units of the Eighth Air Force were the Strategic Air Depots assigned under the provisions of the Bradley Plan. These depots were responsible for the maintenance and repair of combat aircraft. American Air Force Station Watton-Griston in Norfolk was responsible for the maintenance and supply of the fourteen Liberator Groups of the Second Bombardment Division. The base was actually split between two units, the 3rd Strategic Air Depot at Griston and the 25th Bombardment Group at the permanent R.A.F. facilities at Watton. The 3rd S.A.D., comprising the 31st and 46th Air Depot Groups, was based at Watton from July 1943 and came under the control of Eighth Air Force Service Command. To accommodate the 3rd S.A.D. a vast township had to be constructed across the other side of the runway from Watton at Griston. It was called 'Neaton' officially but no community of that name existed. Plywood hutments, steel hangars and shops were constructed and the 3rd S.A.D. utilized existing buildings, like the local church, which was used to conduct regular services together with the civilian services. Griston was adopted as the unit's home while Watton became A.A.F. 376 with its one runway serving both the 3rd S.A.D. and the 25th Bombardment Group.

The 25th Bombardment Group, which was based at Watton from 22 April 1944 until 23 July 1945 used B-24Ds and B-24Hs, Mosquito XVIs and a few B-17Gs on operations chiefly engaged in weather flights over Europe. It was known as the 802nd Reconnaissance Group (P) from 22 April 1944 until it was activated as the 25th Bombardment Group (Reconnaissance) on 9 August 1944.

While plans were being made in 1942 for the build-up of major American air forces in Britain, one immediate concern was the question of advance air depots for the bomber sector. It had been proposed in June 1942 that one mobile air depot should be established for every three operational airfields. General Spaatz planned for twenty small mobile air depots for the entire force. But in August 1942 it was decided to provide only three large advance depots, two for Bomber Command and one for Fighter Command, with additional depots as required. Eighth Air Force Service Command selected Watton and Honington as sites for the bomber depots and these were considerably larger than the traditional mobile air depots on which they were patterned.

In June 1943 active plans were laid to transform Watton-Griston into an Eighth Air Force Service Command Depot, redesignated Station 505. On 23 July the first American contingent arrived. They were joined at the end of the month by units of the 46th Air Depot Group. The Americans were warmly greeted by the R.A.F. contingent who absorbed the newcomers into the general pattern on the base. Cooks and K.P.s were furnished by the R.A.F. Mess-hall and British trucks were provided for collecting American rations. Two of the four C-type hangars, each of 180,000 square feet, were taken over by the Air Corps Supply and Engineering sections. But as the American presence continued to grow conditions became overcrowded and a certain amount of doubling up was necessary. American and R.A.F. Ordnance moved in together, as did the Allied Chemical Warfare Services. Despite the crowded conditions the American and R.A.F. communities operated in relative harmony.

The 3rd S.A.D. was responsible for the third and fourth echelon maintenance, plus all supply functions, for the Second Bombardment Division. Each Air Depot Group was organized, staffed, and trained specifically to service Air Force combat units. The task of the 3rd S.A.D. was to salvage all Liberators which crashed in England. A Field Maintenance Group went to every crash site and salvaged all parts that could be removed. Small mobile field units would go to sites of downed aircraft and if temporary repairs could be made on site, the Liberator would be flown back to Watton for permanent repairs.Those aircraft beyond repair were transported by road to Watton after their lethal cargoes of bombs and ammunition had been removed. These teams always operated under very severe and primitive conditions. It was not uncommon for them to remain out in the field for several months at a time. Some were stationed at emergency landing-strips at Woodbridge, Manston, Catfoss, and any farmer's field where a Liberator might have come to rest. Every single item recovered was returned to depot stock for reissue to the Combat Groups.

The tempo of war called for immediate replacement of damaged or defective equipment and professional-type shops were set up to serve and repair every major component on the Liberator from armament and instruments to propellers and sparking plugs. Every component, system, or major part of the B-24 received specialized treatment by men training on each one. They did a professional job equal to, or better than, factory specifications, under field conditions. Each shop had the appearance of being part of an aircraft factory. Specialized hangars were erected for Aero Repair and Engine Repair while for Depot Supply hangars were set up like huge factory warehouses with each type of class of Air Force materiel together under one roof. Each day the Liberator bases throughout the region would telephone their needs and a fleet of trucks, making two deliveries per day to each Bombardment Group, would leave with supplies.

Although great progress was made the Eighth Air Force still remained heavily dependent upon the R.A.F. for heavy repair work on its engines, air-frames, and propellers at Burtonwood. Such maintenance was performed by R.A.F. units, British civilians, and a few Americans from the aircraft industry.

The Bradley Committee recommended that the Base Air Depots (Burtonwood, Warton, and Langford Lodge) would be called 1st, 2nd, and 3rd Base Air Depots. The intransit depots would be designated as Strategic Air Depots. On 1 August 1943 there were four Strategic Air Depots, located at Honington, Suffolk (1st S.A.D.), Little Staughton (2nd S.A.D.), Watton (3rd S.A.D.), and Wattisham, Suffolk (4th S.A.D.). Because of increasing needs and size of the Strategic Air Depots, they were relocated in June 1944 at Troston (1st S.A.D.), Abbots Ripton (2nd S.A.D.), Griston (3rd S.A.D.), and Hitcham (4th S.A.D.). Towards the end of the war a fifth S.A.D. was located in France.

By late August 1943 a large stock of Liberator parts had arrived at Watton and the Engineering Section was ready to undertake major work programmes. By 1 September the Supply Section was actively engaged in supplying the Second Bombardment Division. Four machine-shop trailer units were activated with four more on 10 September. Medical, Chemical, Signal, Ordnance, and Quartermaster units began depot

Watton-Griston and the runway used by the 25th Bombardment Group and the 3rd Strategic Air Depot. Griston site was located at the bottom right with R.A.F. Watton in juxtaposition.   Noble

functions that month and were distributing supplies to Second Bombardment Division bases. By the end of the month the ever-increasing number of Americans was making conditions at Watton extremely crowded as the R.A.F. was still present. It was decided, therefore, that the American contingent would take over the base on 4 October 1943 while only a small R.A.F. liaison team would remain.

In November 1943 the Eighth Air Force drew a firm line between the echelons of maintenance performed by the

On 2 September 1943 Urgin' Virgin *became the first B-24 to be repaired at Station 505.*   Noble

Strategic Air Depots and the sub-depots which operated from every Liberator base. The sub-depot was to perform more maintenance on aircraft which could be repaired in less than thirty-six hours while those requiring more hours' work were to be turned over to a Strategic Air Depot. Work beyond their capability was to be passed on to the Base Air Depots.

On 18 November 1943, the R.A.F. having departed, Watton faced a large influx of additional units, including the 93rd Supply Squadron and units of the 31st Air Depot Group. By the following month these units had been fully integrated with the 46th Air Depot Group but then came the Bradley Plan. This involved a changeover from organizational operation to a divisional operation and the plan was not readily accepted by the airmen. However the Bradley Plan was a stroke of genius as far as supervision and control of personnel were concerned and eventually became accepted. Among its effects was that all engineering and maintenance was consolidated under one division called Maintenance while all transportation duties and personnel went to Transportation Division.

By January 1944 the 3rd S.A.D. was giving excellent service to the Second Bombardment Division. Repaired Liberators came out of the depot daily while other sections performed vital modifications on newly arrived aircraft from America. Supply Division maintained a steady flow of parts and material to the B-24 bases while the Transportation Division had vehicles roving the country moving supplies and equipment to and from the depot.

In February 1944 the 3rd S.A.D. began moving across the base to the Griston site. By now the Strategic Air Depots were

The 3rd S.A.D. Base Headquarters (centre) with Griston Village (right) and church tower protruding through the trees. Left of centre is the one runway used by both the 3rd S.A.D. and the 25th Bombardment Group. (Note the B-24 at dispersal and very effectively camouflaged hangars in distance.) Noble

performing a large share of the total maintenance work for the Bomber and Fighter Commands. By the spring of 1944 each of the Strategic Air Depots had a strength of 3,500 to 4,000 men. The 3rd S.A.D. performed modifications and repairs to keep the Second Bombardment Division flying. But it was a far from glamorous occupation, as T/Sergeant Wiley S. Noble, assigned to the 31st Headquarters and the Headquarters Squadron Base Ordnance at Watton, recalls: 'We did not receive the headlines in the Air Force papers but we kept the B-24s in the air. Strangely, very few of the B-24 combat people were even aware of our services to their Bomb Groups. However I doubt that the Consolidated Aircraft Factory employees knew as much about the Liberator as our boys at the 3rd S.A.D. did. We made approved modifications to the aircraft and even many unauthorized ones, to produce the most flyable and combat-wise bomber possible.'

This was best illustrated in the case of the *Howling Banshee*. Two Liberators at Horsham St Faith were joined together after one had lost its entire nose section in a crash and the other had damaged its tail section beyond repair in a taxiing accident. Lieutenant Dick Ayers and Lieutenant John H. Blake arrived at Horsham St Faith from Watton and decided to marry the two aircraft. It had never been tried before in England to their knowledge and never by a mobile repair unit such as the 3rd S.A.D. Both sections were too large to be transported to Watton so assembly was completed at the 458th base. Master Sergeant William E. McIver headed a twelve-man repair team which completed the difficult task in only twenty-nine days. The two damaged aircraft were separated at the centre of the

bomb bay and the undamaged halves joined together with specially designed stress plates. It was now mathematically stronger than the original design and the Inspector discovered that less than one quarter of the variations allowed at the factory had been used. Captain Henry R. Miller test flew the *Howling Banshee* and reported that it handled perfectly and cruised 10 m.p.h. faster than the average B-24 of its type!

With the coming invasion and the subsequent increase in missions the 3rd S.A.D. was called upon to make additional efforts. During the week ending 14 June the 3rd S.A.D. Transport Division hauled 3,600 tons of materiel, mostly high explosive, for the Second Bombardment Division Groups. All the drivers carried weapons and 0.50 calibre machine-guns were mounted on the cab roofs and on some jeeps to give convoy protection in the event of air attack. The increase in bombing missions in June was reflected by the greatest ever number of Liberators under repair that month. Twenty-three were in depot on 5 and 6 June rising to forty-nine on 28 June. The Second Bombardment Division had 1,022 B-24s on hand on D-Day but by the end of the month it had decreased to 911. The highest number of combat-ready Liberators in June was 901 on the 13th and the lowest, 643, on 21 June. The 3rd S.A.D. did its part, salvaging forty-six bombers but the Second Bombardment Division lost 101 B-24s in combat.

Despite the increased activity throughout July the number of aircraft grounded through lack of replacement parts was the lowest in the 3rd S.A.D.'s history. During the first week of the month, only 5.6 aircraft were grounded on average per day. By the end of the month it had fallen to 4.3 and on 22 July only

Ground crew who facilitated assembly of the Howling Banshee. Noble

Red Cross clubmobile stops off at Griston near a cle-track and two B-24s — from the 446th (right) and 448th (left). Noble

25th Bombardment Group Mosquito lands at Watton.   Noble

one Liberator within the Second Bombardment Division was grounded through lack of spares! This had been achieved by careful husbandry and by salvage. Eighty-eight Liberators were repaired at Griston in July and were returned to combat duty. Seventy had been battle-damaged bombers while the other eighteen had needed general maintenance.

In December 1944, when the Eighth Air Force Service Command extended its operations to the Continent, trucks and personnel from the Transportation Division crossed the Channel and moved to France, later to become part of 5th S.A.D. The mobile repair crews there sent back almost 1,300 bombers and fighters before VE-Day. Of 1,288 aircraft, valued at about $300 million, all but sixty-seven were returned to England and made airworthy. Wiley Noble recalled that: 'Ours was the best Strategic Air Depot within the Eighth Air Force Service Command and we were so honoured officially by the Eighth A.F.S.C. Commander. Of course I would like to say that ours was the best, as would everyone, but in this case superiority actually did exist with our 3rd S.A.D.'

Probably the best-kept secret at Watton was the true mission of the black B-24s, even though many at 3rd S.A.D. had serious doubts about their alleged 'Pathfinder' missions. Ordnance and Armament sections knew those B-24s did not drop bombs, because there were no bomb racks. Several 913th Signal men knew about the special radio and navigational equipment aboard and the Base Photo Section made facsimile European identification cards and photographed 'civilians' wearing continental clothing. Maintenance Division crews assisting the detachment of 35th Air Service Group personnel with the black B-24s were aware that the aircraft were unusual. Supply Division personnel delivered special supplies frequently. Yet no one 'talked'.

Although U.S.A.A.F. Special Operations from the United Kingdom began in October 1943 with a leaflet-dropping mission by the 422nd Bomb Squadron, the major effort to supply the Free French and patriots in Europe began under the code-name 'Carpetbagger'. The 4th and 22nd Anti-

submarine Squadrons, 479th Anti-submarine Group, flying B-24s, had been disbanded in August 1943. From these two Squadrons came the personnel and B-24s for original Carpetbagger Squadrons. The Eighth Air Force activated the 36th and 406th Bombardment Squadrons in November 1943 and attached them as a sub-group to the 482nd Bomb Group (Pathfinder) at Alconbury. Crews undertook to deliver supplies to Resistance forces in Occupied Europe, using B-24s with only a tail turret providing defensive fire-power. Operations were mounted from Tempsford under R.A.F. guidance from January 1944, while administered by the 482nd at Alconbury, until 27 February 1944. That month several of the Carpetbagger Liberators were moved to Watton. These Liberators had their ball turrets removed and a cargo hatch was installed, called the 'Joe Hole'. 'Joe' was the nickname afforded the secret agents. They dropped through the hole which had a metal shroud inside the opening. Plywood covered the floors and blackout curtains graced the waist windows. The Liberators were painted in a special non-glare black paint and blister windows were installed to give the pilots greater visibility.

The Carpetbaggers were established on 28 March 1944 as the 801st Provisional Bombardment Group and redesignated the 492nd Bombardment Group (H) on 13 August 1944, taking the designation from the recently disbanded Group of that name. The 36th and 406th Squadrons (redesignated the 856th and 858th Squadrons respectively on 13 August 1944) only, operated from Watton, while the main part of the unit, under the command of Lieutenant-Colonel Clifford J. Heflin, had its Headquarters at, and operated from, Harrington.

By the end of May 1944 there were four squadrons of Carpetbaggers with more than forty black Liberators. The Watton Carpetbaggers flew their first mission to France from Tempsford on the night of 4–5 January 1944 and by 1 March that year had completed twenty-nine sorties.

In the next three months the Carpetbaggers completed 213 sorties, most of which were flown to supply the Freedom Fighters in France. During July 1944 all four Squadrons, flying

A black Liberator (left) *and another Liberator,* Booby Trap (right) *undergoing modifications at the Second Base Air Depot at Warton, Lancashire.*
via North

The 3rd S.A.D. band, 'The Continentals', entertaining the men at a noon-time concert early in 1944. Noble

397 sorties, dropped thousands of containers, packages and bundles of leaflets, and sixty-two 'Joes'. From January to May 1944 twenty-five black Liberators were lost in combat and eight others severely damaged by ground-fire had to be salvaged.

Full-scale Carpetbagger operations had ceased at Watton by September 1944 with the occupation of most of France and Belgium. The black B-24s were transferred to Leuchars, Scotland, for operations in support of the Norwegian Underground. The unit was now commanded by Colonel Bernt Balchen, a famous Arctic flyer. Two projects were in operation. The 'Ball' project involved dropping equipment and agents in black Liberators while the 'Sonnie' project involved bringing home American internees from Sweden. 'Sonnie' crews, wearing civilian clothing and carrying passports issued by the American Embassy in London, flew their green-painted Liberators, minus national markings, to Stockholm during the day, while the 'Ball' project Liberators flew at night. There were even ground crews in Stockholm posing as civilians who serviced the Liberators on their arrival. 'Sonnie' crews flew in supplies and mail for the Norwegian Legation, returning with Allied airmen and even Norwegians who finally joined a special Norwegian Army unit being trained in Scotland.

But the operations lasted only until about Thanksgiving Day 1944, at which time the entire unit was transferred to Metfield. But while the green Liberators carried on their operations at the Suffolk base, the black B-24 operations soon ended.

The war in Europe wound down rather swiftly and the tempo at Watton decreased accordingly. During the last six weeks of hostilities the 3rd S.A.D.'s main activity was in returning materiel from the Second Bombardment Division bases to Watton followed by a massive transfer of materiel to the Base Air Depot at Warton and to Burtonwood. It was no secret that the 3rd S.A.D. was earmarked for the Pacific and much of the Ordnance property and equipment (except weapons) was shipped to Luzon in the Philippines. About one-third of the base complement departed in mid July 1945 for the U.S.A. but a larger proportion left on 5 August 1945. However the subsequent announcement that the Japanese had capitulated following the dropping on Nagasaki of a second atom bomb meant that no-one was redeployed to the Pacific. Each man fifty years or older was discharged while the remainder returned to Kelly Field (31st Air Depot Group) or Oklahoma City Field (46th Air Depot Group.) New complements who had not seen service overseas were assigned by the

end of VE-Day and proceeded to the Pacific. All the original 3rd S.A.D. personnel were discharged in October and November 1945.

The last known photo of Glenn Miller, taken on the night of 13 December 1944. Louis Lawrence of the 3rd S.A.D. Base Photo Section was assigned to cover the appearance of the 3rd S.A.D. band 'The Continentals' in a 'Carnival of Music' at Bedford. Glenn Miller was a judge in selecting the top band. This photograph was taken after the final performance. During this photo session it was announced that Miller had to leave for R.A.F. Twinwoods to fly to Paris the next day. The UC-64 carrying Flying Officer John Morgan and Miller was never seen again. Lawrence

Appendix Two
SECOND AIR DIVISION ORGANISATIONAL CHART

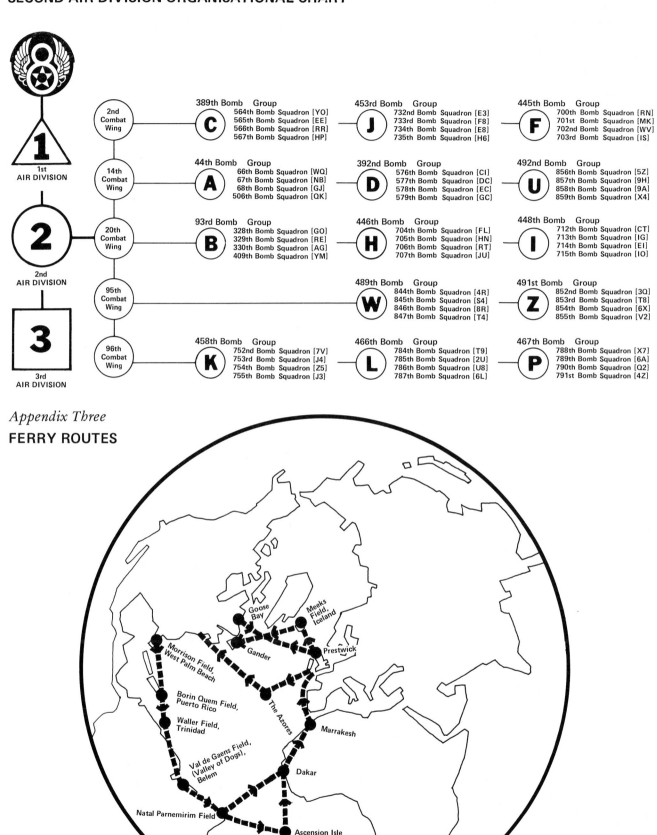

		389th Bomb Group	453rd Bomb Group	445th Bomb Group

1st AIR DIVISION

2nd AIR DIVISION

3rd AIR DIVISION

2nd Combat Wing — **C** — 389th Bomb Group
564th Bomb Squadron [YO]
565th Bomb Squadron [EE]
566th Bomb Squadron [RR]
567th Bomb Squadron [HP]

J — 453rd Bomb Group
732nd Bomb Squadron [E3]
733rd Bomb Squadron [F8]
734th Bomb Squadron [E8]
735th Bomb Squadron [H6]

F — 445th Bomb Group
700th Bomb Squadron [RN]
701st Bomb Squadron [MK]
702nd Bomb Squadron [WV]
703rd Bomb Squadron [IS]

14th Combat Wing — **A** — 44th Bomb Group
66th Bomb Squadron [WQ]
67th Bomb Squadron [NB]
68th Bomb Squadron [GJ]
506th Bomb Squadron [QK]

D — 392nd Bomb Group
576th Bomb Squadron [CI]
577th Bomb Squadron [DC]
578th Bomb Squadron [EC]
579th Bomb Squadron [GC]

U — 492nd Bomb Group
856th Bomb Squadron [5Z]
857th Bomb Squadron [9H]
858th Bomb Squadron [9A]
859th Bomb Squadron [X4]

20th Combat Wing — **B** — 93rd Bomb Group
328th Bomb Squadron [GO]
329th Bomb Squadron [RE]
330th Bomb Squadron [AG]
409th Bomb Squadron [YM]

H — 446th Bomb Group
704th Bomb Squadron [FL]
705th Bomb Squadron [HN]
706th Bomb Squadron [RT]
707th Bomb Squadron [JU]

I — 448th Bomb Group
712th Bomb Squadron [CT]
713th Bomb Squadron [IG]
714th Bomb Squadron [EI]
715th Bomb Squadron [IO]

95th Combat Wing — **W** — 489th Bomb Group
844th Bomb Squadron [4R]
845th Bomb Squadron [S4]
846th Bomb Squadron [8R]
847th Bomb Squadron [T4]

Z — 491st Bomb Group
852nd Bomb Squadron [3Q]
853rd Bomb Squadron [T8]
854th Bomb Squadron [6X]
855th Bomb Squadron [V2]

96th Combat Wing — **K** — 458th Bomb Group
752nd Bomb Squadron [7V]
753rd Bomb Squadron [J4]
754th Bomb Squadron [Z5]
755th Bomb Squadron [J3]

L — 466th Bomb Group
784th Bomb Squadron [T9]
785th Bomb Squadron [2U]
786th Bomb Squadron [U8]
787th Bomb Squadron [6L]

P — 467th Bomb Group
788th Bomb Squadron [X7]
789th Bomb Squadron [6A]
790th Bomb Squadron [Q2]
791st Bomb Squadron [4Z]

Appendix Three
FERRY ROUTES

Goose Bay

Meeks Field, Iceland

Gander

Prestwick

Morrison Field, West Palm Beach

The Azores

Borin Quem Field, Puerto Rico

Waller Field, Trinidad

Marrakesh

Val de Gaens Field, (Valley of Dogs), Belem

Dakar

Natal Parnemirim Field

Ascension Isle

Appendix Four

RADIO NAVIGATIONAL AIDS

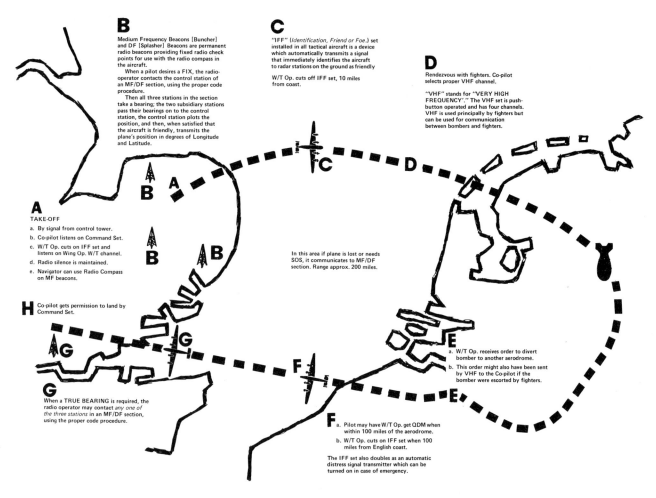

B

Medium Frequency Beacons [Buncher] and DF [Splasher] Beacons are permanent radio beacons providing fixed radio check points for use with the radio compass in the aircraft.

When a pilot desires a FIX, the radio-operator contacts the control station of an MF/DF section, using the proper code procedure.

Then all three stations in the section take a bearing; the two subsidiary stations pass their bearings on to the control station, the control station plots the position, and then, when satisfied that the aircraft is friendly, transmits the plane's position in degrees of Longitude and Latitude.

C

"IFF" (*Identification, Friend or Foe*.) set installed in all tactical aircraft is a device which automatically transmits a signal that immediately identifies the aircraft to radar stations on the ground as friendly

W/T Op. cuts off IFF set, 10 miles from coast.

D

Rendezvous with fighters. Co-pilot selects proper VHF channel.

"VHF" stands for "VERY HIGH FREQUENCY". The VHF set is push-button operated and has four channels. VHF is used principally by fighters but can be used for communication between bombers and fighters.

A

TAKE-OFF

a. By signal from control tower.

b. Co-pilot listens on Command Set.

c. W/T Op. cuts on IFF set and listens on Wing Op. W/T channel.

d. Radio silence is maintained.

e. Navigator can use Radio Compass on MF beacons.

H Co-pilot gets permission to land by Command Set.

In this area if plane is lost or needs SOS, it communicates to MF/DF section. Range approx. 200 miles.

G

When a TRUE BEARING is required, the radio operator may contact *any one of the three stations* in an MF/DF section, using the proper code procedure.

E

a. W/T Op. receives order to divert bomber to another aerodrome.

b. This order might also have been sent by VHF to the Co-pilot if the bomber were escorted by fighters.

F

a. Pilot may have W/T Op. get QDM when within 100 miles of the aerodrome.

b. W/T Op. cuts on IFF set when 100 miles from English coast.

The IFF set also doubles as an automatic distress signal transmitter which can be turned on in case of emergency.

Appendix Five

SECOND AIR DIVISION GROUP ASSEMBLY PROCEDURES

The diagram shows the assembly areas used by each group when an overcast existed.

The unusual concentration of bomber bases in a limited area, and their proximity to one another demanded inviolate adherence to this procedure. Otherwise fatal accidents would result.

Aircraft were required to take-off 30 to 45 seconds apart, sometimes in zero ceiling with less than 500 yards visibility. Pilots knew beforehand the exact headings, speed, and distance separating each plane, and the length of each leg in the pattern they were to fly. For self-protection, all climbed at the same rate to the briefed spot where the assembly pattern took shape. And each group had its own buncher or splasher beacon for control points.

In this fashion they would sometimes climb through as much as 20,000 feet of overcast (80 to 90 minutes of instrument flying) in order to form on top, since assembly had to be made under conditions assuring 1,500 feet of clear air vertically.

Close knit formations were vital if high concentration of bomb impacts and effective mutual defence were to be achieved.

Gaudily painted assembly ships or 'Judas Goats' — war weary Liberators, stripped of all armament — shepherded their flock until the Group successfully formed up on their tails. Monitor ships — normally P47 Thunderbolts flown by high ranking officers — were also employed to 'ride herd' on the formation, using radio commentary instead of flares.

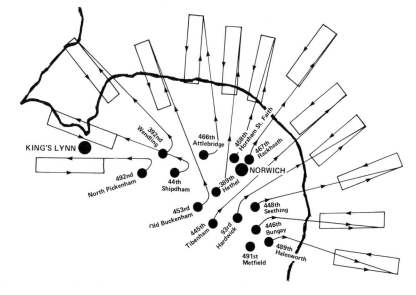

Appendix Six

NORTH AFRICAN OPERATIONS

B-24 aircraft and crews of the Second Air Division carried out operations from North African bases in three major phases: (a) Torch, 13 December 1942 – 20 February 1943; (b) Husky, 2–19 July 1943; Ploesti, 1 August 1943; Post Husky, 13–21 August 1943; and (c) Fifth Army Support, 21 September – 1 October 1943.

On the Ploesti operation, 1 August 1943, carried out from very low level in conjunction with the Ninth Air Force, the oil fields were heavily hit and production substantially curtailed. 30 B-24s of Second Air Division were reported Missing in Action and 17 enemy aircraft destroyed.

Operation	No. of Days Operated	Groups Carrying Out Missions	Aircraft Total Sorties	Aircraft Effective Sorties	Tons Bombs on Targets	Aircraft Missing in Action	Enemy Action Claims Destroyed	Enemy Action Claims Probable	Enemy Action Claims Damaged	Casualties Killed in Action	Casualties Wounded	Casualties Missing in Action
Torch Project 13 Dec.1942 – 20 Feb.1943	23	93rd	273	224	530.2	4	(Unavailable)					
Husky, Ploesti, Post Husky 2 July – 21 Aug. 1943	20	93rd, 44th 389th	989	892	2428.2	54	121	12	35	28	88	420
Fifth Army Support 21 Sept. – 1 Oct. 1943	4	93rd, 44th 389th	191	172	406.6	11	50	3	6	0	4	89
Total North African Operations	47	93rd, 44th 389th	1453	1288	3365.0	69	171	15	41	28	92	509

Appendix Seven

TRUCKING OPERATIONS

The bulk of trucking operations occurred during 29 August – 30 September 1944 when the Eight Air Force supported operations of ground forces by employing over 200 B-24s of Second Air Division and 492nd Bombardment Group to deliver vitally needed gasoline, food, and medical supplies to forward areas.

Month	Aircraft Total Sorties	Aircraft Effective Sorties	Tons Delivered Gasoline	Tons Delivered Medical Supplies	Tons Delivered Food	Tons Delivered Other	Tons Delivered Total Tons	Aircraft Lost Missing in Action	Aircraft Lost Cat E	Casualties Killed in Action	Casualties Missing in Action
1944 August	43	43		27.2	55.7	47.3	130.2				
September	2316	2205	8225.9	154.1	1229.3	14.5	9623.8	2	1	6	12
October	23	23				46.7	46.7				
November	9	9				12.4	12.4			6	
December	10	10				22.3	22.3				
TOTAL 1944	2401	2290	8225.9	181.3	1285.0	143.2	9835.4	2	1	12	12
1945 January	8	8				10.3	10.3				
February	9	9				13.6	13.6				
March	6	6				5.6	5.6				
April	10	10				15.3	15.3				
TOTAL 1945	33	33				44.8	44.8				
GRAND TOTAL	2434	2323	8225.9	181.3	1285.0	188.0	9880.2	2	1	12	12

Appendix Eight

BOMBING ACCURACY

The table gives the average percentage of bombs dropped which fell within 1,000 ft and 2,000 ft, respectively, of pre-assigned Mean Points of Impact (MPI's) on visual missions under conditions of good to fair visibility.

Period	WITHIN 1,000 FT. B17 1st Div. %	WITHIN 1,000 FT. B24 2nd Div. %	WITHIN 1,000 FT. B17 3rd Div. %	WITHIN 1,000 FT. Total Eighth Air Force %	WITHIN 2,000 FT. B17 1st Div. %	WITHIN 2,000 FT. B24 2nd Div. %	WITHIN 2,000 FT. B17 3rd Div. %	WITHIN 2,000 FT. Total Eighth Air Force %
1943 October November December	25	32	27	27	46	58	47	48
1944 January	34	23	41	35	61	48	60	58
February	42	26	46	39	76	49	77	69
March	31	20	39	31	64	36	70	58
April	34	21	32	29	62	43	58	55
May	44	34	33	37	68	64	62	65
June	49	32	35	40	81	62	65	71
July	42	26	44	37	73	56	77	69
August	54	36	42	45	84	65	72	75
September October	29	32	46	38	61	56	72	65
November December	24	24	25	25	54	44	47	48
1945 January	29	34	24	29	59	61	56	59
February	50	57	40	49	80	81	69	77
March	40	45	30	38	76	73	58	69
April	64	58	52	59	91	79	80	85

Index